THE ROADMAP OF BRITISH GHOSTS

For my sister, my endlessly patient proofreader, even when I scare her half to death with my stories

PROLOGUE

So here it is, my third book on ghosts and the supernatural..

When I started this writing malarkey, I thought there might be three, but now there is going to be at least a fourth, because a whole load of witness evidence I have gathered already didn't fit into the themes of the first three anywhere. I'll be starting the fourth pretty soon – my fingers are already itching to get typing!

I still get asked a lot whether I believe in ghosts, and whether I have ever seen a ghost. But even after all this research, I find that my answer is becoming more vague than ever.

That there are phenomena which occur I have no doubt whatsoever. I've personally seen or heard enough strange things to be unshakeable in that opinion. What I am still unsure of – and possibly even more puzzled by than when I started this research – is the question, "What is the cause/explanation for this phenomena?"

I still can't answer that. The stories I gather from people seem to suggest to me that there is more than one answer – and certainly more than one 'type' of phenomena.

For example, prior to writing this, I was fairly certain that the tales of Old Shuck, or Black Shuck, were mostly medieval tales of warning and woe – with no real place in our modern society other than as interesting old myths and insights into the mindset of society in days gone past.

Until I spoke to a number of people who had seen one. Themselves. Whilst awake and sober and going about their normal daily business.

That's led me to wonder whether some of the vague sightings of 'big cats' or 'escaped wolves' you see reported from time to time is actually a modern interpretation of an older type of phenomena...

Ah well. I live in hope that by gathering data like this, and setting it down, I am adding a bit more to the pot for future minds greater than mine to make sense of it all and come up with the answer.

Ruth Roper Wylde
29.12.18

If you enjoyed this book, please leave a review on either Amazon or Goodreads - it helps people to find the book on their search engines.
My other books are: *The Ghosts of Maraton Vale, The Almanac of British Ghosts, These Haunted Times Volumes 1 & 2, and The Roadmap of British Ghosts Volume 2.*

CHAPTER 1 – ENGLAND

BEDFORDSHIRE

ASPLEY GUISE

The first story I was researching relating to this particular lane came from the Paranormal Database website, and simply said that on 09 September 2008 while out running along Gypsy Lane, a witness spotted a dark figure around one hundred metres ahead of him. As the distance closed to around twenty metres, the figure vanished. A friend of the witness also said that his uncle had encountered a phantom woman along the same stretch of road.

When I asked locally for any information some very interesting stories came forward. It's important to bear in mind when reading these encounters that Gypsy lane meets Horsepool Lane as a 'T' junction so the two locations are very close indeed, and that Weathercock Lane is only about half a mile away. Both Gypsy Lane and Horsepool Lane are quite rural roads bordered by open fields and small areas of woodlands, with a few properties that are on the outskirts of the pretty little village of Aspley Guise dotted along them. Weathercock Lane is more in the village proper.

One property along Weathercock Lane is Woodfield House and the legend attached to it relates to the notorious highwayman Dick Turpin, who used to frequent nearby Aspley Woods as one of his hideouts. On dark nights, when the mist is hanging, it is said that the echo of his horse's hooves can still be heard travelling down the lane.

The owner of Woodfield House in the late 1940's was a chap called Blayney Key, who lived at Eel Pie Island, Twickenham. He lodged an appeal against the value of Woodfield House, claiming that he couldn't let it out for rent because it was so haunted. He claimed that Dick Turpin had been an aquaintence of a previous family who had lived at Woodfield House and happened to discover that the head of the family had in fact murdered his own daughter and her lover, by sealing them up alive in a cupboard within the property.

Having such low morals himself, Dick Turpin saw this as an opportunity to blackmail the householder into letting him use the house as a safe bolt hole as well as extorting money out of him. Blayney Key claimed that the ghost of the murdered daughter still haunted Woodfield House, making it a very unpleasant place to live. However, his appeal didn't get very far when investigations showed that the house had been built in 1820, whereas Dick Turpin was hanged for his crimes in 1739 and could not therefore ever have even visited the property!

In reality of course, the fact that this proves it could not have been Dick Turpin who takes a starring part in this tale, does not disprove that the house was in fact haunted by a murdered girl. More likely, it proves that this is a classic case of simply assigning an inexplicable happening to a locally well-known figure. There were certainly highwaymen operating in the area, and at least one version of the tale that I found claimed that the grisly murder actually took place at a coaching inn which used to stand close to the site of Woodfield House.

One witness did come forward to say that she remembered her uncle talking about seeing the ghost of Dick Turpin along Weathercock Lane many years before - she thought it might even have been as far back as the 1940's.

Another witness told me that she was out running late one Sunday afternoon/early evening in December 2015, and her route took her down Horsepool Lane. By the time she reached this part of her run, full darkness had descended.

All of a sudden, there was a yellowish light shining directly above her as she ran and whatever it was seemed to follow her for quite some distance. She was absolutely terrified and could not make any sense of what she had seen. She only ever told a few people about her encounter, not wishing to be seen as crazy, but she knows that something not of this world was with her that night.

She even tried to rationalise her encounter by searching on the internet to see if any of the birds which commonly frequent our shores might have phosphorescent plumage – but of course found nothing to explain what she might have encountered.

Another witness came forward to tell me of his own experience. He recalled that it was about 30 years ago (which would have been in the 1980's) and again was early evening but this time along Gypsy Lane. It was about 7pm and the daylight was just starting to fade into twilight.

He and his friend were walking along the lane talking, when suddenly he thought he saw something float across the road ahead of them. Although vaguely humanoid, the floating shape did not seem to have anything resembling legs, and there was no discernible face or features.

He stopped in fear and asked his friend if he could see the same thing. When they established they were both definitely seeing something they could not explain, the two sixteen year olds took to their heels.

In the comforting light of day the following morning, our witness went back to the scene thinking maybe they had been spooked by some rubbish caught in a hedgerow or some such mundane explanation, but he could not find anything which could maybe have been misinterpreted in the dimming twilight.

It certainly seems as though something haunts these three roads, all within close proximity of one another. If you live in the area and decide to go out walking or running at twilight – have a care. And carry a camera.

BEDFORD – junction of Tavistock Street, Union Street and Clapham Road

Black Tom was a notorious local highwayman who terrorised the roads around Bedford in the late 16th Century. Eventually, the law caught up with him and he was captured and hanged from the gibbet at Union Street in Bedford for his crimes in 1607. He was then buried at what is now the roundabout junction of Tavistock Street, Union Street and Clapham Road. His prosecutors even took the precaution of driving a stake through his corpse's heart, intending to stop him from haunting.

Unfortunately they weren't successful, for there were a spate of sightings of his ghost walking the area with an obviously broken neck and blackened face through the early 1800s. Apparently, he is most often seen in the area close to the roundabout on Union Street. In 1963 witnesses came forward to say they had seen his ghost staggering down the road and then vanishing into thin air as they watched. He was seen again in the early 1990's, but that witness assumed at first that they were just seeing a party goer in fancy dress until he disappeared in front of their horrified eyes.

Given the fact that his ghost is sometimes seen in daylight or during ordinary evening times, it does beg the question as to how many times he has been seen and not recognised as a ghost because people turned away before seeing his vanishing act?

Unfortunately, I was unable to turn up any recent sightings of him.

BEDFORD – Allhallows, near to the HSBC Bank

In 1979 in Allhallows, near to the Midland Bank (now HSBC), shoppers were surprised to see a mediæval friar in his hooded gown calmly walking down the street meditating on his rosary. From the direction in which he was walking, it seems likely he had come from Greyfriars which used to be the site of a priory.

CARLTON TO HARROLD

One lady told me that many years ago, probably around 1974 when she would have been 11 years old, she used to walk from their family home in Carlton through the allotments across the fields over the bridge to Harrold School and back home again.

She explained, "On the way home one night I saw a boy in front of me by maybe 100 yards or so. I thought he was from Harrold School so I ran to catch him up".

As she got closer to the boy she realised he couldn't have been from the same school as her because he was wearing shorts and had a satchel over his shoulder, which would not have matched the uniform of anyone from her school. Curious as to who the little boy was, she carried on running towards him. She didn't manage to catch up with him before he turned right into the field next to the allotments, and even though she was literally only three or four seconds behind him when she turned into the field he had completely vanished.

It was much later in life that she realised that as spooky as the incident was at the time, what with him vanishing so quickly, in actual fact it was even weirder than she had realised. When she thinks back on it, she clearly remembers that she was running and that the little boy was walking.

Logically, and given the distances involved between them, she should have caught up with him before he ever turned into the field.

CHELLINGTON – Carlton Hill

A lady was once pushing her bicycle up Carlton Hill, when she suddenly saw and heard two riderless horses cantering down the lane towards her. She hurriedly stepped to one side and lifted her bicycle clear to let them pass safely, then wondered if she ought to follow them to try and head them off or alert someone, since loose horses charging down a public road like that could easily injure themselves or cause a car crash.

Turning to follow them back down the hill, she was astonished to see they had vanished. She also realised that there was suddenly no sound of them galloping either, which there would have been if they had somehow turned off the lane.

A6 CLOPHILL

One witness recounted a tale told to him by his late father, a steadfast man who had not been known for flights of fancy. The father worked as a lorry driver driving recovery tow trucks. The very nature of that work meant that he was often working shifts late at night or into the wee hours of the morning, and driving up and down all sorts of roads. Despite this he only ever told one tale of experiencing something supernatural, which had left a deep impression on him.

When he was driving a Buckdales recovery truck sometime in the late 1970s, he had occasion to be driving up the A6 road in Bedfordshire. It was around 2am in the morning and he had just passed the small village of Clophill –

perhaps best known for its abandoned and ruined church which hit the headlines in the 1960s and subsequent years for apparently being the haunt of some devil worshippers.

As he drove along on the quiet rural road, which at this point passes some deep woods, he suddenly saw a very elderly lady walking along the side of the road. It immediately struck him as extremely odd that she should be walking alone in the dead of the night in such a rural location. He assumed she must be in some sort of difficulty, perhaps with a broken down car somewhere nearby. As he was, after all, driving a recovery truck he immediately pulled up to the side of the road and put his hazard lights on, intending to offer the poor lady his assistance.

Jumping out of his cab and clutching his coat around him against the chill night air, he walked back along the road he had just traversed. To his everlasting puzzlement, he could find no trace of the lady, and nowhere she could sensibly have gone unless she was prone to plunging through deeply overgrown woodland.

He never wavered in his conviction that he had seen something truly peculiar that night and never embellished on his simple recollection of the event.

CLOPHILL – Great Lane, Old Church Lane, and others.

Between Clophill and the nearby village of Haynes runs a narrow, twisting, quiet rural lane called Great Lane. In 1969 (or 1971, depending which source you read) a man delivering papers in the early hours of the morning by van was driving along Great Lane when he saw a faint glow approaching him along the road.

Not sure what was coming towards him, and given that this is actually a very narrow lane in places, he sensibly stopped his van and waited to see what was coming. To his surprise he saw a cloaked and hooded rider on a horse carrying a lantern. Before he had time to really process what he was seeing, the apparition rode straight though his parked van.

Supposedly, one family living near to the lane got so fed up with the frequent apparitions of the ghost that they upped sticks and moved away.

Another witness described to me her own experiences along Great Lane. She explained that she has had some very strange reactions when out riding her horses in Hill Field, which runs alongside it. She thinks the first time she noticed the strange behaviour of her horses at a certain part of the field would have been around 2005 or 2006.

She explained, "I was riding my completely bombproof and reliable, sensible old mare along the bridle path behind Pedley Wood [accessed off Great Lane on the way to Haynes]. The mare was in her 20's and had lots of experience and would very rarely, if ever, spook or misbehave in any way when being ridden. However every time I rode along that bridle path and came level with the little wooden bridge that crossed through the trees into Hill Field she would always scoot forward and canter into the field. It was almost as if 'something' or someone had poked her backside."

The witness explained that on every occasion she could actually feel her mare's heart pounding, even though there was nothing there and no reason for the animal's clear discomfort. Now obviously, for it to happen once, one could assume a fox or something was close by and although not detectable by a human's duller senses, the horse was picking up on its proximity. Clearly, though, there would not be a fox there every time she and her horse happened to ride past. Perhaps then, one could assume there was something physical there that the horse had taken a disliking to, like maybe a post or tree branch or something, which we with our calmer view just wouldn't notice in the same way.

However, the witness went on to explain that after this particular mare sadly passed away, she rode that way one more time on her next horse, but inexplicably they had a horrible experience there.

She told me, "I was there in around September time of 2009 with two other riders and as we approached that area from the Hill Field side my friend's normally bombproof horse started spooking, and my horse then literally bolted up the hill with me clinging on in absolute terror."

Her horse was so unhappy that at the top of the hill he spun around in a tight circle twice, successfully throwing her off his back before he took off running again. Her third companion was riding our witness' husband's horse and was herself having a terrible time trying to stay on as the normally placid animal bucked and bucked, trying desperately to unseat its rider.

The witness explained that all three of those horses were normally quite reliable steady rides, but on that day they simply went berserk at exactly the same spot near Great Lane where the placid old mare had always balked. Not surprisingly, our witness refused to ever ride a horse at that same spot again.

Another witness came forward to tell me that he recalled there had been some sort of sighting of a ghostly horse in the dirt lane called Old Church Path leading up to the ruined remains of St Mary's church. This path runs parallel to Great Lane. He knew that it was reported by a punk music band called UK Decay, who had visited the site to do a photo shoot for their album cover.

Most people in Bedfordshire who have even a passing interest in the paranormal will have heard of Old St Mary the Virgin Church in Clophill. It is an evocative and picturesque old ruin standing on a hill above the village, which gained notoriety in the late 1960s onwards as it was the subject of a spate of newspaper articles claiming that devil worshippers were using the old ruin for their demonic practices.

Since that time, it has practically been a rite of passage for teenagers and young adults from all over the county to make the nocturnal trip out to the old church to see if they can experience anything otherworldly. I don't intend to cover all the stories there are relating to the church itself, because this is not a book about haunted churches – but the claim of another ghostly horse so close to the same claim on Great Lane was too intriguing to ignore.

I contacted UK Decay, whose guitarist Steve kindly provided their version of events.

"I was in a punk rock band called UK Decay. We completed our second record The Black 45 EP in October 1979 which included some of our new songs with a horror type theme. We needed a cover for the new single and we knew there was this ruined church on a hill in a mid-Bedfordshire village. Someone had the idea that the ruined Church would be a great place for a suitably spooky photograph. So the four of us and a photographer set out in a car to get some shots. It was the end of the month around the time of Halloween.

"We drove to Clophill where the Church was situated on a moonlit and chilly night. We turned off the main road and drove up a winding dirt track that led to the old ruined Church of St Mary's. We parked up near the entrance porch, got out and prepared ourselves for the photos and shone a torch towards the church.

"The graveyard with decaying tombs and crumbling gravestones was completely overgrown and a spooky mist seemed to lurk in the shadows of the sunken path leading to the church's entrance. Back in those days the graveyard was really like a scene from the Hammer House of Horrors. The Church had lost its roof and windows and the tower was crumbling on its upper levels. We were half expecting a crack of lightning and thunder but it was not to happen tonight."

The band walked up the path and through the empty doorway which is the entrance to the ruined church. Steve said, "As the torchlight swept the crumbling walls we could see graffiti, including pentagrams and the clichéd numbers '666' and other stuff scrawled about the walls. Scraped into the floor we could make out a vague hexagram. All the windows had gone, leaving just empty apertures, so all four of us got up onto the bottom of one of the former windows and we posed whilst our photographer clambered among the gravestones to get a decent angle for the shots."

He recalled that they spent about twenty minutes or so creating various poses for the photographer. He said, "We were all in our late teens or early twenties, so I guess we were a tad excitable. As there were five of us there, we didn't feel particularly afraid. We were all enjoying ourselves and having a laugh at first but as time wore on and the fact we were balancing on the window ledge a metre or two high in the dark with the blinding flashes, we soon got a feeling of disorientation. Then someone thought that they had heard movement from within the church behind us. This soon amplified as our eyes blinded by the flashing couldn't see anything and our ears were either playing tricks or there was definitely something moving behind us. In a moment almost spontaneously we all jumped from the wall and we all fled back to the car in blind panic.

"We started the car and quickly headed back down the old hollow track which was sunken with high hedges on each side. Picking up speed and rounding a bend, the car came to a screeching halt as the headlights lit up a magnificent riderless white horse strolling down the lane in front of us. We were puzzled that such an animal was on the loose as the track led to the main road a few hundred yards further down and there wasn't any kind of gate."

Steve said that everyone had pounding hearts as they looked at each other in bewilderment - they couldn't really believe they were seeing a horse calmly walking down the narrow, hemmed in dirt track all on its own late at night. The horse continued walking away from them and disappeared from view around a slight bend in the lane. They followed cautiously in the car, wary of spooking the animal and assuming that they were following an actual live horse. They were wondering whether they ought to try and capture it, in case it wandered out onto the actual village roads they were headed towards and endangered itself and any cars still about at the late hour.

Within moments they too rounded the bend where the horse had just walked, only to find the lane ahead of them completely devoid of any sign of a horse! The lane has high steep sides with fencing and hedging at the top. There are no gateways and nowhere a horse could realistically have disappeared to.

Today there is a footpath off to one side which climbs the steep side of the lane part way down the hill but it does so via a flight of steps hewn into the bank side, which demonstrates how steep the bank is even though the steps weren't yet there back then.

Steve explained how their experience really spooked them all, and they couldn't stop thinking about it and talking about it for days afterwards.

He recalled that he had told the story of their sighting of the mysterious white horse to a local man some years later, who had grown up in Clophill. The man did not seem at all surprised by what they had seen, saying that the ghostly white horse was a well-known legend around the village and reminding Steve that the main pub in the village was even called "The Flying Horse".

I myself visited the church many years ago as a young adult with a group of friends with our first cars. We went late at night and parked the cars up in much the same spot that the band must have done, but about a decade or so later. We messed around inside the church for a while, trying to spook each other out and smoking.

Eventually we got bored with our shenanigans and walked back to the cars, where we stood around discussing where to go next. We had turned the headlights on from one of the cars and were standing in a loose circle in front of it, making use of the light to roll our cigarettes.

We clearly heard the sound of footsteps and jingling, like maybe a man walking his dog and carrying a dog lead would make, approaching us though the dark. Our night vision was ruined by the fact that we were standing in the lit area in front of the cars, so as the sound drew closer we politely moved apart to allow what we assumed was a late night dog walker through our midst. The sound went through the middle of the group of us and on down the lane, but there was absolutely nothing to be seen. I thought 'dog lead' at the time but I wonder now if it might have been a jingling bridle...

Two or three other witnesses from the village also came forward to say that they had uncomfortable feelings of 'something' being along the lane but could not really define what it was that made them feel like that along there. One said that there was definitely something in the area of woods behind the village at the top of the lane called Readshill. Another had heard the story that there was a ghostly horseman who used to ride down the avenue of trees going from Jones' farm along Great Lane towards

Haynes. One lady described a sense of being watched every time she walked down the nearby Back Street.

Intriguingly, another said they had also heard of a ghostly horseman riding between the nearby villages of Wardhedges and Silsoe which are not so very far away as the crow flies. One can't help but speculate whether it is the same entity.

COLMWORTH – Honeydon Road

The original story states that in the late 1980s or early 1990s, five people in a car driving along Honeydon Road were by chance following another car a short distance in front of them. The lead vehicle drove momentarily out of sight around a bend in the road, but to the astonishment of the occupants in the following car, when they themselves swept around the bend just moments later, the lead car had completely vanished. They could find no rational explanation for where the car could possibly have gone.

One witness told me that she had heard a related story back in the late 1980s, from one of the villagers who sadly died in 1990. This older lady had seen the ghostly car on two separate occasions, and described it as a large old fashioned Bentley. The grand old car, dark grey in colour, would approach the junction near The Chestnuts, and then seem to disappear instead of carrying on round the bend towards Bushmead Road.

Another witness came forward to ask whether the car was grey in colour, but declined to comment further – which leaves me curious as to whether they had also seen the same car.

It seems however, that this car has not been seen in more recent times – or if it has, the following cars have not noticed it performing its vanishing act and just assumed it turned off somewhere.

CRANFIELD – Rectory Lane

There is an old legend that a ghostly funeral cortege complete with black plumed horses is sometimes seen passing through Cranfield as a harbinger of death. It has certainly been seen within the last 60 years since one lifelong Cranfield resident told me that her father was walking home from his late evening shift one night and his route took him past where the old Rectory used to stand before it was replaced by newer houses. Hearing a noise, he realised that a hearse drawn by somberly plumed horses was approaching so he respectfully stood to one side and watched as it trundled slowly by and out of sight up the lane.

Wondering which local resident might have passed away, he told his wife about it as he walked through the door. She was in the habit of waiting up for him and making sure he had something to eat and drink before retiring for the night. She pointed out to him the sheer unlikelihood of a fully decked out and decorated horse driven funeral hearse operating at 2am in the morning – and that's when it dawned on him that what he had seen had perhaps been more supernatural than he had at first supposed.

DEADMAN'S CROSS – near Shefford

One witness told me that he had been riding his motorbike just past Deadman's Cross (where the A600 crosses Standalone Warren) at 6am one Thursday in November 2016. He was on his way to work and already a little pushed for time. There were four cars driving along in front of him, but to his astonishment none of the cars seemed to notice what he thought looked like a human hand literally waving at the passing traffic from within a bush!

He rode past without stopping at first, really wondering if it was just his imagination, but quickly became concerned that perhaps someone genuinely had fallen over or been knocked down and was trying to signal for help.

He turned his motorbike around at the first opportunity and rode back to the spot. There he found lying in the hedge an elderly gentleman wearing a smart suit, with his chest decked out with war medals. He helped the poor man up to his feet, asking him if he was OK and what had happened?

The gentleman didn't really respond to his questions, just said "Silly me". Slightly confused that he wasn't getting any answers, our witness stayed with the old man for a few minutes trying to ascertain if he was going to be OK when left alone, but in the end had to leave him or be very late for work.

The whole episode kept preying on his mind though, because something about the encounter and the way the gentleman didn't respond to him just felt off kilter. He did a little research into the area and found a story which said it was haunted by a soldier who was still trying to find his friend who had been killed in the war. Not surprisingly, he remarked that the incident shook him up a little.

I haven't been able to find anything to corroborate his mention of a source story of the ghost soldier, but it's certainly an intriguing encounter.

HARROLD TO LAVENDON

According to one source in February 1998 very early one morning, a local man called Gerald was driving home after a night shift at work. As he came down the stretch of lane which connects Lavendon and Harrold, he saw what he thought looked like an injured pheasant lying in the road.

Thinking to help the bird, he drove on a short distance to find a farm gateway to turn around in.

He drove slowly back towards the bird just as another car coming from the same direction as he himself had originally, also appeared to have swerved to avoid the bird and had come to a stop in the road at a slightly crosswise angle. The driver of the second car had climbed out and was looking towards the bird, which was some twenty feet away from his car. He was a young man, wearing a grey jumper, jeans, and a wooly hat. As Gerald drove round the young man and the pheasant, the feeling of something slightly surreal and uncomfortable about the whole scene started to creep over him, and he decided he wasn't going to stop after all.

He knew he had to turn back around and go back past the scene, however, in order to continue his original journey, so he once again turned his car, this time some sixty feet or so from the injured bird.

As he turned his car, he immediately realised that the bird, the man, and the car had all vanished: even though there simply was neither time nor place for the other car to have gotten out of sight in such a short span. He also realised that part of what had made him uncomfortable was that as he had maneuvered his car past the young man, the man had remained stock still, not even reacting to the presence of another car.

I couldn't find any other witnesses who had ever seen anything odd down that stretch of road. I can't help but wonder if this was one of those time slip type of events?

HOUGHTON REGIS – Drury Lane

This long-reported story is said to go back at least as far as the 1930s. The most common version says that a couple walking home in Houghton Regis one night saw a young girl ahead of them. It was quite a cold night, but she was wearing what looked like a summer frock and was barefooted. She was walking towards them, but turned into Drury Lane before reaching them. They were concerned for her welfare and hurried to the lane to ask her if she needed help only to find she had completely disappeared.

Most versions of the story say that she is the apparition of a little girl who was tragically killed after being run over by a car whilst she was on her way back home from Sunday school.

Another version says that one person has explained that during World War II his grandfather was on fire watch at The Chequers pub in Houghton Regis. He explained, "He and my Nan lived in Drury Lane and one night my Nan was hurrying down to the pub with his evening meal plated up for him, which she didn't want to get cold."

Due to the blackouts regulations in operation at the time because of the war there were no street lights and the nights were really pitch black. The witness said, "My Nan rounded the corner at the bottom of the lane and carried on towards the pub. A young man was standing at the bus stop, which used to be situated where the layby is now.

"He took one look at her as she loomed out of the dark, and took to his heels and ran for his life. Nan thought it odd but thought no more about it. The next day she was told the story of a young lad being scared by a ghost rushing at him in the dark, or I should say, just a pair of white shoes running towards him. She then realised it was her he had seen, dressed all in black except for a pair of white plimsolls. She never ever saw him at that bus stop again."

Curiously, another witness came forward to say that she had heard that there was a ghost of a girl there who used to be seen crossing the road and disappearing with only her white shoes showing fully in the dark. Could this be where story and reality are merging together to form an urban myth?

Several people came forward who had heard the story of the young girl killed in her Sunday School dress, and several said they had heard that she had been seen by many people over the years. One witness had heard a version where the haunting was only at a certain time of the year. Curiously yet another version came to light, this time that an American couple staying in the village in the 1970s had seen her crying and walking up the lane in the pouring rain. They had followed her to try and help but she had disappeared, and they later found that she had lived in a cottage close to the Green but had died when a fire broke out.

And finally, yet another witness came forward, but this time to tell me about a male entity seen down the same area but in St Andrew's Lane just off Drury Lane. He was seen by a group of lads many years ago, and ran backwards and forwards across the lane before he called out to them each by name, leaving them absolutely terrified.

One researcher found that in 1933 there was a murder of a young mother in Houghton Regis by her husband and she was found stabbed and dying at the top of Drury Lane.

KEMPSTON – Church End

I have lumped together several ghostly tales all related to this small area, as there is always the possibility that they are all linked but local urban myth has ascribed them separately.

Kempston today is a small town attached to the side of the large county town of Bedford. Originally however, it was a cluster of small hamlets which is still apparent from the remaining outlying areas called collectively 'Kempston Rural' and including Kempston Church End, Kempston Box End, Kempston Green End and so on.

There is a small lane on the edge of Kempston itself called Church Walk, which wends its way across the fields to All Saints Church in Kempston Church End. Beyond it are fields and the River Great Ouse. Part of this area is known as Ladies Walk, and is said to be named predominantly for the twins Sophie and Frances, who used to walk together through the picturesque and tranquil riverside meadows together hand in hand. So happy were they then that their ghosts still re-enact this and walk hand in hand along Ladies Walk.

In life, Sophie and Frances were twin daughters of John Cater, who owned Hastingsbury Manor in Kempston. When their father died their brother, also John, inherited the manor. However, he died sometime after 1749 and without any heir to pass the estate down to. Accordingly, his property was bequeathed to his three sisters, May, Sophie and Frances. Sophie and Frances both married in 1796, Sophie to Robert Sherbourne and Frances to Reverend Oliph Leigh Spencer. The three sisters sold the Manor in 1801 and since Reverend Spencer is not listed at All Saints Church, it is possible they were not living in the area after their respective marriages.

Also in the fields around this spot is said to be the ghost of the Green Lady, who is thought to have drowned in the river but there seems to be very little to say who she might have been in life. Apparently she is particularly fond of appearing to children and scaring them, and also sometimes to seem to flow out of the mists of the river.

One recent witness to the ghost explained, "Firstly I must state that I didn't believe in ghosts, I had no reason to as I'd never experienced any sort of supernatural phenomenon. Neither, must I add, had I mocked it as I like to keep an open mind on things. As a child growing up and going to school in the Kempston rural area I had heard of the legend of the ghost of Kempston mill known locally as the green lady. The story went that a young woman had gone for a walk with her child, a little girl, along the river bank down at mill meadows. The child had fallen into the water at the start of the old mill race and her mother had jumped in to save her. Both had drowned as the sides of the race were too high to allow the poor lady to drag herself and her daughter to safety."

Although he was aware of the legend from childhood his own experience came much later, when he was a young farmer working on the land around the Kempston Mill area. He told me, "My experience came when I used to farm the river meadows at Kempston Mill in approximately 2001. I was mowing hay down there in late August after a wet July which had put us behind with the haymaking. I started mowing the 40 acres in the morning [using a tractor pulling a mower] that day but I had a fence post go through the mower which bent various parts [of the machinery] and forced me to stop. I returned home, mended the mower and returned to the meadows later in the day to finish cutting. Darkness crept in and I kept going, spotlights switched on all over the tractor and Radio 1 screaming out through the speakers."

He explained that by 11.30pm he only had some last small bits to finish alongside the mill backwater, and thought if he pushed on he could probably get it done in another twenty minutes or so.

He said, "In that particular part of the field there is a cutout in the river bank where the cows used to go down to the water to drink. I was mowing towards this cutout and in full view of the headlights I saw the figures of a woman and a young girl standing in front of me. Needless to say the brakes were applied pretty sharpish and I stopped with the pair standing full on in front of me lit up by the tractor's lights. They were wet and bedraggled, both wearing dresses with weed caught in their hair and parts of their clothing. They slowly turned and walked down the bank and into the water where they disappeared. After a few minutes when I'd come to terms with what I saw I carried on to the end of the swathe and with the tractor lights shining on the water, got out and had a look."

Despite his definite bravery (I am not sure I would have wanted to get out of that tractor!) there was nothing to be seen down beside the water where they had disappeared. Although he worked there many times more over the years before finally moving out of the area to another part of the country, he never saw the figures again. Even today, he describes how the encounter didn't really frighten him so much as intrigue him, and left him with a definite belief that ghosts do in fact exist.

Another witness said that having seen a ghost fourteen years ago in the same area with two other adults and several children all present, she developed a lasting interest in ghost hunting and intrigue about the paranormal.

A final tale for the area says the ghost is that of Lady Snagge who wanders looking for her lost son, and yet another version says it is the ghost of a young girl whose lover was murdered during the English Civil War in 1642 to 1651. Whatever the original truth behind the tales, it seems likely that the haunting is still active, since two witnesses came forward who had seen it in recent years.

MARKYATE – the A5 near the PACKHORSE INN

There is a tale that in 1958 a minibus was returning to Surrey carrying the members of a cricket team from Kenwood Manufacturing Co., who had just played in a match at Milton Bryan. As they were coming down the A5 close to the Packhorse Inn, their vehicle was involved in a head on collision with a car. Sadly, three of those on board the minibus were injured, and a further two died.

Since then, it is said that the ghost of at least one of the cricketers can sometimes be seen standing on the edge of the road close to the Packhorse Inn (which currently operates as a Chinese food takeaway). On one occasion in 1973, it is claimed that the ghost actually stepped out into the road in front of an oncoming taxi. Although the poor taxi driver hit his brakes in alarm, he could not stop his vehicle from apparently passing through the figure of the ghost. Although he did stop to check, he could not find any explanation for what he had seen.

One witness told me that she remembered the story of the cricketer's ghost being seen by the taxi driver appearing in the newspaper, and that if she remembered rightly it was at about 1am in the morning that the ghost was reported. She also explained how she lived in one of the cottages not far from the A5 back in the 1970's, and she recalls that one evening her brother was coming home from Luton riding his scooter when he saw what he thought at first were two youths playing in the fields near the turning for Slip End (this is only a half mile or so from the Packhorse Inn).

They were showing as white in colour, but he just assumed that was his headlights washing the natural colour out the way headlights sometimes do. Within an instant, however, the two figures were immediately in front of him and he had to swerve violently to avoid hitting them, losing control of his machine as he did so. A car travelling behind him on the road stopped to help him pick himself and his scooter up off the road, but neither he nor the car driver could see any sign of the figures he had swerved to avoid hitting.

It does seem to beg the speculation whether it wasn't two youths showing up as white in his headlights he saw, but actually two men dressed in cricket whites?

The same witness also recalled that her grandmother, who lived in the cottages there, used to describe how she was hanging washing out in her garden one day when she suddenly heard the clattering of hooves and the rumble of carriage wheels go by down the road, accompanied by a high pitched and loud sound of a lady laughing.

The grandmother was always sure she had heard the ghost of the infamous lady highwaywoman, Lady Ferrers.

A507 MILLBROOK - Woburn Road

This short section of road, where the A507 Woburn Road passes the tiny village of Millbrook, seems to be incredibly haunted with a variety of phenomena reported over a great number of years. The most well-known ghost is perhaps that of Galloping Dick. He was a highwayman who made his home in an area known as the Sand Pit near to the A507. I have heard various descriptions of where exactly this was ranging from the area near to Millbrook Station (which is over a mile away from the village itself) now known as Rookery Pit, to a small depression in the wooded hillside virtually next to the roundabout which gives access to the village itself. Personally I would discount Rookery Pit as being 'too young' a feature to have been the home of a highwayman, unless there was some sort of pit there before the current one. The earliest Ordnance Survey map lists an area called 'Blacklands' not far from the shallow depression on the hillside which is also a possibility. I've also discovered a narrow, steep-sided wooded cleft in the hillside just above Boughton End, very close by as the crow flies, which looks like it might have made an ideal hide out for a highwayman as it is shallow enough to ride in to at one end if the vegetation were cut back.

The stories for Galloping Dick say that it is just the sound of his galloping horse that can be heard, anywhere on Sandy lane passing through Millbrook from the A507, right on down all the way to Millbrook Station. I'm always a little skeptical of this kind of identification – if all that is heard is a galloping horse, then who is to say that it is the ghost of a particular highwayman as opposed to the ghost of anyone who might be riding a horse pell-mell? I have also come across other sources which attribute the sound at Millbrook to the highwayman Black Tom, who is generally more famous for haunting in Bedford town around 12 miles away.

Interestingly, about three miles away there is another galloping horse ghost, and although this one is attributed to Lady Snagge who was the lady of the local Manor (see the entry for Wood End), I can't help but wonder if it is actually the same ghost but just misidentified? That one was felt as it passed by in the middle of the night by two brothers walking home within the last thirty years which might suggest the haunting is still at least partially active.

Another often told tale of this part of the A507 is that one night a mother and her child were walking along the path leading out of the village and onto the main road when suddenly a pile of small stones rose up in the air and proceeded to fly about like a little swarm of granite bees. Although no date is given to the story, from the context I think it is quite an old tale.

On another occasion a man was followed by a strange and inexplicable ball of light which emerged from a hedgerow, pursued him for a short distance and then mysteriously disappeared. There was also a more modern tale of a ball of light experienced about two miles from here by two men cycling home down through The Thrift wood at Wood End late at night.

The Vicarage in Milbrook was also haunted – as detailed in a letter dated 1945 from a former Vicar of the Church of St Michaels and All Saints in Millbrook.

And finally, there is a legend locally that this same stretch is haunted by a Black Shuck – one of the devil dogs of English folklore – and also by a coach and horses which rattles down the lane unseen but heard. The Shuck along here is said to be as big as a calf, and legend tells us it once terrified a local woman so badly that she died three days after the encounter.

The Luton Paranormal Society visited the village on 28th September 2012 and conducted a night time investigation, which they have written up in very thorough detail and which you can find easily online.

They started their investigation at the shallow depression next to the A507, but as its sides are quite steep and overgrown with nettles they felt it wasn't safe in the pitch dark. They moved on to the ruined chapel which stands barely visible only a scant few yards from the busy A507, but hidden by the woods and undergrowth. Here they conducted a séance and felt they were given a number of different names including 'Martha Humble' whom they believed might have been jilted at the altar there.

They then walked down the road through the village and up the steep footpath to the Church of St Michael and All Saints, which has an amazing panoramic view over the Vale of Marston. They encountered some strange lights from within the church itself and thought they caught a glimpse of a male figure and later a female figure wearing a hooded cloak. Sadly they were unable to record evidence of either Galloping Dick or the Black Shuck.

Interestingly, a few miles further down along the A507 as it gets close to Beadlow Manor, a man driving home one night a few years ago saw a knight on a horse cross the road. He has no rational explanation for what he saw.

MILTON BRYAN – Mags Lane

There is a source story which can be found online which says there is an entity on Mag Lane, near Hockliffe. In fact, the lane referred to is called Mags Lane, and is in Milton Bryan, a picturesque hamlet not far from Hockliffe, but definitely not part of it.

The story goes that the entity has been nicknamed Headless Mag and is thought to have been a local witch. Her misty form is supposed to drift along the road looking for people to scare. One source I found says she usually appears as an ordinary mist which gradually takes on a more substantial form.

I have been unable to find any corroboration for this old tale.

PAVENHAM

A lady cycling home along the road by Pavenham in fairly recent years was suddenly horrified to see a large white dog literally materialize out of nowhere in front of her bike. Completely unable to stop in the short distance offered by its sudden appearance, she braced herself for impact – but the bike passed straight through the dog as if nothing was there.

My friend and I conducted a night investigation there in August 2018 but with no results to report.

RISELEY

There is a story that a local farmer passing near Eastfield Corner, which is on Buryfields Farm near the airfield, suddenly heard the sound of a galloping horse approaching him. Stopping to look about he could see nothing, but the sound of the beast crashing through the hedgerow right next to where he was standing assaulted his senses – accompanied by the rush of air as if the horse had just passed in close proximity. But still, there was nothing to be seen.

One witness described how in February 2000 on a cold but clear day she and her husband were out walking their dog somewhere in the fields between Bowers Lane and Keysoe Road. Their intention had been to walk a circuitous route, cutting back across the fields. However, their path took them alongside the field they intended crossing, with a thick hedge separating them from the view of the field.

She explained, "We could hear what sounded like a very big angry horse, neighing and galloping right behind the hedge. We were discussing if it was safe to walk through the field as it seemed the horse was reacting badly to our dog, and decided we would take a look and probably walk back rather than risk it. When we got round the corner and looked in the field it was totally empty."

Another witness told how he was standing outside his house on the High street in Riseley in 2017 when he heard the sound of a horse trotting down the road, coming towards him. It was very late in the evening and so a very unusual time to hear a horse out on the roads in this day and age.

He turned to look to see who was coming and to his surprise, although he could clearly follow the sound as it went past, there was nothing to be seen of any live horse and rider. He says that prior to this he never believed in ghosts but now he does: especially because the sound was crystal clear and definitely not being caused by anything mundane.

Yet another witness remembers actually seeing the apparition, early one morning many years ago although she could not remember precisely when. It was a horse and rider, but surrounded in a slightly unreal orange glow. The pair galloped on past and out of sight, but our witness was aware straight away that she was seeing something otherworldly.

And finally, another witness remembers coming home to the village late one night in a car, and being startled by the apparition of a horse running across the lane in front of her car. She described how it was more of a sort of outline of a horse, than a solid figure of one.

There is also said to be the ghost of a man who walks the path across the meadow by the village, and possibly a ghostly horse and carriage which approaches the village from the west. Another witness told me that they once saw the ghost of a young boy standing beside the road as they were returning to the village one night. They only realised it was a ghost because they stopped the car to check if the child was OK, but he had disappeared.

My friend and I conducted an investigation along the lanes around Riseley in March 2018 and again in August 2018. We didn't have any really documentable experiences, but there is certainly one spot which has a very heavy atmosphere and where we both thought we could see something large moving around behind our car in the dark.

SALFORD

There is an account that in July 2009 at around 11pm at night, a man who was driving his girlfriend home to nearby Cranfield had to brake sharply when his car headlights illuminated a figure standing in the road. Although they only saw it for a few moments before it moved out of sight into the bushes at the side of the road, they described the ghost as wearing a scarlet jacket and a pale colored tunic which seemed to be bloodstained down the front of the chest. They said the figure had black 'Cavalier-like' hair. I presume they mean longer curly hair, as was the fashion at that time.

Actually, both Cavaliers and Roundheads wore jackets and tunics of any colour they could lay their hands on - there was no such thing as a 'uniform' then. They tended to distinguish themselves from each other on the battlefield by either wearing an insignia of some kind, or by wearing coloured sashes across their chests. Typically, Cavaliers would wear a red coloured sash, so perhaps this was not a bloodstain they saw at all but rather the coloured sash.

I have not been able to find any other accounts for this stretch of road.

B1042 SANDY – Potton Road

There is an account that in 1997 the occupants of a car driving along Potton Road saw a skinny woman in modern day clothes walking a small dog. They thought nothing of it for a moment - until she stepped out straight in front of their car. Horrified, they braced themselves as the driver slammed his brakes on, even though he instinctively knew that there was no time for the vehicle to come to a safe stop and that inevitably the woman and her poor pet were going to be hit.

Astonishingly though, the car passed straight through the figure, which immediately faded away. This seems to have been a one off event as far as I could find out.

SHARNBROOK - Mill Road / A6 roundabout

One witness told me that he had heard that on the roundabout at the end of Mill Road in Sharnbrook, there is the ghost of a man who was killed in a road accident there.

It might relate to a time before the roundabout was built, when apparently there used to be a dangerous dog-legged junction there.

He had heard that it is sometimes possible to see the man standing beside the roundabout at 2am in the morning, on the Riseley side of the road. He himself had often driven across the roundabout in the wee small hours of the morning on his way to the airport to catch early business flights, but had never seen the ghost.

My friend and I drove around it from every possible approach one morning in August 2018 at close to 2am, but there was no sign of the ghost. We did notice that since all the roads approaching it are not lit, and the roundabout itself is, then tired eyes making the adjustment from dark to light could easily mistake the various signs, posts and bushes as something standing there.

STANBRIDGE - Station Road / Peddars Lane

The original account of this hitchhiker ghost is an extremely well known one. The story is that a van driver named Roy Fulton picked up a young, dark haired hitchhiker with 'a long face' one evening in October 1979. He asked the young man where he wanted to go but the man didn't answer, just pointed ahead. Roy turned back to look ahead as he pulled out onto the road, then once he was safely in motion glanced across to his quiet passenger with the intention of offering him a cigarette. To his astonishment, the man had vanished.

I visited the road in March 2018 and saw nothing strange. I did think it was a slightly odd location to be picking up a hitchhiker, even given the fact that in 1979 the local bypass was not yet built. The nearby A5 is (and was in 1979) the main road, and seems a more likely place to try and hitchhike from.

One witness came forward to tell me that she had grown up on Station Road, opposite the intersection with Peddars Lane. The version she had heard in the 1980s was as follows, "He was picked up by a kindly motorist on a dark, stormy, rainy night. After the hitchhiker got in the car, they drove off, but the mysterious passenger didn't speak even when the driver asked him if he wanted a cigarette. The driver started rooting around in his door panel to find his cigarettes and, flipping the pack open, turned to his passenger to offer him one, only to find to his astonishment that the hitchhiker had vanished. The driver stopped his car and looked around, and although the passenger seat was wet from where the bedraggled hitchhiker had sat, he was nowhere to be found."

She went on to say, "I have a vague recollection of him being seen just one more time walking in a storm by a driver who claimed he passed him quite slowly then when he looked for him in his rear view mirror the apparition had disappeared."

Another witness said he knew the story well when he lived around there, and although he walked or cycled down the stretch of road on numerous occasions, he never saw anything untoward.

There is a video online of a full interview with Roy Fulton - search for Arthur C Clarke's World of Strange Powers 3.

WOOD END – Wood End Lane

Wood End is a tiny hamlet just outside the village of Marston Moreteyne. The lane leading to it is said to be haunted by the apparition of a headless horse and rider galloping madly down the road. The legend concerns Lady Elisabeth Snagge, whose effigy lies in Marston Church alongside that of her husband Sir Thomas Snagge. He was a

Member of Parliament and a wealthy landowner residing at Moreteyne Manor in the village.

Apparently Elisabeth Snagge was riding down the lane at speed one night having visited her illicit lover at Brogborough, when she was decapitated by a rope strung across the lane by some footpads, who then mercilessly robbed her body of its jewellery and finery before slipping off into the night.

Since then she can sometimes be seen riding pell-mell down the lane, without her head, but other times people hear just the sound of galloping hooves late in the night, or sometimes it is just the sensation of a horse swishing past at speed.

In truth it was unlikely to have been Lady Elisabeth Snagge, as she had seven children by her husband and then outlived him by 43 years which would put her as a dowager in her eighties when she apparently took a nocturnal ride to meet a lover. That seems a little far-fetched even for a quite sprightly octogenarian.

It is possible however that whoever she was, the ghost no longer rides, as I did find one reference that the Rector of Cranfield was called to the lane and put the ghost and her steed to rest with the use of a bell, book and candle (an old rite to lay a spirit).

There was one witness though, who told me about his experience on a road close to Wood End Lane, Beancroft Road. In the late eighties or early nineties, when a teenager, he and his brother were walking back towards the main farmhouse at Beancroft, having finished their work on the farm late in the evening. As they approached Beancroft Lane, they heard the sound of a rushing horse, and something large rushed past them. Even today, the farmer cannot fully articulate what it was that rushed past them in the dark – he says it was more that he sensed it was a horse and rider rather than clearly heard or saw it. Whatever it was, it thoroughly spooked the two of them, and they took off running for home.

BERKSHIRE

A329 BRACKNELL - Ascot Road (or various others)

This is a somewhat elusive story. Somewhere in this vicinity there is said to be the ghost of a policeman wearing an old fashioned high collared uniform who is only seen when car headlights illuminate him, showing his badly scarred face. He is variously listed as being near the railway arch between Martins Lane & Whistley Close in Bracknell, or on the A329 between the town and Ascot.

Yet another source claims it is at the junction of the A30, the A332 and the A329, but since I can't find anywhere that all three cross, I think we can discount that one. The A332 and A329 seem to cross at the Heatherwood Hospital roundabout, just a short distance along the A329 from Whistley Close, so it seems to me this is the most likely area in which to find this ghost, if he is still active. Unfortunately, no-one came forward to tell me that he is.

BRACKNELL – Quelm Lane

Quelm Lane is a bridle path running for quite a distance through the northern part of this town. Some sources say its name might relate to an old name for a gibbet, but the old English word 'cwealm' actually means slaughter, murder or death. It could relate to an old battle site, then, or a notorious highwayman's route? Certainly, Quelm Lane itself is probably a very ancient trackway, perhaps even dating back to prehistory, since there is a standing stone on it known as the Quelm Stone.

The legend is that the lane is haunted by a phantom rider on a huge black (some sources say white) horse who likes to scoop up any children he comes across and spirit them away, never to be seen again. This smacks much more of either the Wild Hunt, or Herne the Hunter type legends, and given the antiquity of the lane itself, is probably the remains of a very ancient tale. Today though, the sources claim that dogs still don't like to walk down Quelm Lane.

So next time I'm passing through that area, I'll try to find time to walk my dogs along it and see if they react, since I was unable to find any witnesses to either confirm or deny that claim.

A338 HUNGERFORD

This stretch of road claims to have no less than three ghosts and at least one of them is said to appear in broad daylight.

In 1957 a motorist saw a lady riding a galloping horse across the road, who promptly disappeared once she reached the other side. The same area is haunted by a spectral coach being pulled at breakneck speed by four horses and also by a hooded man riding a bicycle. One source claimed that the occupant of the coach was the same lady ghost as the one riding the horse, although how you would determine that without stopping the coach and looking inside, I'm not sure!

Unfortunately, I was unable to find anyone who had actually seen anything along there.

HURST - Tape Lane

The legend here is the age old tale of unrequited love. Supposedly the lane is named after a local lass called Molly Tape, who became romantically involved with a local farmer called Dick Darval. Dick was quite fickle in his affections though and soon tired of the girl, leaving her broken hearted and desperate enough to take her own life by hanging herself from a tree in the lane which now bears her name.

It is claimed that her ghost can still be seen running down the lane wearing very little in the way of clothing, and some sources state that this happens most often around Easter time. There is also supposed to be an old rhyme about the story in which it says Molly tried witchcraft in order to win back her lover's affection, but I was not able to find a full copy of it anywhere.

Historically, there was certainly a farming family called Darvall in the area and their farm was known as Darvall's farm. George and Richard Darvall were listed as residing there in 1854 and another Richard Darvall was listed in 1860, so one of those could perhaps be the 'Dick' Darval of the tale. There do not appear to be any records of poor Molly, nor actual sightings of her ghost though.

A34 NEWBURY, and surrounding roads

It has been quite widely reported that the construction of the A34 Newbury bypass in the late 1990s disturbed a mass grave containing the remains of both Roundhead and Cavalier soldiers. Since then, it is claimed that the ghosts of these Civil War troops have been reported manifesting as shadowy entities.

One witness told me that as a teenager in the 1980s, he went down Cope Hall Lane towards Skinners Green Lane late one night, and to his horror, saw what he described as a Cavalier on horseback crossing the road. He knew it was a ghost without a doubt, because the current road surface was at the horse's knee height! He has hated that road at night ever since.

These two lanes are just alongside where the A34 now lies, and so it is possible that the building of the A34 might have 'stirred things up'.

Another witness came forward to say that he had been told a story by colleagues in the Police Force. During the construction period of the new bypass, very early one morning, they had gone to make a routine check with the civilian security guards for the construction site that everything was OK. They found the guards in quite a traumatised state. When they asked what the problem was they were told that the men had witnessed an army of Civil War soldiers marching through the woods next to the site.

A third witness told me that she recalled her father, many years ago, saying that he had seen a headless horseman coming down the hill past Littlecote House, which is about 13 miles away as the crow flies.

Even closer, about 4 miles away, another witness saw a headless horseman wearing a flowing cloak coming down the hill past the ruined medieval Donnington Castle. He and his friend were parked there late one night in the 1980s, and as he put it, they didn't hang around long enough for it to actually reach them! He says that to this day, his friend won't talk about the experience at all.

One lady told me that her sister also saw something at Donnington castle, in the early 1980's. She and a male friend were sitting in his car, again in the car park of the castle (obviously a popular spot for youngsters!). They noticed a little light up at the castle itself, swinging gently side to side. Fascinated, they watched as the light came down the hill from the castle towards them, wondering what it could be. As it got closer, they made out the image of a man 'dressed in olden day clothes' holding a lit lantern which swung from side to side as he walked. Sadly for the ghost researchers amongst us, they too did not hang around to confront what they were seeing. She was apparently very shaken up by the whole incident when she got home that night.

Nearby, in Newbury itself, Cheap Street is said to have the ghost of a Quaker lady who haunts late in the evenings who is possibly connected to the Quaker burial ground on that street.

BUCKINGHAMSHIRE

BENNET END – Road between village and Radnage Bottom

Bennet End is a tiny hamlet to the north west of High Wycombe, set in a very picturesque landscape of gently rolling hills and woodlands. Some sources claim that a phantom coach and horses can sometimes be seen late at night making its way down the road between this hamlet and nearby Radnage Bottom.

One witness told me that he had lived in Radnage for his whole life and had never even heard the tale of it, and another said he had lived in Bennett End from 1947 until 1955, and despite walking the lane at all hours of the night he never saw or heard anything. Another concurred, saying he had lived in the hamlet for 38 years and had neither seen nor heard anything of it.

Another witness, whose father was the historian for Radnage, told me that the road was once an old coaching road from London. She had only ever heard of ghosts at Radnage Bottom Farm, but used to feel very scared riding the horses down the lanes back to their stables. She said that there was a story that Radnage Bottom Farm was haunted by King John (d. October 1216 a.d.)

Apparently in 2014 a metal detectorist unearthed a 'groat' which she thought might be from King John's time. It must have been a little later in date though, as the first English groat was minted some time after 1272 a.d., in the reign of Edward I. (European Groats are a little earlier).

Another author gave me permission to use the following from his own research, which covered the track which runs from Bennett End along the valley bottom towards the farmhouse below Stokenchurch Village Hall. It would have been around 1985 when he had this experience and he told me, "Across the valley on the left the large wooded area reportedly had a headless horse rider. I was with a friend on the edge of these woods making a camp out of branches on a hot summer day the way kids like to, but we stopped when we heard a horse rider going along the valley.

"It was one of those very still days during the school summer holidays with the sun beating down, no breeze could be felt and the air was dead still. You could see for miles along the valley's dirt track in the bright sunlight and clear air. We distinctly heard a horse rider for several minutes going the full length along the track that ran straight for at least a mile along the bottom of the valley, we both stopped and sat to watch, we could clearly hear the horse clopping along the valley floor with the track in full view, but we never saw anyone, we were intrigued, but never did we feel any fear."

He thinks that it just sounded like a horse which was walking quite fast – he didn't believe there was any sound with it to suggest there was also a carriage.

A413 CHALFONT ST PETER – Amersham Road near the Greyhound Inn

There is a story that on misty nights an old fashioned stagecoach pulled by a team of ghostly horses can be seen clip-clopping along this road. The coach then vanishes as it pulls up outside the Greyhound Inn. One source claimed that the coachman can be seen wrapped up in a thick cloak, and that he turns to look at the Inn just before the whole apparition disappears.

Certainly this Grade II listed Coaching Inn has been in use for more than 600 years: so there will have been literally thousands of coaches and horses which travelled that route and pulled up at the Inn. Unfortunately, however, I was not able to find any recent sightings of this apparition.

CRYERS HILL - road leading to FOUR ASHES

This lane, which runs between Cryers Hill and Four Ashes in Buckinghamshire, now has a large modern day crematorium sited on it. In September 1986 car driver Mark Nursey was being followed along the lane by his girlfriend Allyson, who was driving her own car. They both saw a strange figure standing at the side of the road, close to the turning for the crematorium. It was about 5'11" tall, but seemed to be stooped over so that neither its head nor hands were visible. It seemed to be wearing a dark green jumper or tunic.

Once their story was reported, another witness came forward and was reported in the local newspaper The Star of October 17th, 1986. "ANOTHER witness of the phantom of the forest has recalled his terrifying ordeal. The seven-foot tall green ghost was seen by warehouseman Phil Mullett just yards from where 21-year-old Mark Nursey saw the figure on Four Ashes Road, Cryers Hill, near High Wycombe.

"Mark's sighting, reported in the Star, September 26, happened just before midnight by Hughenden Garden of Rest on the road. His girlfriend Allyson Bulpett also saw the ghost. When Phil, 28, of Dashwood Avenue, High Wycombe, read the account he realised Mark had seen the same figure he saw eight years previously. Phil said: 'It gave me quite a shock to read it. The account was so close to my own. It was about 9.30pm when I drove into Four Ashes Road and on turning my car lights on full I saw this green person appear from the right hand side of the road. It drifted out to the centre of the road and turned towards me. It waved its arms, not to frighten but as if to warn me to keep back. It drifted into the hedge on the other side of the road but as I got closer it came out again to the centre, turned and lifted its arms. I knew I was going to hit it. I think I cried out or shouted something.'

" Phil braked and although he must have hit the figure when he got out to look there was nothing there. He said the figure was bright green but appeared to have no legs or hands. The body was solid and it stood about seven feet tall. Instead of a face there was just a misty grey round shape."

Some sources have speculated that this might have a connection to Herne the Hunter type manifestations, and may be connected to the leyline that runs close to the spot. I have not been able to find any more recent sightings.

A40 GERRARDS CROSS - Area around the Bull Hotel

On February 10th 1984 the newspaper The Bucks Free Press reported the experience of a Mr Dave Robson.

He said that he was walking home along deserted country roads about midnight as he had done many times before after finishing work at the Bull Hotel, Gerrards Cross. At one point he was startled by an owl's screech, which made him stand still and listen.

To his surprise, he heard the sound of a horse trotting towards him. He waited as it approached, wondering who could be riding out at that late hour of the night. He was horrified when out of the darkness there came the faintly luminous figure of a mounted highwayman. He described him as dressed in a big cloak and hat, and carrying a gun. The vision rode past him and vanished close to a group of nearby trees. There is no corroboration for this sighting that I could find.

A418 HADDENHAM, the turning for the village

There is a story that the ghost of a man will sometimes appear at the side of the road here and if he does, you should take it as a warning that something bad is about to happen. The story dates back to the murder of a young husband called William Noble Edden in 1828. He was walking from the market at Aylesbury back to his home in Thame, but as he passed Haddenham, he was set upon by thieves and murdered. Curiously, his wife claimed to have had a vision of the murder and accused one Benjamin Tyler. With no evidence other than her vision, the matter rested there for nearly a year.

However, then another 'witness', Solomon Sewell, came forward who claimed that he had seen Benjamin Tyler strike William Noble Edden dead using a hammer. At first, the matter was still taken with a large pinch of salt, since even Solomon's mother was prepared to testify that he was a simpleton who would say anything he was told to say. The autopsy had shown that death was caused by something breaking his ribs and crushing his liver, causing internal bleeding.

Mrs Edden testified that she had sent for Benjamin Tyler to come and touch the corpse, but he had refused to do so. This was based on a centuries old superstition that if a murderer later touched the corpse of his victim, the blood would rush forth out of the body and thereby confirm the identity of the murderer.

At first Tyler was released, but he then somewhat foolishly at best and with sinister callousness at worst, set about taunting those who had testified against him. In 1830 he was re-arrested, and this time Sewell was tried alongside him, and both were found guilty of the murder. They were hanged on 8th March 1830. In his speech, Tyler reiterated his innocence, and said that his "life had been taken away by false swearers". Allegedly, Sewell's body was subsequently dissected at St Bartholomew's Hospital, London and the surgeons reported that the brain of Sewell was diseased and bore the appearances of those of persons who had been insane. In their opinion the disease had existed throughout the lifetime of Sewell.

I can't help but wonder why Mrs Edden wanted Tyler dead...

There is also a tale that in late summer in 1994 a driver travelling along this road saw a stagecoach and horses coming towards him, but with no apparent coachman handling it.

One witness sent me a photo he had taken a few years back whilst walking along a leafy bridle path close to that turning. It was early evening, but still broad daylight when he took the photo – but in it there is a misty form in the right hand corner showing what looks like a creepily leering face.

A4128 HIGH WYCOMBE – White Hill

In December 1936 a lorry driver and his driver's mate reported hitting a man dressed in a black cloak (like a monk's habit) in cold misty weather one night along this stretch of road. When they saw the figure on the road they were horrified when they realised it was too late to avoid hitting him because of the steep descent of the hill. They watched helplessly as the figure went under the front of the truck. When they screeched to a halt and ran back to look, they could not find any evidence that anything had happened. The police were duly informed but the officer told them that several other people had recently reported the same story along the road.

One witness told me that he had heard of the original story, and said that over the years the reports have still sporadically come in of a figure being run over or narrowly missed on White Hill. He said that he had heard other reports of people seeing a wispy white figure in that area.

He pointed out that given the geography of the area, it was quite likely a haunt for highwaymen in times gone by, looking to relieve wealthy merchants of the money they had made at Wycombe market. A highwayman might be as likely to wear a dark cloak as a monk.

HIGH WYCOMBE - Cock Lane

There is supposedly the ghost of a lady dressed in grey who either walks or floats along this road in High Wycombe. She was seen in the early 1980s, and then again in January 1994 according to some sources. On both occasions she mysteriously vanished when the witness glanced away or turned back to look at her.

When I asked locally, no-one came forward with any more recent sightings.

HIGH WYCOMBE - Loakes Road

Loakes Road in High Wycombe is just a short residential street today, but on maps it looks like it might once have been part of the route of an old drover's lane or something similar.

It allegedly has the ghost of a lady riding her mare, eternally following the route she took in life just before she was thrown from her mount and died. There are no recent accounts of sightings.

A404 HIGH WYCOMBE to AMERSHAM

In 1971 Steve Bond and his wife were driving home towards High Wycombe along the A404 quite late at night. As they came to the Holmer Green Road / Penn Road junction, their car's lights picked up the figure of a stout man wearing a sports jacket and with a bandaged head standing in the road.

Steve swerved to avoid him, and as he did so, they both realised that the apparition had only a sort of greyed out smudge where his face should have been. Furthermore, the car which happened to be following theirs took no evasive action at all, suggesting that they didn't see any figure.

One witness came forward to say that just before Christmas 2017 her husband had seen a man walking a dog along the same stretch of road but a bit further down, and he had come home to tell her that he was not at all sure that what he had seen was in fact a real person walking a real dog.

Several witnesses told me that there are often fatal accidents along this stretch of road, and one told me that she had heard that the nearby woods are supposedly haunted by Civil War soldiers who can be seen from the road at night.

NASH

When I was asking about the various ghosts around Buckinghamshire, one witness wrote to tell me his own experience. He was unsure of the exact date of the incident, but remembered that it was at the time when the gas pipeline was being laid across the fields past Bletchley, just southwest of Milton Keynes. He thought it must have been at least twenty years ago or more, which would put it in the mid 1990's at the latest. He had a passenger with him in his car, and the day was bright and sunny. He pulled up at what was then the Nash / A421 towards Bletchley crossroads, waiting for his opportunity to pull out into the traffic (today there is a roundabout there).

He and his passenger were quietly chatting when their attention was caught by a lady on a horse trotting down the road. She was wearing Victorian style clothing and sitting side-saddle, with a small dog trotting obediently alongside.

They only had a moment to wonder at her attire and riding position, when to their horror instead of stopping at the crossroads, she simply carried on going completely oblivious and without even looking at the massive Pentus Brown and Sons lorry which was bearing down on her. The poor lorry driver obviously saw her as he braked so hard he almost jackknifed his lorry, and came within a few short yards of actually hitting the woman, her horse, and the dog.

To everyone's astonishment, neither the woman, nor the horse, nor the dog reacted at all to the commotion or the sight of a massive lorry skidding to a halt almost close enough to touch them – but carried on their way as if they were completely oblivious. The lorry driver was obviously very shocked and was swearing profusely as he set off again.

SEER GREEN

Another witness wrote in to tell their story. Many years ago, some friends of theirs had been over to visit them where they lived in Seer Green. The friends had a pleasant visit, then left in the evening to drive back to their own home in Uxbridge.

There was a husband, wife, and their two young sons in the car. The wife was driving and they had not gone very far (towards Chalfont St Giles) when suddenly a horse dashed across the road in front of them and through the thick hedge to the side. She slammed on the brakes, breathing hard at the near miss, and her two sons piped up from the back seat that they too had seen the horse.

It could conceivably just have been a runaway horse, even given the time of night, but on that particular stretch of road the hedges are just too thick and dense for a real living horse to pass through.

A421 TINGEWICK – Dual carriageway between Tingewick and Buckingham

The source story I found claims that on 17 January 2016, at 10:35 (not sure whether this is a.m or p.m), a driver travelling along the short span of dual carriageway which bypasses Tingewick saw two figures cross the road in front of him. One seemed to be quite tall, whilst the other was short and seemed to be wearing loose baggy clothing of some kind. The two figures reached the edge of the road and disappeared. At first the driver assumed there must be a hidden gateway or whatever there, but as he drew level, he realised there was absolutely nowhere the figures could have gone – since there was nothing there except a blank expanse of roadside verge.

One local farmer then came forward to tell me that their land used to be an old airfield, and that it runs alongside that stretch of road. They are aware that they have a ghost in their fields whom they refer to as the Shepherd, but in reality she thinks he is probably the ghost of a wartime pilot.

He doesn't appear very often, but every now and then they will get a distinct feeling of a presence behind them. Sometimes there will be a pervading feeling of something being wrong which they have learned to go and check out since he is always right – there *is* something urgently needing their attention. The family tends to say 'thank you' to him when this happens.

Towards Christmas time in 2017, one local person who knows she has a sensitivity to ghosts was driving along the road to drop a friend off in Tingewick after they had been out together for a Christmas meal. When they pulled up outside the friend's house, they sat chatting for about 40 mins, before the friend bade our witness good night and got out of the car. It was after 11.30pm at night but as the driver went to pull away, she strongly sensed someone sitting in the back of her car.

Glancing in her rear view mirror, she could faintly see in the dim light that someone was indeed sitting on the back seat but everytime she turned around to get a proper look, there was no one there. She carried on driving out of Tingewick and along the A421, heading towards Brackley. As she neared the roundabout, she suddenly felt the spirit move into the front seat and sit alongside her. If she used her peripheral vision she could make out that a man was now sitting in her front seat, but if she turned to look properly, there was no-one there. When she touched her hand to the gearstick, she could feel her arm grow cold with his proximity. However when they reached the roundabout to turn for Brackley, he suddenly left the car - as if he was not able to travel any further.

An older witness told me that during her childhood in Tingewick, where she had been born and raised, she and her friends from the village would run around in the woods playing. They became quite accustomed to the sound of marching soldiers coming from within the woods. This would be especially noticeable around dusk in the summer evenings, when they would hear the shouts of the men as well as the sound of them marching - always just far enough away to be out of sight. They never dared to camp out in the woods even as they got older. She told me that 8pm was their limit to be in there because after then, the place seemed less welcoming and they always sensed an uncomfortable feeling steal over them, as if they were being watched.

As she grew older, she would be driving home to the village from Bicester, and on a handful of occasions saw a misty figure cross the bypass from the woods, and then just disappear. She was never close enough to the figure to make out whether it had any distinctive look or features.

So if you are using the bypass to skirt Tingewick - keep an eye out. You might just be lucky.

TURVILLE - Dolesden Lane

The story here is a well-documented one. Mary Blandy was the daughter of Francis Blandy, a wealthy solicitor and well respected gentleman. Naturally, she was sought after as a suitable hand in marriage, but she set her cap for one Captain William Henry Cranstoun who courted her for a number of years in the late 1740's.

At first Mary's parents thought highly of William Cranstoun and encouraged him, impressed by the fact that his father was Lord Cranstoun, a Scottish peer.

However, Mary's father then received information in 1751 that Capt. Cranstoun was already married. Not surprisingly, he was absolutely furious at how his daughter had been deceived and wanted her to end the relationship. However, the fickle Captain managed to convince Mary and her mother that his marriage had been a sham which would be very shortly annulled. He made several trips to Scotland in order to get the marriage annulled, but each time there seemed to be a reason why he had not been successful in doing so.

In actual fact he had tried and failed already to annul it. In 1746 he had gone to court to legally disown the marriage but his wife denied his claims, insisting that their marriage was in fact legal and presumably providing sufficient proof to back up her claim. On 1 March 1748, she had been granted a decree in her favour, with an annuity payable by William for herself and for their daughter which would last until the daughter herself was married.

Mary's father Francis Blandy became violently ill shortly after making his feelings about the whole business known and died in August 1751. His relatives and servants were very suspicious about the sudden manner of his death and brought in the authorities. Mary was arrested on suspicion of his murder and the trial was held in February 1752.

She claimed that Captain Cranstoun had supplied her with a powdered tonic to give to her father, telling her it would make him feel more favourably about her plan to be wed to her Scottish suitor. Despite her fevered claims of innocence right to the bitter end, Mary was found guilty of murder and was sentenced to hang on 6th April 1752.

There was never any evidence that Captain Cranstoun was involved in the murder, and he himself fell ill and died later that same year.

Mary's ghost has been reported haunting the lanes around Turville and Hambleden. The most common sightings are those of the ghost of a woman in old-fashioned clothes with a rustling dress being seen on Dolesden Lane near Turville. She has also been seen riding a white horse through Churchfield Wood

I could not find any recent stories of sightings of this murderous lady's ghost.

CAMBRIDGESHIRE

ALCONBURY – North Road

There is an old tale that the road which runs between Alconbury and Alconbury West (The old Great North Road) is haunted by the spirit of a murdered drummer boy, who can be heard at sunset walking along and drumming.

Apparently, in 1796 two sailors were making the long journey home from Plymouth to Cambridgeshire. One was Gervase Matcham, the other a man called Sheppard and when the pair stopped overnight at Woodyates on the Salisbury Plain in Wiltshire, a sudden storm blew up and rattled the eves of the old Inn as they sat there supping their ale. Matcham suddenly went mad, running around the room frantically leaping over the trestles and tables, begging his friend Sheppard to save him. When Sheppard finally managed to calm him, Matcham poured out his sorry tale.

In 1780, the then much younger Matcham had enlisted in the army, and met Quartermaster Sergeant Jones, whose young son Benjamin Jones was serving as a Drummer Boy. One day, Matcham and Ben were sent off to Diddington Hall to collect money kept there for supplies from their base in Huntingdon. On the way back, they stayed overnight at Alconbury, where Matcham began to think about the large sum of money the young boy was carrying and how it might set him up for life.

He attacked the hapless lad and slit his throat, taking the money and fleeing. Eventually, as the years passed, Matcham joined the Navy and now found himself back in England and once again heading towards Huntingdon. He claimed that he had just seen the ghost of the young boy and that the ghost would not leave him alone. Matcham was duly taken to the authorities, where he was tried and found guilty of the murder of young Benjamin.

Ever since he was murdered, the tale goes on to tell us, the poor drummer boy still walks the road in Alconbury forlornly tapping away on his drum...

Of course, there are some rather major holes in this story. For one thing, why would one pay for an overnight stay in Alconbury, if one were travelling to Huntington from Diddington? For a start, the two are only 7 or 8 miles apart and easily achievable even on foot. But to get to Alconbury you would have to carry on past Huntington by another six miles - so you would not be travelling that route in the first place. Furthermore, what on earth was the ghost doing wandering off down to Wiltshire to haunt the Salisbury Plain? Why wait all those years if he was able to travel and haunt anywhere that Matcham happened to be?

Perhaps unsurprisingly, no-one came forward to say they had seen or heard the ghost. Curiously though, this same stretch of road is reportedly the haunt of a nun who steps out in front of cars and causes them to swerve, and yet another story claims that there are three ghostly cars that can sometimes be seen here crashed and burning.

B1052 BALSHAM, Wratting Road

This stretch of road is reported to be haunted by a strange creature which one local told me is known as the Shug Monkey. Other witnesses had also heard of this entity. For the most part, it appears as a large black shaggy dog in proper traditional Black Shuck style, except for the fact that its head is bald and wide-eyed, resembling the head of a monkey more than a dog. It also has a tendency to leap out in front of cars either running on all fours like a dog, or running on its hind legs like a monkey can.

One witness told me that the best place to encounter it is said to be along the lane which runs from the bottom of West Wratting Road across the fields to what used to be Padlock Farm. The lane is overgrown now, but you can just make out its route on Google Maps if you work your way back across the fields from Padlock Road towards West Wratting Road. One source says that this used to be known as Slough Hill Lane.

When our witness was at school in the 1960's, he used to cycle home to Balsham from West Wratting after visiting his friend on a Saturday night, and although he never saw anything, he would sometimes hear very strange noises late at night along there that he can't really account for but they certainly made him peddle faster.

HORSEHEATH - Money Lane

Money Lane, one witness explained to me, is a bridle path just off the B1307 opposite Park Farm, which then crosses the old railway.

Supposedly, on the night of a full moon, a disembodied voice can sometimes be heard floating along this lane saying, "pick up your spade and follow me". It's possible the tale grew up because there was a horde of Roman silver coins found along there in 1854.

Nobody had any experiences of this to give me, but one witness had heard another old tale of the witch buried in the centre of the village close to the cricket pitch. For some bizarre reason, she is known as Daddy Witch. Whenever it rains, the patch of road above the site where she is buried is said to remain dry.

B1050 LONGSTANTON

There is one source (that I could find) which claims that someone driving home to Longstanton along the B1050 once saw a shadowy figure standing at the side of the narrow road. He swung his car slightly wide to give plenty of room but as he passed the figure, he suddenly realised that where its face should have been was just a blank space. Horrified, he looked in his mirror as he swept on past only to realise the figure had disappeared completely.

Unfortunately, there is neither a date, nor an accurate location, and I have not been able to find any corroboration.

M11 - Area close to junction 13 (near Cambridge)

Apparently on 27 June 2015, a motorist travelling up the M11 watched a dark figure cross the busy motorway. The figure was walking casually as if it were completely unaware of the traffic around it. The driver was convinced that no-one corporeal could have crossed the road without an accident occurring.

I have not been able to find any other sources or accounts to corroborate this story.

A1 PETERBOROUGH - close to Wittering

There is a source story that a man and his wife were driving along the A1 close to Wittering when they suddenly saw a lady wearing what they described as '1950's clothing' and carrying a bag, who dashed across the road ahead of them onto the central reservation.

It's unclear why they thought she was a ghost and not just someone who likes to dress in older style clothing, particularly since the source story does not mention her disappearing or any such peculiar thing, it just describes what to me sound like the perfectly normal actions of a normal living person who just happened to be wearing slightly odd attire. That being said, some witnesses did however come forward to tell me that there was a lady killed along this stretch of road in the 1980s, and she has sometimes been seen standing in the central reservation.

PETERBOROUGH – Sutton Heath Road

One source says that in 2007 a man travelling along this stretch of road saw an apparition of a man driving a horse and cart cross the road ahead of him from right to left – even though there was heavy shrubbery on the side of the road which would have completely prevented any real horse and cart from passing through. He stopped to look for an explanation of what he had just seen, but there was nothing to be found.

Although no-one came forward with anything to say about that particular apparition, one witness did tell me that there used to be a hump backed bridge along that stretch of road, which went over the old railway line. Although the hump backed bridge has now been flattened out and straightened, he recalls that many years ago there used to be tales of a ghost along there, and it was a known accident black spot.

SNAILWELL – Chippenham Road

There is a story that in 2012 a man driving home in thick fog along this stretch of road on a November evening on his way home from work at 5pm encountered a U.S Airman walking slowly down the middle of the road. The apparition was clearly not corporeal, as it was glowing slightly and seemed utterly oblivious of the car and its occupant. There is unfortunately no corroboration for this somewhat eerie account.

A142 STUNTNEY

On one side of the A142 lies Stuntney Old Hall, a completely renovated Jacobean Manor House where Oliver Cromwell's parents once lived, which is now used as a sumptuous wedding and party venue, hotel, and restaurant. On the other side of the main road lies the actual village itself.

If you happen to be driving along there at dusk, you might be lucky enough to see the ghost of an old lady who hurries across the road carrying a basket.

WEST WRATTING - the junction of High Street, Mill Road, and the Common.

One source states that there is a ghost of a lady in white who can sometimes be seen walking alongside the road here, picked out by car headlights as they pass her. I was not able to find any other references to this ghost.

WHITTLESFORD - Whittlesford Road

I found an account that said this area is haunted by three gentlemen wearing Victorian style clothing. It claims this ghostly trio has been seen twice but I was unable to find any other sightings to corroborate or add to the tale.

The first witness saw these three Victorian gentlemen standing in the road but caught only a brief glimpse because their appearance startled his horse, which threw him. The source account does not give a date for this occurrence, but since the witness was riding, it is perhaps an older tale from at least the early 1900s or older.

Then in January 2005, a car driver reported three male figures dressed in Victorian clothing walking across the road in front of his car. The vehicle went straight through them, leaving the witness feeling deathly cold and very shaken.

There is also an old tale, written in 1905, which tells how in the early 1800's the villagers dressed up as ghosts to scare three lads who had decided to go ghost hunting at the church.

CHESHIRE

A529 AUDLEM – Audlem Road leading to Corbrook Court

According to one source, in October 2001 Barry Cooke and a friend were driving from Audlem, along the A529 towards Corbrook Court. It was late at night – after midnight – and they suddenly noticed a man standing in the road whom they thought was 'a bit strange looking'. As they drove past him, he seemed to bend down so that he could stare into their car. They were a little spooked to say the least, and wondered if what they had seen was a real person or a ghost.

Apparently, Barry was driving the same road, this time alone, exactly one year later and saw the figure again. Although he tried to find out if anyone else had ever seen the apparition by making a plea in the local newspapers, he had no luck. Sadly, neither have I.

BUNBURY – College Lane and School Lane

Local legend says there is a ghostly horse and rider on College Lane, leading out of Bunbury, and a ghostly dog sometimes seen on School Lane. Unfortunately – this was all I could find about them.

A50 CHURCH LAWTON – Liverpool Road West

On 9th September 2011 during the evening, a car driver saw a figure walking along the pavement with its head down. He only caught a glimpse of it picked up in the headlights of an oncoming car, but as his own headlights reached the same spot, there was no sign of the figure at all, anywhere along the road.

B5074 CHURCH MINSHULL – Swanlow Lane

On 15 December 2004 two people travelling by car along this stretch of road close to the cemetery after midnight saw the figure of a woman in a red scarf. Her face did not look natural, seeming to have dark sunken eyes as they drove past, and she was dressed in clothing from a few decades earlier. Eerily, she remained utterly motionless as the car approached her and drove by her.

KINGSLEY – Hollow Lane

The source for this story describes it as being 'on the road towards Frodsham, near the cemetery'. From the description given, I don't think it is likely to be Frodsham Cemetery, since that is on the other side of Frodsham from Kingsley. It seems more likely that it refers to the churchyard and graveyard next to St John's Parish Church, which is divided by the B5153 Hollow Lane.

In 2014 a car driver saw a hooded figure without any visible legs, by the edge of the road. The apparition drifted across the road, yet the oncoming traffic appeared to be oblivious of its presence. When I asked locally, no witnesses came forward with any recollections of this entity, although one mentioned that there are steps by the roadside along there.

KNUTSFORD – Tatton Street

This ghost was seen on 9 October 2009, at around 10.30 at night. The source account lists it as 'Tatton Mile Road' which I could not find, but there is a Tatton Street. The car driver had his car's headlights set to full beam as he drove along and the lights picked out the figure of a man standing in the road with his hand out in front of him, as if gesturing for the car to stop. The driver was looking straight at the figure, wondering whether he should stop or not, when the image inexplicably vanished right in front of his eyes.

I could not find anyone else who had experienced anything strange along this road.

TARPORLEY – (possibly) Birch Heath Road towards Tiverton

The source story says that in September 1971 Mr Presick was driving along a small lane between Tarporley and Tiverton and found himself slightly lost. To his relief, through the gathering twilight ahead, he spotted a man walking a small dog. Pulling up alongside the man, he wound his car window down and asked for directions. He noticed that the man and his dog both seemed to be straining forward as if leaning into a strong wind despite the fact that it was a completely calm night.

The man ignored his request and sensing there was something slightly odd about the pair, the driver gave up and drove on. As he left, he glanced back in his mirror only to find both man and dog had completely disappeared.

I was unable to find any other sightings of this ghost.

WYBUNBURY – A51 London Road

In October 1996 the Nantwich Chronicle carried the story of Trevor Madline, who was travelling along this stretch of road in his car. He came across a hitchhiker wearing vintage leather motorcycle clothing, but didn't think too much of it because there was a vintage motorcycle meet in the area at the time. He stopped and offered the man a lift, who gratefully accepted and climbed into the passenger seat. To his astonishment, a few miles further on he realised his passenger had completely disappeared from the moving vehicle.

There are no other sightings of this hitchhiker as far as I could find, although it does follow the classic hitchhiker ghost modus operandi.

CORNWALL

BUDE

There is an account of a car seen around the lanes of Bude in 1984, which was there one moment following the car in front and which had vanished the next. The driver believed he might have seen something paranormal and speculated as to how often ghost cars are actually seen and people don't realise it.

Personally, I'd be more likely to speculate that it had turned off into a gateway, unless I had taken the time to go back and ascertain there were no gateways or turns?

A30 BOLVENTOR

Curiously though, and not so far away as the crow flies, there is a tale from the 1970's, (when the A30 was still a small A road and not the multiple laned highway it is now), of another man who also encountered a ghostly car. It overtook him as he drove along and he had time to notice that it was an old fashioned open topped car, with four young men in it singing boisterously. Some years later, he met another driver who claimed to have seen exactly the same car and occupants just the night before, but some miles away from the first location.

Nevertheless, these tales give off a strong impression of 'urban myth' and I was not able to find any corroborating witnesses.

CALSTOCK

One source claims that the roads around this small village are haunted by a group of miners wearing old fashioned outfits and carrying candles. When I asked, however, no-one local came forward who knew anything of the tale.

CAMBORNE

One author described the experience of a witness who had written to him. She had been walking her dog up the steep and narrow road 'off Tehidy Road which runs alongside Red River and then up to join the main road'.

About 20 yards in front of her she suddenly noticed a lady who was just mounting her bicycle, about to ride down the hill towards her. She glanced down for a moment to pull her dog in close and out of the way but when she looked back up, the woman and her bicycle had disappeared. There was literally nowhere she could have gone, without either passing the witness, or turning around and pushing her bicycle up the steep hill.

This was in broad daylight, in the middle of the afternoon, and the cyclist was wearing a grey cardigan and a hat.

B3266 CAMELFORD TO BODMIN

One writer says he was driving along the Bodmin to Camelford Road one November afternoon in 1984, when he saw the ghost of a cyclist. The Bodmin to Camelford road is most likely the B3266, but seeing as the two towns are around 13 miles apart, this account does seem rather unnecessarily vague if it's true. Surely he would remember where exactly along that length he had seen something?

He states that visibility was good and he saw the cyclist quite clearly coming towards him down the road. However, one second he was there and the very next, he simply was not. The author turned his van around and went to check on what he had seen. He could find no trace of any cyclist even though he was sure there had not been enough time for the cyclist to reach the next side turning along.

Several witnesses told me that they had lived along this road for a great number of years, and none of them had ever heard or seen anything of this ghostly cyclist. One witness said that there is a gentleman who regularly cycles that route and has done so for years; he wondered if it might be a case of mistaken identity.

Strangely, one witness told me she *had* seen a ghostly cyclist, but further up the road towards Davidstow, in 2017. He was riding an older style bicycle with a blue parcel strapped onto the back of it. As she glanced at him and took in these details he suddenly disappeared right in front of her eyes!

One lady told me that there is another ghost close to this road at the nearby Stannon China Clay works, close to the Stannon Stone Circle. Apparently this ghost is known as the Glug Woman, and to see her is sure to bring bad luck in her wake. Her husband and his mates, when much younger, had gone up there messing around one night and on their way back down from the hill, he glanced in his rearview mirror and saw a lady in a ragged grey outfit. He described her as wearing a hat and carrying an old fashioned lantern. He got out of his car and looked for her, but there was no-one to be seen. The poor man had a terrible run of bad luck after that which lasted some years.

Another witness came forward to say she had heard of a hitchhiker ghost along that stretch of road, and yet another explained that her mother is a paranormal investigator who once saw an elderly man crossing the road ahead of her as she returned home from a ghost hunt at Bodmin Gaol. She slowed her car down to give him time to cross, glanced away for a split second, and when she glanced back he had disappeared..

Curiously, another lady wrote to me to say that one summer afternoon at about 4.30pm, she was driving from St Breward to her job in Camelford. Her route took her down one of the tiny side lanes just off the B3266 and she had just passed the entrance to Pendavey Farm. She glanced in her mirror and was astonished to see a young man running down the road behind her car. He was very slim and lean in build, and was wearing a collarless shirt and brown trousers with braces on. He chased after her car for a moment or two, but then just disappeared even as she looked at him.

She said that funnily, the thing she remembered most about him was how very clean he looked! She thought the attire he was wearing was reminiscent of the late 1800s or early 1900s.

She also recalled that a Frenchman was once killed close to here riding his bicycle, and wondered if that had anything to do with the ghost I was originally asking about.

B3274 CARTHEW to St Austell

A lady wrote to me to tell me about her own harrowing experience with a haunted road. She was a passenger in a friend's car and they were travelling along the B3274 heading into St Austell. All of a sudden, with no warning at all, a man wearing a tan coloured jacket suddenly stepped out in front of the car on the passenger side where she was sitting.

As she screamed in horror, the car hit him (there was really no chance for him to be avoided, he literally seemed to step out of nowhere straight in front of the car) and he rolled up over the bonnet in front of her and dropped out of sight back on the passenger side of the vehicle.

The car driver panicked and slammed the car brakes on, coming to a skidding stop. As soon as they were stopped however, it quickly became apparent that the driver had only reacted by slamming the brakes on because our witness had scream so awfully. The driver had not seen anyone, nor felt the impact on the car.

There was, in fact, no man lying in the road by the car either.

A39 DAVIDSTOW

A gentleman mentioned to me that a friend of his can see the ghosts of three hanged men at the turning on the A39 just north of Davidstowe, which heads towards Tintagel. He says that at night, apparitions can regularly be seen at that junction.

HELSTONE (near Camelford)

One author writes of his own experience in October 2001, on the roads between Helston and St Teath. He describes the road as being a lane, so I am guessing he was on the B3267. It was around 4.30pm, in broad daylight with good clear weather. He saw a grey van heading towards him in the narrow lane, so pulled over into a suitable passing place to allow it through. As he waited for a moment, watching the van approach, it suddenly vanished.

LISKEARD – Between Park Fenton and Lake Lane

A lady wrote to me to tell me of her own experience of the supernatural. She explained, "In May 1990 I travelled to Liskeard in my camper van to visit a friend. He was living with part of the so-called 'Peace Convoy' on the old Maudlin Farm site that ran to the south of Lake Lane, Liskeard. I parked up nearish to his coach, right on the edge of the encampment.

"That evening I decided to cook us a meal so I went off to my van. It was dark by then, the curtains in my van were closed and I was playing music as I cooked. I distinctly remember it was Sinead O'Connor, singing 'Nothing Compares 2 U' and I was cooking spaghetti bolognaise.

"Out of the blue I was aware of a strange feeling. Somehow I just knew 'something' was swarming over my van, sort of inspecting it – and me. Not something physical, it felt more like some kind of electric energy, but I knew I was safe if I stayed inside.

"I felt that whatever it was wasn't harmful, just inquisitive, although I was still petrified. However I couldn't leave the van, or look out, as I didn't want to see what was out there. The 'energy' remained for around a minute and then it was gone. I immediately ran out of my van to my friend's coach to share the story and said to him, "Something really weird just happened!"

"My friend's face turned white – completely ashen. He responded, "Don't tell me.... I know what happened." He was clearly a bit agitated."

My witness told him he could not possibly know what had just happened to her, and proceeded to tell him. It turned out he'd originally put his coach exactly where she was parked and had a similar experience, although he'd fallen to the floor. He said that another person had also parked in the same spot and the same feeling happened to him, but he looked out and saw red eyes looking in. He subsequently moved his vehicle to another spot too.

She explained, "My friend then told me we were actually living on an old abattoir site. My van was parked right next to the (now derelict) slaughterhouse ... it was literally just a few feet from my van. Indeed, I have found mention of a slaughterhouse on a 1963 map of Liskeard and it's right where my van was parked.

"It turned out that several other people had apparently also seen the red eyes and another person had seen a procession of ghostly figures (although it's unknown whether they were animal figures or human) down nearby Lake Lane. Needless to say I immediately moved my van and I didn't have any other problems during the few days I was there."

A30 MITCHELL

The original story I found dated back to 1965, when the A30 would have been a much quieter road than it is now as it would have been the old A30 before the modern day bypass was built in its place. Apparently, a car driver saw a young girl dressed in Victorian clothing run across the road in front of a lorry. It looked to him as if the lorry must have hit the girl, but neither the lorry nor any pedestrians reacted at all, leading him to believe he had just seen a ghost.

One witness wrote to tell me about his own experience, but on the new A30 just as it passes the town. He, his mother and a friend were travelling home from Treliske hospital in early 2016 after being with his son who had unfortunately been in an accident earlier that same day. It was late at night, probably a little after midnight, but there were still other cars on the road.

Suddenly, they all saw a dark human shaped shadow drift across the carriageway in front of their car. The sight of it caused his friend, who was the driver that night, to slam his brakes on hard. The shadow seemed to just drift right through the crash barrier as if it wasn't there. It passed onto the other carriageway, where the lights of another car coming towards them should have illuminated it if anything solid was there. Instead, there was nothing at all to be seen. All three of them saw the shape, but could not think of a rational explanation for what they had seen.

PENZANCE

There is a legend that a coach drawn by headless horses sometimes rattles its way through the older streets in Penzance, and that to see it is unlucky.

I rather suspect that it is just that though - a legend. It was probably originally told to keep people tucked up fearfully in their houses at nights whilst local smugglers or ne'er-do-wells got on with their night's work!

B3314 PORT ISAAC

The source story I found described how a lady driving out of Port Isaac and heading along the B3314 in the rough direction of Tintagel pulled over to the side as she thought she had just hit an animal which had darted out in front of her car. She looked in her rear view mirror to see if she could see it laying in the road, intending to get out and try and do something for the poor thing.

Instead, to her horror, she saw a woman standing there staring at her. She just had time to realise the woman was wearing Victorian style clothing when the apparition disappeared. Needless to say, she stayed in the car and drove off!

One witness told me that she had never heard of a ghost along that stretch of the B3314, but further south along it near Trewornan Bridge there is supposed to be a carriage complete with headless horses.

Another witness came forward to say that in April 2018 her son had seen something on the B3314 just outside Delabole. He was riding home from work on his scooter at about 11pm at night, when he suddenly saw a white haired figure in the road in front of him.

The figure was so close that he had no opportunity to brake or swerve and his scooter seemed to hit it. Shocked, he looked behind him in his rear view mirror and could see the figure still standing there. Probably braver than I would have been, he pulled up and put his scooter on its side stand. Turning round to call out to the person, he discovered to his horror there was nothing there. Not surprisingly, he was still very shaken up when he arrived home.

A3058 QUINTRELL DOWNS

I found a source story which stated that a couple caught in heavy stop/start traffic on the A3058 by Quintrell Downs in early 2001 watched in idle boredom as a middle aged, ordinary looking man wearing dark trousers and a pullover and carrying something in his hands, crossed the road between the lines of cars ahead of them. Boredom, that is, until the figure reached the opposite kerb and simply vanished into thin air!

Another witness wrote to tell me of his own experience quite close to there, on the A392 between Hendra Holiday park and where it crosses the A3058 at Quintrell Downs. He explained that this happened around twelve years ago, which would put it in around 2006 or so. It was around 11.30 at night and he was driving from the Newquay direction towards Quintrell Downs. His friend was with him in the car, sitting in the passenger seat.

As they came up to the turn off for Chapel Farm they saw a man walking down the middle of the road heading towards them. He was wearing a black suit and pale coloured shirt, resembling a tuxedo or formal evening wear. He had an extremely pale face. As they approached and passed him they slowed right down for safety, but our witness says he was feeling annoyed that someone would be stupid enough to walk in the middle of the road at night like that. As they passed, he glanced in his mirror, but the man had disappeared.

His friend started shouting in a panicky voice, "Oh my God! Did you see that? There was a guy!" He agreed with her but told her to quieten down, as actually he was trying not to panic himself. They took the road towards St Columb Minor, then headed back towards the Treloggan area of Newquay to pick up his girlfriend from her workplace at a tavern.

They picked his girlfriend up at midnight and both explained to her what they had just encountered. She thought it might just have been some drunk wandering down the road, who was perhaps trying to find his way back to the holiday park. They decided to go back and see if they could see him.

They drove back, but found themselves unable to get to the same spot. In the intervening hour or so there had been an accident close to Trencreek and the A392 was shut because the two vehicles had collided head on. They had to turn around and go back the way they came and although they did stop and ask one of the bystanders whether they had seen the man in the suit, the drivers were too shocked really to talk about what had happened.

A few weeks after this incident the passenger from that night in the car, who worked in a local shop, was chatting to one of her regular customers, and was told that there was a death close to that spot some years ago when a young man returning from a party was killed on the train track.

They have often wondered in the intervening years whether it was his ghost they saw that night, and whether the two cars actually collided because one of them swerved to avoid hitting him.

Curiously another witness told me that when she does the school run, walking along Quintrell Road to Nansledan School, she often hears the sound of disembodied footsteps behind her.

Another witness came forward to say she didn't know anything about that particular area, but her father (who passed away in around 2007) used to talk about the headless horseman ghost he had seen down towards Trevellas.

B3306 ST JUST – close to the Lands End Airport

This apparition was seen in 1994. A couple who were holidaying in the area were driving their camper van along the B3306 close to the Lands End Airport. It was around 7pm on a Sunday night and Alison, who was driving, suddenly caught sight of a figure out of the corner of her eye. She slowed down to pass the person as their van was quite wide and bulky, but then couldn't see the figure anymore. Before she had time to gain speed again or really think about what had just happened, a silvery white shape drifted across the road in front of them, moved up into the air to a height of around 15 feet above ground, and then dropped down out of sight behind a hedge.

Her boyfriend, who was sitting in the passenger seat, also saw it and joked that they might just have seen a ghost. When they arrived at their campsite they asked their friend whether he had seen anything as he had been travelling behind them in his own camper van. He too had seen the white shape rise and then swoop down behind the hedge.

Ghost, or Barn Owl on the hunt? They show up as silvery white shapes crossing lanes at night...

A3071 ST JUST – towards Tregeseal

It is said that on stormy nights, you can hear the sound of a carriage and horses along this stretch of road. I could not find anyone who has actually heard it though, although I guess there's not much call these days for walking lonely stretches of rural road in the middle of a storm!

A39 ST KEW HIGHWAY

This village is actually bisected by the A39, and one witness tantalisingly told me that he had heard people say this stretch of road is haunted. When I tried to follow it up with him he declined to give any more detail sadly. Another witness chimed in to say they had heard of that too.

CUMBRIA

A6 BARROCK GILL – Low Hesket near Carlisle

This is a very gruesome tale. Allegedly, on this lonely stretch of road, a notorious local highwayman was hung for his crimes. Unfortunately for him the rope was not tight enough and the drop not sufficient to kill him, and he was left dangling alive from the rope crying and moaning. A passing coachman heard his cries and took pity on the wretched soul, ending the man's suffering with a shot from his pistol.

Supposedly his cries and moans can still be heard.

I wrote to the nearby pub, the Rose and Crown, and they were very helpful with their response. They explained that in 1777 the highwayman John Whitfield was gibbeted (not hung) alive on Barrock Hill outside of Carlisle. Gibbeting a man was to hang him in a small metal cage which enclosed his body, and despite popular assumption was actually usually only done with corpses – not with live people. The Rose and Crown sent me the following quote, written around a hundred years after the event:

"Although there are several Gallows Hills in Cumberland and Westmorland, there only seems to be one place which has retained any particular story, and it is thus told in Mr. William Andrews' third book relating to punishments:- 'It has been asserted by more than one local chronicler that John Whitfield, of Cotehill, a notorious North-Country highwayman, about 1768 was gibbeted alive on Barrock. He kept the countryside in a state of terror, and few would venture out after nightfall for fear of encountering him. He shot a man on horseback in open daylight; a boy saw him commit the crime, and was the means of his identification and conviction. It is the belief in the district that Whitfield was gibbeted alive, that he hung for several days in agony, and that his cries were heartrending, until a mail coachman passing that way put him out of his misery by shooting him.'

"There is a contemporary record of the execution to be found in the St. James's Chronicle, for August 12th, 1768, as follows: 'Wednesday, John Whitfield, for murdering William Cockburn on the Highway, near Armithwaite, was executed at Carlisle, and afterwards hung in Chains near the Place where the Fact was committed.' It will be seen that the record makes no mention of the culprit having been put into his iron cage when alive but rather says that he was executed, and *afterwards* hung in the gibbet, and one can only hope that there is nothing beyond tradition to support the assertion."

It was actually very common to take the body of a murderer back to the site of the murder, and there display it hung in gibbet chains. These chains would sometimes hang for decades as the corpse slowly rotted away. Gibbet chains were sometimes more like iron cages which closely enclosed the body, so that it was forced to remain upright as it slowly rotted. Other times, they were chains hooked through the strongest muscles and joints of the dead body in order to preserve it in its natural shape as it hung for as long as possible.

Let's hope that the poor man was actually dead when he was put in his gibbet and this is just a fanciful story which arose afterwards. There is of course a lingering doubt that he could conceivably have revived somewhat if his execution at Carlisle was botched, only to find himself already gibbeted.

BARROW IN FURNESS – Clive Street

There is a report that on a rainy night in 2008 a man and his daughter were driving along Clive Street, which is not far from the Docks Museum, when a man crossed the road in front of them from left to right. The driver slowed his car down a little to give the man time to cross the road, but even as he did so the figure just vanished from sight right in front of the car. Both the driver and his daughter clearly saw the man disappear, and even though they stopped the car and looked around, there was no-one to be seen.

I haven't found anyone else who has encountered anything strange in this area.

A685 KIRKBY STEPHEN – between the town and Ravenstonedale

There is a local legend that the evil Lord Wharton was struck blind (some say by God, for punishment for his sins) as he travelled home and as a result his ghost, still dressed in his finery but looking bedraggled, now wanders about on this stretch of road, hoping to find the mercy in death that he never showed anyone in life.

There is a possibility this refers to Thomas Wharton – 1st Baron Wharton (1495 – 1568), who was much hated locally since he had the town of Wharton demolished because it was spoiling his view of the valley.

LEECE

Leece has its own strange story to tell. A couple driving through the village one evening had to quickly stop their car, to avoid hitting the large black creature that was calmly sitting in the middle of the road and blocking their passage. They could not give any explanation for what it could have been, because even seated it was around 6 feet tall with bright yellow eyes.

DERBYSHIRE

A511 BRETBY - Mount Road and Ashby Road East

On February 4th 2015 the Derby Telegraph reported the following account, from a lady called Lisa Fisher, who was recounting what she had seen on Monday 2nd.

She was driving towards Bretby Hall around 2pm in broad daylight, and had just turned into the lane off Ashby Road that leads up to the Hall itself. This would be the lane by Keepers Cottage Lodge.

As she turned into the lane she noticed a young woman with black hair standing with a bicycle by the side of the road a short way ahead. The woman was dressed in old fashioned clothes - a floral fitted dress and a hair net. The bike itself was quite old-fashioned, with a wicker basket on the handlebars. The lady seemed to watch the car as it drove past, but the driver thought nothing of it really until she glanced in the rear view mirror after passing the figure, only to find she had disappeared.

On February 26th of the same year, the newspaper carried a second report from a lady called Janet Fielding.

Janet was driving down Mount Road, which is about half a mile or so from the first sighting, and on the other side of the Hall near the Garden Centre at the end of that lane. It was around 4pm and raining quite heavily. She noticed a lady walking by the side of the road. The lady was again black-haired, wearing a floral dress and a hair net. As Janet passed, the lady turned and stared at the car in a way that made Janet feel slightly creeped out. It was also noticeably incongruous to be wearing a floral dress out in the rain.

I haven't been able to find any other accounts.

BURBAGE BRIDGE – Layby on Ringinglow Road

This remote and picturesque road runs across the moors, and there is a popular beauty spot with two parking areas at Burbage Bridge.

There is a report that in December 2016 two people parked up intending to stay overnight in the layby in their camper van. They were just settling themselves in for the evening when they distinctly heard the sound of a horse's shod hooves immediately outside their vehicle, even though there had been no sound of its approach which surely in such a quiet and remote location there would have been.

The sound seemed to go away for a while, then return, and this time something large seemed to brush up against the side of their van, rocking it slightly. They climbed into the front seats of the van and drove a short distance away, then turned the van around to shine its lights across the moors to see what had been bothering them – but there was nothing to be seen.

I haven't found anyone else who has experienced anything along that stretch of road.

A514 CASTLE GRESLEY – Cadley Hill

In winter 2011 a motorcyclist approaching the Cadley Hill roundabout at about 10pm noticed a white 1970s style car heading towards him and turning on the roundabout. Turning his head to watch and make sure the car was not going to cross his own trajectory, he was just in time to see the vehicle vanish right in front of his astonished eyes.

CHARLESWORTH – Chapel Brow and Monks Road

The original story I found stated that in the late 1990's, four people travelling in a car heading towards Charlesworth down Monks Road towards Chapel Brow, watched the semi transparent figure of a lady described as 'wearing Victorian dress complete with ruff' cross the road and pass through a gateway.

Now this in itself contains an intriguing inaccuracy. Ruffs are pieces of clothing which were very popular in England in the Elizabethan age - centuries before the Victorians. Their original purpose was to be an article of clothing worn around the neck, which could be removed and laundered separately from the rest of the garment, and thus served a role rather akin to a fashionable 'bib' in being designed to keep the clothes underneath it clean. Over time its form and significance developed, becoming much bigger and more elaborate and sometimes made out of expensive lace materials. At one time in the fashion, the bigger and more elaborate the ruff the higher social standing of the wearer was considered to be. The fashion waned over time, and by the early 1600s had largely started to disappear.

So either our ghost was not wearing a ruff, but perhaps a lace collar more appropriate to Victorian dress which someone has incorrectly named as a ruff, or she was not wearing Victorian dress but the witness just guessed it as such, or else someone somewhere along the repetition of the story has mixed up Victorian with Elizabethan. It might seem an unimportant detail of fashion - but it sets the possible dates for our ghost nearly three hundred years apart.

Local witnesses were able to tell me that they had heard of a tunnel leading from the house at the top of Chapel Brow through to the church yard on Monks Road. They thought the house might once have been an Inn named something like 'The Coffin and Cradle'.

From this description, I was able to ascertain that there was indeed an Inn occupying the site of what is now Nos 44-46 Town Lane which was called 'The Cradle and Coffin'. Town Lane leads into Chapel Brow. I was also able to find that there was an underground tunnel from this pub into the Chapel's graveyard, which was on Chapel Brow. The tunnel has now collapsed, but one witness recalled that as a child of around 7 years of age they had tried to venture into it, even though there wasn't very much of it left. They got scared of the dark eerie passage though, and bolted before venturing too far.

One witness remembered being told that coffins used to be made in the upstairs attic room of No 46 Town Lane, and once completed they would be lowered down the outside of the building to a waiting horse and cart using ropes and pulleys. It seems very likely that is the reason for the strange name for the pub – since a cradle is another name for a pulley system.

Another witness told me that there had been some gruesome murders on High Lane which branches off from the junction of Town Lane and Chapel Brow.

It seems that there was a 62 year old farm labourer named Albert Edward Burrows who lived on High Lane. He had a bigamous marriage with a young lass called Hannah Calladine during the First World War whilst working in the munitions factory. In December 1919, once she bore his child, she arrived on his doorstep determined to live with him whether he liked it or not, bringing with her a daughter from a previous relationship. He had been found out for his lack of honesty, and had served a short prison sentence before the courts ordered him to look after his mistress and child. Not surprisingly, his poor wife moved out of the house in disgust. She then claimed maintenance from him, leaving him unable to make ends meet on his meagre wages trying to support two dependents and the children.

The story says that on 11th January 1920 he took Hannah and their son for a day out on Symmondley Moor. I'm not sure about the timing of this, since if she only arrived in December how was there time for a court case and a prison sentence?

Whatever the truth of the dates, once he got them up on the moors he murdered them and threw their bodies down an abandoned mineshaft. The following day he disposed of Hannah's young daughter in the same way. Somehow, he patched things up with his wife and they returned to living together. For the next three years Burrows callously wrote to Hannah's mother pretending that she was still alive.

On 4th March 1923 police received a report of a missing 4-year-old boy, Tommy Wood, who lived close to the Burrows' house. For several days, police and neighbours searched for the boy, even employing trained Bloodhounds to try and follow his scent. Burrows was questioned by police on 10th March, when he gave a statement which roused their suspicion that he was trying to plant a trail of false evidence to lead them to believe Tommy had drowned in the heavily flooded brook.

They found witnesses who had seen Burrows with Tommy, and when they interviewed him again on Monday 12th, he changed his statement, saying he had taken young Tommy out rabbit catching on the moors but Tommy had left to go home alone. The police decided to search out on the moor and soon discovered the sexually assaulted body of the missing boy hidden in the abandoned mineshaft. Burrows was seen watching the proceedings from a hidden spot on the moor, and a crowd of angry villagers and police chased after him. He was captured and arrested and the police continued to excavate the air-shaft. Eight weeks later in May they discovered the remains of Hannah and her two children.

Burrows was found guilty of his heinous crimes and was

hanged on 8th August 1923 at Nottingham Gaol. One wonders if it was the ghost of Hannah which was seen on the road? As a poor farmer's wife in late 1919, she was unlikely to be wearing the latest fashions, so was perhaps more likely to dressed in a more conservative, Victorianesque type dress? Perhaps with a small lace collar?

DERBY - Agard Street

In January 1862, Eliza Barrow was beaten up by her boyfriend, local boxer Richard Thorley who at the time was aged 26. He believed she had been flirting with some of the soldiers at the nearby garrison. Although this wasn't the first time he had been violent towards her, she decided it would be the last and broke up with him, returning to her home and shutting him out.

Later that night, furious at her defiance, he broke in and slit her throat with a razor. He was convicted of her murder and hanged in April of the same year outside nearby Derby Gaol. It is said that his ghost can still be seen wandering this lane wearing chains and dressed in blue.

I haven't been able to find any actual sightings of him.

DERBY - Ascot Drive

Curiously, this road is supposed to have both a headless man haunting it, and a vampire who smells like rotting fruit! I haven't been able to find any detail on either haunting, and certainly no-one has come forward with their own experiences, or even any suspicious puncture wounds..

DERBY - Chester Green

Chester Green is an area within the city of Derby, just north of the city centre. There is a tale that the sound of a Roman army marching can be heard here. This kind of urban myth always raises suspicion with me. How many of us could *really* listen to the sound of marching men and determine from sound alone what army and what era we were listening to? There is a street called Roman Road in the area though, so perhaps this is an old folk memory from the area that has been handed down?

Whatever the truth, it is hidden in the mists of time now as I could not find any recent accounts.

A623 EYAM - Between Eyam and A6 Chapel en le Frith bypass

The original story I found was that in June 2013 a car driver became uncomfortable when his own vehicle was tailgated along a country road by a dark, older model sports car. He was getting quite annoyed by the arrogant driver behind him, but as they reached the A6, the sports car accelerated and overtook him, much to his relief.

A short lived relief though, because just a short distance ahead of him, the sports car suddenly disappeared. He was left shaken and unable to give a rational explanation for the experience. I could not find anyone else who had seen anything on that particular stretch of road.

B6521 EYAM - towards Stoney Middleton

Every report I could find of this haunting lists it the same way: that a squeaky bicycle with a ringing bell has been heard approaching various witnesses at speed. The witnesses move out of the way and turn to see where the sound is coming from, but nothing can be seen. All the reports say that a few people have reported spotting the phantom cyclist, who quickly vanishes from view.

Sadly, none of the reports say who has reported it, or when, or to whom - leading me to think this is just an oft repeated urban myth. I was not able to find any actual accounts of this phenomenon.

HANDLEY

The tale of this ghost or entity, is a little strange and creepy to say the least. Sometime in the 1970s Dilys Twyford and her three friends were driving through Handley in the evening, when they suddenly all saw what looked like a young child sized person wearing a dirty white smock type garment standing at the side of the road. They couldn't be certain quite what it was in terms of age or gender, because the thing was not only headless, but was waving its arms about in a weird wobbling way – as if there were no bones or joints in them.

One witness told me that he used to have to ride his motorbike down this road on his way to work in Matlock. Very often, he would get a strange feeling as he rode along that stretch. He described it as a sort of 'off' feeling – like a heavy depressive atmosphere that would clear as soon as he hit the open road a little further on. The feeling was so prevalent that for the summer of 2016, he took to riding his bike round the longer way round to avoid the stretch of road.

A couple of witnesses came forward who remembered being told the tale of Peggy Lantern, an alleged ghost in the surrounding area and nearby villages, when they were children. The story went that Peggy, heartbroken when her fiance ditched her for another, went off one night to jump off the bridge and kill herself.

Having reached the bridge she changed her mind, and decided to go on home. Unfortunately, as she crossed the railway line, she was struck by a train and killed. The only whole part they found was the smashed lantern she had been carrying to light her way.

The thing that always bothers me with that kind of myth is – how does anyone know she changed her mind, or what she was intending in the first place? Surely if she had said to someone, "Right, I'm off out to throw myself off the bridge", they would have stopped her from ever going out in the first place? She didn't survive to tell anyone why she was out or what subsequently happened, so all we really know for sure from that story is that she was out, and was struck by a train. To complicate the myth a little further, one of the five steam locomotives that ran the line in that area was called Peggy.

As you leave Handley Lane and join Clay Lane closer to Clay Cross, there is a small turning called Mill Lane. Close to it is the tunnel entrance for the railway line. One witness told me that as a young man, he used to walk down Mill Lane frequently and on numerous occasions he would hear weird noises and sounds coming out of the tunnel after dark. It would have been in the early 1960s and the sounds he could hear were the sounds of someone quietly sobbing. It would scare him so much he would sing loudly to drown out the sound and sometimes would just speed up and literally run away, even though in those days the lane was pitch dark.

On one horrible occasion, just as the quiet sobbing started up, he felt a hand gently stroke the back of his hair. As he says, that night, "I ran like the devil".

B6001 HASSOP – Eyre Arms public house, and road passing the pub

Supposedly this stretch of road has quite a plethora of ghosts: a Cavalier soldier whom motorists sometimes have to swerve to avoid, a horse drawn carriage, and a mysteriously disappearing pedestrian into whom a car crashed in the 1980s.

Sadly, I have been unable to find any more detail than that on any of the hauntings, and no-one came forward with any actual sightings along the road.

A6013 LADYBOWER RESERVOIR

The source story I had found for the A6013 stated that a motorcyclist came across a horse pulling a cart with a high back and sides, being led by a man holding a large whip. As the biker slowed to overtake the cart he was momentarily blinded by an approaching car. From this, we can assume the encounter must have taken place at night. When his vision had returned to normal after a few seconds, he discovered that the cart had vanished, even though there was nowhere it could have turned off or been concealed.

When I asked for witness accounts, one lady came forward to tell me that on Christmas Day evening in 2003 her and her husband were driving home when they both suddenly saw the apparition of a bride standing beside the road on Snakes Pass, just past the reservoir. They both saw it and both exclaimed out loud, "What's that?" at the strange figure as they passed. They have never been able to figure out a logical explanation for what they saw that night, even though they were left quite shaken and spoke about it afterwards.

B587 LOUNT – Nottingham Road, near the Household Recycling centre.

In the early 1980s, one account claims that a driver thought he had run over a teenaged boy who ran out in front of his car, leaving him no time to take evasive action. A search of the area found nothing - not even any damage to the vehicle. I haven't been able to find any information other than this simple statement.

There are so many of these types of vague accounts of hitting something that I can't help but wonder if they are all urban myths grown up from one or two actual accounts from elsewhere.

SMISBY - Forties Lane

Forties Lane is a quiet rural lane which is quite heavily tree-lined in places. There is a tale from 1967 which describes a ghost seen walking the lane wearing a long length open jacket with many small buttons, paired with a waistcoat, tie, short trousers with stockings and a top hat. This probably describes the fashions of the mid to late 1700's into early 1800's.

Curiously - the report describes the ghost as 'walking in silence'. It seems a strange thing to comment on, as I really don't see many reports of ghosts who walk along chattering or making much noise!

I haven't been able to find any actual accounts of sightings of him, though.

WHALEY BRIDGE

The original source story I found told of the ghost of an old lady seen in the back of a taxi in 1974. She was wearing a black coat of some sort with a white blouse and sporting a black bow. The taxi driver only noticed her as he was driving. He did not notice her get into the car, nor get out of it, since when he pulled over and turned around to speak to his mysterious passenger she had disappeared.

When I asked whether anyone else had experienced anything paranormal in the area I got a lot of interesting answers. One man remembered that in his childhood there was talk of a dark female figure who haunted the road by Cadster Wood. Another lady came forward to tell me that her father had actually seen the female ghost at Cadster Woods. Yet another witness recalled that many years ago the farmer near Cadster Woods said he had spoken to the ghost and was shunned by the local folk because of it. One person thought that the ghost was actually known as the Cadster Boggart.

Another witness told me of a ghost that haunts close to the A6 to the north of Whaley Bridge in an area known as Disley Tops. There is a standing stone there called the Murder Stone and he said he had seen the ghost of a man there. The stone is so called following the callous murder of William Wood there in July 1823, who was walking home from market with a sum of money in his pocket, and whose murderers stove his skull in using stones. There are apparently legends about the Murder Stone, such as if you lay fresh flowers there in the evening, they will have been removed by morning, or if you try to fill in the hollow in the ground next to it, the next day it will once again be smooth and empty.

One lady told me that even today, she won't drive up over Disley Tops if she is on her own. However, the landowner near the Murder Stone told me that she is out on her land at all times of day and night around there and has never seen or felt anything.

There was another account given to me of a local tale from years ago of a headless horseman in the same area.

Yet another gentleman wrote to say, "I was driving home in the early hours about 3am when I was twenty years old, past the big lay by going up Long Hill around the tight left bend. There's a wood on your left and there was a large ball of light which was lighting the whole wood up in a blue colour. I stopped the car and wound my window [down] to see if there was any one [there with it] and there was no one it was just floating along. It was about four feet tall. I spoke to my brother about it the next day and he'd seen it going over the fields near to where Shallcross Manor used to stand".

From his description, it is apparent he was driving on the A5004 Buxton Road at the time, heading to the south away from Whaley Bridge. He told me this must have been in 1993 as he recalled he was driving in his red Volkswagen Golf GTI when it happened.

A lady responded, saying her mother had seen the same thing on the opposite side of the fields where the old manor used to be (it was torn down in 1968) around fifty years ago, by the 'Swingfield' on Elnor Lane. Yet another lady recalled always feeling very nervous around that same spot when she used to play there as a child – the fields around the manor itself were no problem, but the spot near Elnor Lane and the woods used to frighten her.

I was then told that the behind the 'Swingfield' up Elnor Lane were once the engine house and work sheds for the High Peak & Cromford railway line, complete with a winch house to pull up and lower down the railway carriages transporting coal and quarried stones from one canal line to the other.

Another witness recalled stories from his childhood of a ghostly soldier riding a horse up the old Manor Road, as well as there being a headless dog and the ghost of a woman in white, carrying a bowl of blood! Just to the north of the old site of the Shallcross Manor is Bings Wood, and another witness recalled being told stories of a faceless male spirit who haunted there.

A6187 WINNATS PASS

There is a story that this lonely windswept pass is haunted by the ghosts of two lovers, who were murdered here by robbers in times long past.

I spoke to one witness who had often walked this pass, and had sometimes heard footsteps on the wind and the sounds of cries from the rocks above the road.

DEVON

CHERITON CROSS – route of the old A30

There is an account that one October evening in 1969, a Mr Potter was driving along the A30 near Cheriton cross, heading east, when his headlights picked out a pale coloured Great Dane dog standing stock still in the middle of the road ahead of him. Although he braked sharply, he was afraid he had hit it, but when he got out to look there was nothing.

Clearly, if it had been a real Great Dane he had hit, he would have known about it as that would have been a heck of a thump. Unfortunately, this seems to have been a one off sighting. I always wonder with this sort of sighting though, if in other times this might have been classed as a sighting of a Shuck? They're more usually cited as dark coloured, but still?

A379 GARA BRIDGE – Modbury Road

In 1967 a gentleman driving from Modbury to Gara Bridge saw an old 1920s style Daimler Landaulette approaching him from the other direction. Just before the vehicles should have met and passed each other, the Daimler disappeared.

A week later, the same driver saw the same car again, and again it repeated its vanishing act. Allegedly, he was told by other locals that it was quite a common occurrence.

It seems the haunting went on for a while, as it was seen again in 1975, but unfortunately I have not had anybody come forward who has seen it since then which tends to suggest the apparition might have faded away.

A386 GREAT TORRINGTON

There is a published account that in 1976 a family were staying in a holiday cottage on the A386 as it passes through Great Torrington. On their last day, the family was woken just before dawn by the sound of what they described as a group of motorcyclists going past the house in a roaring crescendo. The sound stopped as suddenly as it had started. The mother of the family also heard strange voices calling out and saw a peculiar orange light reflect on her bedroom wall.

Since then, it is widely reported as the 'sound of battle' that they heard and linked to the battle that was fought here during the English Civil War, when the munitions store exploded.

Personally, I struggle with that as an explanation for the sounds. I don't think I would ever liken the sound of a group of motorcycles going past as being similar to the sound of an explosion, nor the sounds of battle generally.

Either way, I haven't been able to find any other accounts of this phenomenon.

HOLCOMBE

Whilst researching for this book, I found repeated mentions of the same account of the ghost of a middle aged man who would try to flag down motorists using a torch in Holcombe, Devon. As I researched, I became more confused because several of the stories mentioned the Heatherton Grange Hotel as being close to where the apparition was reportedly seen. I already knew from my research that the Grange Hotel was associated with Wellington in Somerset, and is now called the World's End pub. Holcombe and Wellington are some 35 miles or so apart and in different counties, and yet the various source accounts I found spoke about the locations as if they were close together.

I've eventually discovered that the accounts *should* refer to Holcombe Rogus - a small village in Somerset near Wellington. So for the full account of this rather active ghost - go to the chapter on Somerset and look at the entry for Wellington. I've just included it here in the Devon section in case anyone was looking for it here - because everywhere else lists it as Holcombe in Devon.

LAPFORD

Sir Thomas Beckett was brutally murdered on 29th December 1170 in Canterbury Cathedral in Kent, yet his spirit is said to haunt this small Devonshire village many miles away. He can supposedly be seen galloping through the village on a white horse on the anniversary of his death: purportedly because one of his murderers came from around here and Beckett is on his way to confront the man.

I have not been able to find any actual sightings of this particular ghost so it seems very likely it is just a myth with absolutely no basis in reality, but just a story using a very tenuous link to this historic tragedy. Alternatively, maybe this is one of those situations where someone did once see a ghostly figure on a horse and ascribed it to a suitably famous historical figure? I am often very persuaded that most of our so-called famous figure ghosts are actually cases of mistaken (or even deliberately misconstrued) identity. After all, the story is so much more tantalising if it's someone famous, isn't it?

A more plausible local ghost is that of John Radford, the vicar of Lapford from the 1860's. He murdered his curate and was consequently tried for murder. The jury, consisting entirely of his own parishioners, found themselves morally unable to condemn their Vicar to the gallows. As a result, in spite of overwhelming evidence that he was guilty of the murder he was acquitted and returned to his duties as Vicar of Lapford where he remained until his death in 1867. One can't help but wonder what the curate had done that the vicar felt moved to murder him, and the villagers felt moved to turn a blind eye? Or what hold the Vicar had over his flock that they daren't go against him?

It was apparently the Vicar's wish to be buried in the chancel of the church and he threatened that if this was not carried out, he would haunt the village. He was buried outside the vestry door and so he kept his threat and became a ghost.

In 2007 a biker wrote to the village website stating, "I was staying with a group of Bikers at the Malt Scoop last year. We'd had a good night drinking and had camped out [at the] back of the pub. About 2.30 am I awoke with a splitting headache (beer induced I assume). Anyway I decided to take a walk down the hill towards the A377 to get some air. I set off on my walk down the left side of the road and was almost immediately greeted by the sight of a vicar or man of the cloth walking up the hill on the right side. I say vicar because it was just the impression I got from his dark robe type attire. The man passed on the other side of the road and appeared to go into the church gate. I thought little of it other than to think it a little late for the vicar to be about. I continued down as far as Barris and then walked back up on the other side of the road without seeing another soul.

"The next day I actually enquired of one of the locals as to whether somebody in the village had died as I'd seen the vicar in the early hours and assumed he must be on a mission of mercy of some sort. The local said they hadn't heard of anybody dying and actually weren't sure if they had a vicar at the church at the moment. No mention of a haunting was made. I've been to Lapford many times in the past and have never heard of the vicar haunting until now.I thought no more of this until I read the account of Vicar John Radford on your site today."

A379 SHALDON BRIDGE

Shaldon Bridge near Teignmouth is reputedly haunted by the ghost of a young boy, after a discarded pile of clothes clearly belonging to a small boy were found on the bridge which no-one ever claimed. There is also the ghost of a local schoolmaster who was blown off the bridge whilst walking across it during bad weather many years ago. The original bridge was built in 1827, so presumably both ghosts must post-date that.

When I asked if anyone had any experiences there I received this fascinating account, "I distinctly remember the encounter as if it was last night – it was that vivid. I moved from London to Shaldon with my parents when I was six and so spent most of my formative years in the village.

"I was actually 19 years old at the time of this event and had just returned from living in London where I had spent a couple of years working in the capital. I had been to see a girlfriend in Teignmouth and had decided to walk home during the early hours of the morning – we had in fact had a row. It was quite normal in those days to walk into Teignmouth to meet friends or girlfriends – in fact, quite often, I would take the ferry over in the early evening and walk back across the bridge or cadge a lift with a friend.

"On this occasion I was alone, sober and it was roughly around 2.30 am. It was a very clear, cold and crisp night with little or no wind. I had walked across and was about 50 yards from the start of the stone wall element of the bridge. I suddenly heard what I can only describe as a 'pppssssssttt' sound which was repeated every five seconds or so. I looked around and worked out that this distinctive sound was coming from the direction of St

Peter's Church. I stopped and watched intently as a small white cloud two or three feet across and four or five feet off the ground was slowly working its way along the road, right to left towards the Dolphin Court flats. I watched it for several minutes until it just disappeared. It had no form whatsoever, just a cloud/mist like appearance.

"When I had plucked up enough courage to continue home – my route took me along the riverside – there was a very strong smell of electrical burning in the air. I can't say that I was terrified – just on edge as if something weird had just happened rather than 'seeing a ghost'.

"Whilst writing this short account, I have suddenly remembered a vague memory of another odd experience whilst walking over the bridge – this time in the opposite direction. On this occasion, I remembered seeing someone walking behind me – nothing odd about that – but when I turned around again, the individual had just disappeared. I remembered thinking at the time – was there someone really there, had they jumped or had I just imagined it? I thought no more about it thinking that it was just my mind playing tricks."

DORSET

B3157 ABBOTSBURY between Abbotsbury and Portesham

One source reports that at around 2am on a summer's morning in August 2014, a driver travelling this rural road had to stamp hard on their brakes as a shadowy figure ran in front of their car. The driver then watched as the figure slowly disappeared, its legs being the last thing to evaporate before reaching the side of the road.

I haven't been able to find any other reports of this entity.

B3081 BOTTLEBRUSH DOWN – Sixpenny Handley

The first written account for this ancient ghost that I have found came in 1956, purportedly in a letter from the archaeologist R.C.C.Clay to the collector of ghost stories, James Wentworth Day. In the letter he recounted an incident which had happened some years before, in 1924.

Clay was driving home from an archaeological dig he was conducting in the area at twilight one evening. As he slowed down for the crossing of the modern road and ancient Roman Road, he suddenly noticed that there was a horseman riding at full gallop, who swerved across the field and for a few moments rode parallel to Clay's car.

The rider had bare legs and wore a long loose cloak and he appeared to be riding his horse bareback and without bridle. Clay believed that his clothing looked to be from the late Bronze Age. He did not see where the horseman went when he lost sight of him. Apparently, when Clay was asking around, an old shepherd told him that many people had seen the phantom horseman.

One witness did come forward when I asked locally to tell me that she remembered being told years ago that there is the ghost of a soldier on a white horse who gallops across the Downs, so it seems some version of the story is still told, even if no-one has seen the horseman in recent years.

A348 BOURNEMOUTH – Millhams Lane, and surrounding Longham area

The area around the A348 bridge by Longham is haunted by a ghostly white woman (or grey, depending on which source you read). It is said that she died when she was hit by a horse and cart whilst she was walking along the road, which would likely make her a ghost of more than 100 years' antiquity. One version of the story says she tries to entice men to jump off the bridge, but that sounds like it might be a mash-up of older tales of water elementals by bridges.

Branching off the main road just past the bridge itself is Millhams Road and one witness told me via social media that her husband had some spooky experiences along that stretch of road. This sparked some debate about whether it is called Millhams Lane or Millhams Road - the general consensus seems to be that it is known locally by both names.

Several witnesses remembered being told the tale of the grey lady when they were children and being terrified they might encounter her - and at least one remembered she was the white lady.

There is also an account from 1972, when a cyclist travelling along Millhams Road early one February morning suddenly caught sight in the beam cast by his bicycle lamp of a figure in a grey cloak or cape crossing the road ahead of him, which vanished almost as quickly as he had seen it.

I also came across a suggestion that this is just a myth that was actually started to disguise the smuggling that was going on in the area, centred on St Andrew's Church which is sited along Millhams Road.

Local children used to dare each other to ride their bicycles down to the church and through the graveyard as it was known to feel so creepy at night. One witness recalled her mother speaking of tunnels going from St Andrews Church for miles underground – and that would certainly tie in with the smuggling suggestion. The witness' uncle had tried exploring them when he was a boy.

BRADFORD PEVERELL – Roman Road

The legend is that during summer months, at midnight, you can see the spectral visitation of a coach and horses repeating its last fateful journey, when it careens off this road and crashes into the River Frome, killing all aboard and the horses too. Some versions of the tale say it was the boggy land between the river and the road which was the doom of the poor travellers.

There are no recent accounts of this visitation, sadly.

BRIANTSPUDDLE – Rogers Hill

This account dates back to 1983, before the modern A35 dual carriageway which now sweeps up Rogers Hill was built. The story goes that a police officer patrolling the area by car at night approached a bend in the (old) road and spotted a single headlight coming from the other direction. The officer dipped his headlights but on turning the bend, found that the other light was nowhere to be seen.

Apparently this apparition of mysteriously vanishing headlights had been seen several times over the years prior to this. I wonder if the advent of the new road has brought an end to this phenomenon, as there seem to be no recent accounts of it.

Just south of the village is Briantspuddle Heath with its famous geological feature Culpeppers Dish. The dish is a sinkhole, probably caused by the fine sandy nature of the soil here. There is also a tale that four spectral figures can be seen walking along the lane over the heath carrying a coffin.

BRIDPORT - Gipsy Lane

There is a report that claims there have been several accounts of a lady wearing Edwardian style clothing seen walking along this lane. She is said to be coloured completely in grey. Her skin, clothes and hair - every part of her a uniform grey. I spoke with the gentleman who runs Bridport Ghost Tours, but neither of us have been able to find anything more about this account, nor anyone who has actually seen it.

B3162 BROADWINDSOR - coming from Drimpton

Broadwindsor is a small picturesque village nestled between the two highest hills in Dorset. It has an old ghost story attached to it - that one is supposed to sometimes see a hearse pulled by four black horses heading from the Drimpton Road into the village. It is followed by a large crowd of silent ghosts, and the whole spectacle vanishes just as it reaches the church.

This is possibly a folk memory of the funeral of a local dignitary, and has perhaps faded out with time, for certainly I could not find any actual sightings of it.

A35 CHARMOUTH

There is a report of a lady driver and her friend travelling the A35 heading out of Charmouth towards Bridport along the A35, one September night in 2004. They suddenly saw the figure of a woman in white sweep across the road ahead of the car, and both noticed the temperature within the car suddenly plummet.

Unfortunately the account gives no more detail than that and this is quite a long stretch of road, so it is hard to know exactly where this might have occurred.

CHIDEOCK - North Road

One old tale tells of two men walking home to Chideock down North Road when they suddenly saw the apparition of a black dog ahead of them. It turned into the churchyard and disappeared. There are two churches along here, so it is hard to tell where this relates to specifically and either way, there are no current accounts of anything along here that I could find.

HORTON

On one of the lanes running through Horton, there is supposedly the ghost of a young boy from around the time of the English Civil War, although it's not clear why that connection has been made. He supposedly darts in front of the traffic and quickly vanishes but I have not found anyone who has actually seen him.

B3078 KNOWLTON - towards Hinton Martell

The village of Knowlton has a fascinating ruined church standing inside the remains of a stone circle and earthworks. The church was originally built in the 12th century but is now just a shell. It seems likely this and the surrounding lanes are paranormal hotspots, as there have been a lot of sightings over recent years.

In July 2013 a family out ghost hunting one evening captured a video that showed what could be a human figure walking across the screen. The figure is very faint but with a slight blue sheen to it.

In August 2016, some other visitors took photographs of the church and captured faces in the windows.

There is supposed to be a horse and rider who sometimes ride across the site and straight through the church as if it were not there – which would possibly make this a phantom from the era before 1099 a.d. (which was when the church was built).

There is also the phantom of a woman kneeling and weeping outside the church and she is also sometimes seen walking down the lane. It is thought she might be the ghost of a nun.

One paranormal investigation group found themselves suddenly encompassed by a strange mist with the faint sound of disembodied voices coming from within it. Another group, using a Spirit Box, captured the phrase, "I'm the Devil" when investigating the church.

Yet another family of visitors saw a tall figure in black stride across the ruins in front of them and suddenly disappear – in broad daylight. I suspect this location is well worth a visit if you are hoping to catch a ghost.

LODERS – Yellow Lane

This curiously named rural lane boasts its own ghost. It is said to be haunted by a headless coachman, who was supposedly decapitated when his speeding coach hit an overhanging tree branch.

This sounds more than a little far-fetched, and I have not been able to find any actual sightings of the spirit.

LYME REGIS - Near Trent Manor House

This is a slightly curious entry and should probably be listed under 'Trent'. According to one source (and one source only) the stretch of road close to Trent Manor House, near Lyme Regis, is haunted by a coach and horses which vanished without trace many years ago. I'm presuming from that, there was a coach and horses which never reached its destination - rather than the haunting itself vanishing? Either way, the location description also leaves a lot to be desired. I can't find a Trent Manor House near Lyme Regis.

There is a Trent Manor House near Trent, also in Dorset - but it's nearer to Yeovil than Lyme Regis (even though Yeovil is in Somerset). This makes it virtually impossible to look for modern sightings of it - unless someone reads this and knows where to find more information?

SYMONDSBURY - Lane between village and Bridport

One account claims that on 'the country lane' between Symondsbury and Bridport, there is the ghost of a young crying girl. She is said to vanish if approached. It is difficult to pin the location down, since there are several lanes that could be described as 'between' the two places.

Curiously, close to Symondsbury there is also an ancient holloway - a drover's track from bygone years which over the millenia was gradually worn down until it was lower than the surrounding landscape. Perhaps it is this location which harbours the sad little spirit?

The relatively modern word 'holloway' derives from the ancient 'hola weg' - literally meaning 'sunken road'.

WEST LULWORTH

There is an account that Coach Lane in West Lulworth is so called because it has its own ghostly horse and carriage. Sadly for that story, there doesn't appear to be anywhere in West Lulworth called Coach Lane today – perhaps someone will be able to tell me that it used to exist and where it was?

DURHAM

B6278 BARNARD CASTLE

I have included the following account out of curiosity, although it doesn't really fall into the category of 'ghost'. In June 1977 a local young lad of sixteen called Mark was riding his motorbike along the B6278 near to the village of Lartington, quite late in the evening. As he rode, he noticed two spots of light behind him which he naturally just assumed was a car coming along the lane and slowly gaining on him. Sure enough, after a few moments a Jaguar car came up behind him, so he pulled over slightly to allow it to pass.

At that moment however, a strange pinkish purple hazy glow enveloped both of the vehicles, making the witness think of ultraviolet light. Simultaneously, his motorbike engine started to die, fading out as if it was losing power: not coughing and spluttering the way it would if it was losing fuel.

Mark was astonished to see his leather jacket start to steam slightly from an unknown heat source, and realised as well that although his bike engine was sounding as if it was not revving properly anymore, the bike itself was actually continuing to move forwards uphill.

After a few moments, the phenomena dissipated, and both vehicles came to a stop. Mark got off his bike and went over to the Jaguar car to speak with the driver, who confirmed that his car had also behaved in the same way as Mark's bike - continuing to move despite the fact that the engine seemed to be dying out.

Neither driver could explain what had just happened to them. When Mark later arrived home he realised that actually there was around a half hour of time missing that he simply could not account for. He also developed a sort of sunburn over the part of his face that had not been covered by his crash helmet.

I have not been able to find anyone else with experiences along that stretch of road – but if you know of something – email me.

A690 BRANCEPETH

According to one researcher, in January 1995 a lady was driving to work when to her absolute astonishment she saw a small man – only a few inches tall – climbing the grass verge at the side of the road. She slowed her car right down and watched the diminutive figure for a couple of minutes from just a few yards away. She described it as moving with a strangely disjointed action – a bit like a puppet would.

Tantalisingly, the researcher mentions they have a second sighting of something similar in the same area by a paramedic which they will record in due course – but I have been unable to find that anywhere. Although not strictly a ghost or a haunting in the conventional definitions these accounts still hold interest. Are the same stretches of road subject to strange phenomena as well as hauntings?

A167 NEWTON AYCLIFFE

This curious entry might just relate to the longest running hitch-hiker type ghost. The story is that in 1698 the body of a woman was found floating in the nearby River Skerne. Since then, a forlorn ghost of a woman dressed in white has been seen around the area, often frequenting the A167 which runs alongside the river in places. She is seen particularly around the North Briton area of the village, but right on through and up to Rushyford.

Apparently she was sometimes picked up by stage coaches travelling the old road - and even today she will sometimes hitchhike a ride in a passing car!

One gentleman wrote to the Birmingham Society of Ghost Hunters in 1978 detailing an encounter he had with her whilst on his way to a 2am shift at the nearby mine. He said it was a fine moonlit night and he saw a woman in a white coat and bonnet float across the road with no legs, "at the junction of North Street and William Street." There is a North Terrace in Newton Aycliffe, but no William Street that I can see - which tends to cast a rather big doubt on that particular account!

A688 STAINDROP

There is a legend that if you drive along the A688 the short distance between Staindrop and Raby Castle, you might see the phantom white horse carrying his bloodstained rider across the adjacent fields at full gallop. The pair disappear by apparently sinking into the hillside. It's not clear from the accounts where exactly this is, and unfortunately no-one came forward with any recent sightings, which tends to suggest this is an ancient tale which either never was, or is not now, an active haunting.

That being said - it is a curious village name, for one with a ghost with blood stains....

ESSEX

AUDLEY END - Audley End Road & Chestnut Avenue

Audley End House is a spectacular Jacobean mansion, with a befittingly magnificent arched gateway on its main entrance topped by a white stone lion. Appropriately named the Lion Gate, it was built in 1786 a.d., replacing an earlier gate which had stood there since 1616.

There is supposed to be a ghostly coach and horses which emerges from the gate, turning right and going over the humped bridge, before joining the main road and then turning right onto Chestnut Avenue. As with most ghostly carriages - there do not seem to be any recent sightings.

BASILDON - Church Road, coming in from Cray Hill

This one road has a very unusual number of hauntings and possibly tomfoolery relating to it. It apparently has an active spirit who once threw some men over a bush as they returned from the local pub, and also the ghost of a small girl who was killed by a cart back before there were any cars on the roads. When I asked for information, I was given a lot of detail about its third ghost - the Red Monk.

So-called because of the way it glows faintly red in the moonlight, this figure seems to have been first reported in 1964, when it crossed church road and disappeared as it entered the churchyard. There was a spate of these sightings, but then in 2004 it was reported in the local paper that some local jokers had come forward to say it had been them all along. They claimed that they had used a powerful torch with a filter to project the figure onto the early morning mists to frighten people.

Several people locally told me they had lived on or near the road for all of their lives, or for a great number of years, and had never heard of this ghost at all. One remembered that the derelict Manor House at the corner of Rectory Road was said to be haunted, but thought that was probably just down to it being a derelict building and therefore gaining a reputation.

One chap said his mother was frightened once by what she thought was a ghost glowing white in the night – but it turned out someone had just dumped an old fridge over the graveyard wall!

Curiously, one witness said that as well as the Red Monk, there was also supposed to be the ghost of the Grey Nun. She was supposed to appear if anyone ran around the church four times.

Several others remembered hearing stories about the ghostly monk when they were younger, and that people were scared to walk this road at night for fear of seeing it. One remembered that the local factory even took to providing a minibus for evening shift workers who were not wanting to come in for their shift for fear of having to walk past the Red Monk! They dismissed the later claims of it being a prank achieved by shining torches onto the mists, pointing out that there weren't any houses along here back when the sightings were most prevalent in the 1960s, so there was nowhere for pranksters to have been shining a torch from...

So – you decide – a spate of true hauntings, or a prank not admitted until nearly thirty years after the deed?

BRADFIELD

There is a tale that on moonless nights you can see the ghost of Sir Harbottle Grimston, 2nd Baronet, being driven around in his fancy horse and carriage. A respected gentleman and scholar of his time who was heavily involved in the politics surrounding the English Civil War, he died in 1685 as an elderly man in his eighties, which was a very good age for that period. Quite why he should still be parading around is unclear and perhaps his reasons, as well as his ghost, have been lost in the mists of time since there are no reported actual sightings.

There was also a report in the 1940s of a ghost seen standing in the middle of the lane in the village – which might be related to the ghost of a farmer who is said to still walk the fields around this area.

BRAINTREE – Stubbs Lane

In 2009, a lady walking with her two children close to where Stubbs Lane passes Millenium Way encountered a weird mist hanging about 3 meters off the ground in a vaguely humanoid shape.

CANEWDON – Larkhill Road, near Puelsey Hall Lane

This delightfully rural area is reputedly haunted by a Crusader. The Crusades, which were pilgrimages to the Holy Lands, are generally thought to have happened between 1096 a.d. and 1295 a.d. so this would be quite an ancient ghost if still active.

One witness explained that he had heard of a medieval ghost along there who had frightened a cyclist, and that he had also been told that on the anniversary of the Battle of Assandun (18th October 1016), the cries and screams of the dying soldiers can still be heard at night.

Another person recalled being told of a ghostly horse and rider cantering around that area at night. She had lived in a cottage at the top of the hill and remembered as a child in the late 1970's often hearing the sound of galloping horses in the night, for which she has never had a rational explanation.

Yet another explained that she had been told the area was so haunted because two ley lines cross near Hyde Wood Lane.

It seems possible to me that these are all just one haunting, but ascribed to different periods in time by the knowledge level and mindset of any given witness at the time? A mounted soldier or knight type figure, and echoes of battle, seem all possibly related to me?

And finally, one witness said the ghost she had heard about was a grey lady, seen in Gardners Lane down where it meets Anchor Lane, whereas another had heard of a dark mist seen in that same location, and yet another had heard of a headless ghost there.

CHELMSFORD - Patching Hall Lane

One source reports that in the 1970's a tall pale figure wearing a top hat and cloak was seen by a group of teenagers hanging about together. The figure frightened them enough to make them run off, but as one looked back he saw the figure actually vanish.

Some local witnesses who had grown up around that area in the right era had not seen or heard of anything, even though they spent a lot of time on the grounds of Patching Hall after it was demolished.

One witness had heard that someone had drowned in the pond at Patching Hall and subsequently haunted the area, but others believed there was no actual pond on the grounds - just a natural spring which did not form enough of a pool for anyone to be able to drown in. Patching Hall used to stand where the Courtlands blocks of flats are now.

Another lady told me that her property in Patching Hall Lane used to be haunted by a young boy, who would run from the dining room area through to the front door. In recent years, they had some extensive remodelling done to the house, essentially completely changing the floor plan, and this seems to have laid the little ghost to rest as he has not been seen since.

FAULKBOURNE – Witham Road

There is an account that a ghostly cyclist has been seen, "on several occasions, wearing a billycock hat, who peddles furiously at living cyclists as if intending to knock them over before vanishing". He is said to be dressed in clothes from the 1800's and riding a suitably ancient period bike.

The phrase 'billycock hat' is a nickname for a bowler hat and was in common usage as a phrase in the early 1900's – which is rather later than the ghost. Whatever period it was actually from, nevertheless I could not find any recent accounts of this figure.

GREAT WAKERING – Star Lane

Star Lane runs between Poynters Lane and Southend Road, and lies more or less in between Great Wakering and Shoeburyness. Apparently it is named after an old public house that used to be there. It is supposed to have a Black Shuck who haunts along its quite short length. I will be honest and say that I thought Black Shucks were an old tale relating to the Viking war dogs or hellhounds, and probably just a matter of myth handed down over the centuries.

To my astonishment however, one witness came forward who said that she and her friends actually encountered this frightening apparition in nearby Barrow Hall Lane (just the other side of Southend Road).

Then a gentleman told me that years ago his father was riding on his bike along Star Lane one night and he could feel the presence of something following him. He looked around and saw two red eyes in the dark behind him. His father was a farmworker, and was cycling home after harvesting, one August night in the 1960's.

Given its height and the appearance of the eyes he thought it might be a dog but although he called out to it, he could not make out any shape. He got back on his bicycle and set off again, only to have the same thing happen. In total he stopped four times and tried to see the dog which was following him, but could only ever properly make out its eyes. Black Shucks in English folklore were often said to have glowing red eyes.

There is also an audio account recorded for the BBC by Lesley Cripps who twice saw the Shuck in the 1930's whilst out hunting at night, but in his version the dog was black and white.

Another lady told me that in 2014 she was driving down Star Lane, and glanced in her rear view mirror. Imagine her shock when she saw the face of an old lady staring back at her!

Curiously, another witness told me that many years ago his father was walking the family's pet dog up nearby Little Wakering Hall Lane, when he noticed a lady walking towards him. To his surprise, his normally friendly dog seemed nervous of the approaching lady, growling softly as his fur stood up on end. His father said, "Good Morning" to the lady as they passed each other but she did not acknowledge his greeting. He took a few more steps, wondering if she had refused to answer him because she had been offended at the way his dog growled, and looking down thoughtfully at his pet.

He suddenly realised that he could see the footsteps he and his dog were taking marked out clearly in the heavy frost. There were no footprints where the lady had just stepped. Slightly startled, he looked up and behind him, only to see that the lady had completely vanished!

Yet another witness mentioned that his brother had a lady friend who rode a motorcycle and she would always refuse to go via Star Lane because she had seen a man standing by the side of the road once, and when she glanced back at him in the mirror he had vanished.

It might be a good idea to take a camera with you if you happen to be walking down there after dark.

B1052 HADSTOCK

Next to the village of Hadstock in Essex there used to be the airfield of RAF Little Walden. It was opened in 1944 and used by both the Royal Air Force and the USAAF. It was closed in 1958 and today is just some abandoned buildings used for farm storage, with fields across what used to be the runway and grounds.

It is claimed that one American pilot was tragically decapitated in a flying accident here and since then he has haunted the road close to the site, seen standing at the side of the road thumbing for a lift. A team called Shadow Paranormal conducted an investigation there in January 2014 which they recorded and posted on YouTube, where they were able to read out the list of names of airmen from the site who had lost their lives in the hope of sparking a response via their EMF recorder. They did capture an EVP (Electronic Voice Phenomena) that they thought said, "Please help me. Heal me".

One viewer on that video post mentioned that their Mum had seen him in 1978 when she was driving back home alone at 2am on a foggy night. I drove the road with a few friends in November 2018 but we didn't see him, sadly.

HIGH LAVER

High Laver is a very small village, with around 500 inhabitants. Its main claim to fame is that the philosopher John Locke is buried there, having spent his last few years living in the household of Sir Frances Masham until he died in 1704.

However it is Abigail, Baroness Masham who is the subject of our ghost story here. Once a year on Christmas Eve, she is said to drive her coach past her old home of Otes Manor in High Laver and gaze at it longingly. In historical record she was said to be a plain woman, born Abigail Hill, who although of good birth fell on temporary hard times when her father ruined his branch of the family financially. She was lucky that her cousin Sarah raised her out of penury by finding her a place in the household of Queen Anne.

Much to Sarah's chagrin, over the ensuing years Abigail rose to the position of one of the Queen's favourites and closest confidantes – usurping the spot from Sarah herself. There were even rumours as to the exact nature of the relationship between the Queen and Abigail, but that is perhaps more down to the spiteful jealousies of court gossip.

Abigail married Samuel Masham, and it was through him that High Laver became her out-of-town residence. After Queen Anne died Abigail retired from court life and lived out her days at High Laver, dying on 6th December 1734 and being buried at the church there.

There don't seem to be any records of actual sightings of the ghostly carriage.

A1060 LITTLE HALLINGBURY – Junction at the bottom of Church Road

Little Hallingbury boasts a possible location for the burial place for Queen Boadicea, but it's probably a more modern ghost that is said to haunt the lanes. There used to be a palladian manor house here, and the park which it occupied is still largely extant, although not open to the public and partly laid to arable now.

However, in the 16th century it was owned by the de Morley family, and there is a tale that Lady de Morley haunts the lanes thereabouts, forever paying back her perfidiousness in lying about Queen Catherine Howard in order to allow King Henry VIII to have his Queen beheaded.

The only De Morley who was around for Catherine Howard's time was one Lady Rochford – real name Jane Parker – who was the daughter of the 8th Baron Morley. In reality, it was Anne of Cleves, one of Henry's earlier wives that she made accusations about, agreeing the marriage was unconsummated and therefore Henry could legally put Anne aside as not 'truly' wed to him. Lady Rochford was part of Catherine Howard's household at court and was in fact imprisoned when Catherine was. She was beheaded on the same day as the Queen, so it might be that her ghost haunts because of how unfairly she was treated.

In 2010 a motorist driving this road had to swerve to avoid a floating dark figure which then vanished. It's hard to say whether there is any correlation between the older tale of Lady Rochford and this more modern sighting or not.

MERSEA ISLAND – Dawes Lane

There is a story that a couple out for a pleasant stroll in broad daylight saw a woman wearing a long dress and matching bonnet walking towards them. Curious about her dress, they were watching her when she turned aside and started to walk through a corn field. Just as the couple noticed that she did not seem to be disturbing the tall crop at all, she suddenly vanished right in front of their terrified eyes.

A witness told me of her own experience on that same stretch of road when she herself was about 18 years old. She was driving off the island itself and going via Dawes Lane. At the end of the lane she went to turn left onto East Mersea Road, which led to the causeway. As she went to make the turn she saw a really frail looking old lady standing beside the road. The lady caught her eye because of her bedraggled appearance with long grey hair. As our witness turned to look at the figure properly, however, she suddenly realised the 'lady' was completely transparent.

Not surprisingly, and in the witness's own words, "I was too scared to stop and investigate further so I put my foot down and carried on and got the hell outta there quick!"

MERSEA ISLAND – East Mersea Road, onto The Strood

In the same vicinity of the two hauntings above, but just around the corner on East Mersea Road itself, there have apparently been a number of sightings of ghostly Roman soldiers. Mersea Island was used as an outpost garrison by the Romans when they occupied Britain, and they will certainly have used the same spit of land now turned into the causeway called The Strood to gain access and egress.

According to legend, there is a centurion who patrols this road and out onto the Strood but he is still marching on the old level of road – and is therefore only ever seen from part way up his legs!

Some drivers have caught a glimpse of him in their car headlights and anyone walking there might hear the sound of his marching steps behind them. Sometimes, it is the sound of fighting men and clashing swords that can be heard. One woman reported being followed by the ghostly Roman soldier when she walked home alone there late one evening.

Another pair of witnesses from the late 1940s reported being out at night in a row boat on the stretch of water near the Strood. Suddenly both saw the centurion marching along his eternal route. They beat a very hasty retreat.

NORTH SHOEBURY - Poynters lane, near junction with Wakering Road

The public account of this ghost says that on 29 July 2006 at around 10pm at night, a lady motorist had to swerve her car to avoid hitting a man wearing a striped polo shirt and casual trousers who stepped out of the hedgerow straight in front of her car. Cross that she had nearly hit him, she looked in her mirror to see where he went - only to realise there was not a soul in sight. I was not able to find anyone else with any experiences along this stretch of road.

STANWAY - Turkey Cock Lane

One account says that a ghost wearing a long raincoat steps out of the hedge part way down the lane, walks towards the old London Road (now the B1408) before slowly fading from view as he walks. I wasn't able to find anyone who has actually seen him.

THORPE LE SOKEN - Tan Lane

Just south of Thorpe Le Soken, there is a turning off the B1414 called Tan Lane. Apparently, several drivers have braked sharply along this road to avoid the bearded man with a top hat and walking stick who takes a stroll down the lane. Occasionally he is seen walking with a lady – but there is no record of who they might be or why they haunt.

Slightly curiously, and probably unrelated (but who knows?), Sir William Gull, physician to Queen Victoria, came from Thorpe Le Soken. Some historians have put forward the theory that he could be a candidate for the identity of the infamous murderer Jack the Ripper. Sadly, no-one came forward to say they had ever seen the pair or felt anything down that lane.

TOLLESBURY – Prentice Hall Lane

Wrongly cited in most source accounts as 'Apprentice Hall Lane', this ghost actually belongs to Prentice Hall Lane just outside Tollesbury. It is a lonely, rural stretch of road branching off from the B1023 and leading towards the waters of the estuary.

Late one night in June 2007, a driver and his friend suddenly spotted what looked like a lady lying curled up on her side in the middle of the lane. She looked to be quite young, was wearing dark clothing and high heeled shoes or boots. She lifted her head and raised her hand as the car approached. They immediately stopped the car and rushed to give aid to the stricken lady, only to realise that she had completely vanished.

The B1023 along the same stretch is also said to be haunted by a Black Shuck – one of the demon dogs of folklore. He was supposedly last seen in the earlier years of the 20th Century, when a midwife who regularly had to cycle the route at strange hours of the night would often encounter him. Sometimes he would be lying in the road (which has curious echoes of the lady ghost above) but other times he would trot alongside her bicycle for a while before disappearing. Probably the same Black Shuck was also seen by another cyclist in the 1960s along the nearby B1026 by

Tolleshunt D'Arcy. As he watched, it disappeared before his eyes.

GLOUCESTERSHIRE

AVENING - Road between village and Minchinhampton

There is supposed to be the ghost of someone who committed suicide who waits along this piece of road. It's difficult from the source story to tell how old this tale is, since there is very little detail given. Certainly it was a long held belief that anyone committing suicide was doomed to remain earthbound, so the tale could be quite old.

Curiously though, I did find a witness who had experienced something very strange along that stretch of road. In November 2013, our witness was driving home from Malmesbury at about 1am in the morning on a clear, cold, typical winter's night. There was some ambient moonlight, and it was quite a crisp, still night. As he drove near Minchinhampton golf club, he suddenly saw a slim, middle-aged woman wearing just a dress (no coat or warm scarf for the chilly night) trying to flag him down and looking very distressed. He immediately pulled the car over and wound his window down to ask her what was wrong and if she needed help.

She suddenly wasn't there. His experience has left him profoundly interested in the subject of the paranormal.

Interestingly, in the same area the Black Shuck has been seen on numerous occasions.

B4226 CINDERFORD - St White's Road

St White's Road is sometimes haunted by the misty white form of a lady keeping pace with anyone foolhardy enough to walk along the road. She is supposed to be the ghost of the founder of the local hermitage, who still likes to keep a protective eye over travellers passing through her domain.

CLEARWELL – Church Road turning onto Stowe Road

In the late 1960s a husband and wife driving from Trow Green towards Clearwell were forced to slam the brakes on in a hurry and perform an emergency stop, to try and avoid the man carrying a shopping bag and walking stick who was suddenly standing in the middle of the road. With no sign of the man when they came jerking to a stop, they were afraid they had knocked him over, and immediately jumped out of the car to investigate.

There was no-one there, and nowhere he could possibly have moved to that quickly to have simply been out of sight. His apparition doesn't seem to have been seen since that I could find.

B4632 CLEEVES HILL – towards Prestbury

There is a record of a lady who was driving home towards Cheltenham one summer's evening, when she suddenly noticed a funeral cortege passing slowly through the field on her left. The hearse was being drawn by black-plumed horses, and all the mourners following behind on foot seemed to be in Victorian style dress. She was so surprised at the incongruous sight, that she turned her car around and went back to have another look - but the procession of mourners had completely disappeared.

I wasn't able to find any corroboration for this story, and something about the original account niggles as odd. It says that the lady was in the Cleeve Hill area travelling towards Prestbury, and the field was on her left. She was on Southam Road. She turned her car around in Noverton Lane to go back and have a look.

The trouble is, Southam is a village between Cleeve Hill and Prestbury. Prestbury is where Noverton Lane is. So, if she drove all the way from Cleeve Hill, through Southam and on to Prestbury, BEFORE turning around in Noverton Lane and driving all the way back, why is it even faintly surprising that the funeral cortege wouldn't be there any more? Of course it would have moved on in that amount of time.

Why could it not simply have been an actual funeral cortege with a themed funeral? Not three months ago, I politely pulled my car over to allow a full Victorian style hearse complete with amazingly beautiful black-plumed horses to be 'walked out' of the street where the deceased had lived and even took some photos as it went past with all its dignified solemnity.

Other versions of the same account I found said she saw the cortege in the fields near Mill street in Prestbury, and that would make much more sense as to why she thought it disappeared more quickly than possible: and yet it also begs the questions as to why there are so many differing and vague versions of where this supposedly happened.

B4228 COLEFORD - towards Bream

One author has mentioned that there is a legend of a coach and horses galloping wildly down this country road, and that on occasion its sudden appearance has caused cars to crash. Unfortunately, I have not been able to find any corroboration for this haunting at all.

B4234 COLEFORD - towards Cinderford, close to Waterloo Screens and Pond

One account tells the story of a Mr Bolter driving home along the B4226 from Coleford to Cinderford one night when it was raining quite steadily. As he passed the Waterloo Screens, his car headlights picked up the figures of a man and boy holding hands as they crossed the road in front of him. He slowed down to allow them plenty of time to cross, but the figures simply vanished before they reached the kerb on the other side of the road.

He later found out that a man and boy had been killed there some twenty years previously when hit by a horse and cart. Presumably, although no date is given, then this tale must be from possibly the 1960s or even earlier if one assumes the lane was often used by horse drawn carts just twenty years earlier?

When I looked for more recent witnesses, a gentleman came forward to tell me that his mother had seen a vintage horse and carriage crossing the road just there sometime in the 1980's. She was on her way to the shop 'Quicksave' at around 6pm to pick up a few bits and pieces, so certainly not thinking of anything otherworldly at that moment. The evening was already dark so it must have been the colder months of the year.

He was also able to tell me that the Waterloo Screens are part of the Waterloo mines, and they were an area where the coal was graded and sorted. From his description of the sighting, it is more likely both sightings must have been on what is now called the A4136. He was also able to tell me that many people claim to have seen the ghost of a miner in the woods there.

A429 FOSSEBRIDGE

The source story I found for this says that in 1997 three men travelling along the A429 close to Fossebridge reported that they had seen a vintage style motorcycle and sidecar ridden by a man wearing no crash helmet, which had suddenly disappeared after pulling up behind their car.

I was pointed in the direction of the local 'ghost expert' when I asked for information, and he very helpfully told me that the machine was a World War II era vehicle, when motorcycle and sidecar outfits were in very common usage as dispatch vehicles. He is aware that it has been seen just outside Moreton in the Marsh (around 16 miles roughly north of Fossebridge) heading into the town just before the railway bridge. It is also seen in Bourton on the Water (almost exactly halfway between Fossebridge and Moreton In the Marsh) just by the turning into Lansdowne.

It seems fairly reasonable to assume it is the same one, and our expert points out that there were a lot of airfields around this part of the Cotswolds during the war, so it would have been a common sight to see one of these making the rounds at that time.

A429 MORETON IN THE MARSH - Fosse Way

In October 2005 a couple were driving south away from Moreton in the Marsh at about half past nine at night. They suddenly saw the top half of a human figure float across the road in front of them - they could not make out its head or legs, but it seemed to be wearing a light grey jacket of some description. The way it was moving made them think of a horse rider but nothing could be seen of any spectral horse.

Curiously, another lady also wrote to me who was working as a community nurse in 2008. Her patch covered a large area of the North Cotswolds, and she recalls one day heading back towards Moreton in the Marsh up this same stretch of road when she suddenly saw a large horse and rider standing stock still in front of her. The pair were utterly motionless - making her think immediately of a statue rather than living beings. She lost sight of them for a split second, but quickly realised that there was no gap or break in the hedgerows that they could have ridden away through. To this day, she feels there was something oddly otherworldly about the encounter.

There is also another account of a driver along the A429 heading towards Stow on the Wold glancing into her rearview mirror and seeing a horse and rider leap out into the road just behind her car - so close that for a moment she genuinely thought the horse would hit the back of the car.

She had just long enough to register that the rider was wearing an old fashioned black cape, when the pair suddenly vanished into thin air.

I wonder if all of these relate to the same entity, covering a certain defined area?

A44 MORETON IN THE MARSH

A local expert on ghosts, who runs a tour on the subject under the name Bloody Bourton Walking Tours, told me about a tale he was told some years ago. He was working in a shop in Bourton when an old couple came in and picked up a flyer for the tour. The old gentleman turned to his wife and said it might be useful to talk to the person who led these tours to see if he knew anything about what they saw.

Our witness spoke up and explained that they were already talking to him, and asked what they had seen. Although the wife was reluctant to say anything, as everyone else they had told laughed at them and told them they were mad, the old gentleman proceeded to tell their story.

He said that a few years previously they were travelling east from Moreton in the Marsh just past the Fire Service College when they suddenly saw a World War II style plane literally just hovering frozen in the air: like a snapshot in time rather than an actual flying plane. Although they had hurriedly turned the car around to get a better look at it, it had disappeared. Our expert was able to reassure them that they weren't mad – they had seen the ghostly Wellington Bomber which has been known to frequent the area.

B4068 NAUNTON

There is a report that on 26th August 1998 an anaesthetist driving down the road at about 10pm suddenly saw a lady standing beside the road wearing a cream coloured sleeveless dress and with shoulder length dark hair, worn loose. She gave him a slight wave as he approached and he was so surprised to see her standing alone there on the country lane he thought she might need help, so pulled up next to her. As he put the car into parking mode, he glanced away from her for a moment, but as he glanced back and started to wind his window down, he realised she suddenly wasn't there anymore. Although he got out of the car and scanned the field with his torch, she was nowhere to be seen.

In April 2000 a security guard driving the same route saw a misty white figure cross the road ahead of him. It was around 6ft tall, and made him think of a monk in the brief second he saw it before his car seemed to pass straight through it. One witness did come forward to say that she recalled a lot of speculation at the time the haunting was originally mentioned as none of the locals believed it was true. She doesn't think anyone else has ever seen anything along that stretch of road.

RODBOROUGH COMMON – Butterow Hill

There is a narrow, winding lane running part way up and along the steep escarpment of Rodborough Common, called Butterow Hill. As it joins the more populated area of Minchinhampton Common, it passes The Bear of Rodborough Hotel. There is a story that on cold, misty, winter nights, a coach and horses complete with headless coachman rides along this stretch of road. The lane gets its name from the Butts (straw targets) used for archery practice in centuries past.

B4020 SHILTON

Another witness wrote to me to say that in the early 1970s her father saw a ghost as he was driving along the B4020 where it goes past Shilton. She couldn't unfortunately recall exactly what it was he had seen, but it was the one and only time in his life he ever saw a ghost, and he was always adamant that he was sure he had seen it. I thought it was worth mentioning in case anyone else has seen something along that stretch?

A429 STOW ON THE WOLD

In autumn 2006, two friends driving saw a man dressed in Victorian style clothing complete with top hat walking along the A429. They probably would not have thought much of it, except they returned along the same stretch a couple of hours later, and saw the same figure walking in the same place! On this second pass, they actually saw him disappear, leaving no doubt that they had encountered something supernatural.

There are also accounts of an old lady seen walking the road, but only in wet weather. Cars drivers have either slowed down to offer a lift, only to find they can't see where she has disappeared to, or glanced in their rear view mirrors to realise they suddenly can't see her anymore.

A438 TEWKESBURY – Church Street

There are a lot of ghosts in the ancient town of Tewkesbury, but one particular pair of spirits were spotted by a couple out walking one evening in 1982. The two sad little child ghosts were stumbling along on crutches and wearing old fashioned clothing including knickerbockers. They turned down a side alley in front of the astonished couple, but when the couple rushed to look for them, they had completely vanished, even though the side alley turned out to be a dead end.

I wasn't able to find anyone else who had ever spotted them.

UPPER SWELL – small lane towards Lower Swell

One witness wrote to me to say that when he was a boy, he used to live close to Stow on the Wold. One evening he was cycling home, and was passing down the small rural lane which runs between Upper Swell and Lower Swell. To his astonishment, he suddenly came across a group of soldiers in some kind of uniform riding horses across the road. He stopped his bicycle and watched them pass – they seemed solid and real and were accompanied by the noises you would expect from a small group of mounted soldiers. He said he was not far from the woodlands which are known as Bloody Jims.

A local ghost tour leader also wrote to me to say that Roman soldiers at Upper Swell are often seen crossing the road here, but on foot, and that they head to the burial mound (The Upper Swell Long Barrow). On one occasion, they were even seen marching along the road.

B4234 WHITECROFT – New Road towards Lydney

One source describes a woman dressed in black who is sometimes seen pushing an old fashioned pushchair in front of her as she crosses this road, always disappearing before she reaches the opposite kerb. Unfortunately, not only is the source completely vague about where on this 3 mile stretch of road this occurs, but I wasn't able to match the sighting with any others.

WINCHCOMBE - Lane below Belas Knapp Long Barrow

In 1956 according to one source William Hunter, an RAF officer, had been playing sports one evening in August and decided to take the scenic route home. His chosen route took him down the lane which runs along the side of the hill just below the Long Barrow of Belas Knapp. This stretch of road is heavily wooded in places and steeply sloped above and below the road.

As he drove, he suddenly saw a light moving up the hill through the woods towards the road he was travelling down. As he and the mysterious light converged on a collision course, he realised that the light was actually a glow surrounding a strange looking figure in a blue cloak, which was gliding along in a most unnatural way. The blue robed figure actually seemed to pass through the bonnet of his car even as he braked sharply to try and avoid it, and continued unperturbed on its way up the hill.

GREATER LONDON

A116 ALDERSBROOK ROAD

In 1993 four people were travelling in a car along Aldersbrook Road, when suddenly an Asian woman ran out in front of the vehicle, looking terrified and distressed.

Curiously, as two of the occupants of the car screamed, thinking there was going to be an impact even though one never occurred, the other two looked completely puzzled at their companions' commotion – since they had been completely unaware of the apparition.

A2 BEXLEY

As the very busy A2 roars its way into London between the Bexley Heath turn-off and the Black Prince turn-off, keep your eyes peeled for the two ghostly airmen that have on occasion been seen standing silently on the hard shoulder. They look like they are dressed from World War II, and one description says that one of them seems to have a wound near his throat.

Apparently they were most recently seen in 2008, and some people have speculated that the ghosts come from a bomber which crashed near here during the war, killing the crew.

BLACKHEATH – Hare and Billet Road

Even in the busy metropolis of today, this road is still bounded on either side by open grassland, passing as it does across one corner of the heath.

It also harbours the ghost of a lady who committed suicide. Desperately unhappy in her marriage, she took a lover and for a time found some happiness: until the lover jilted her. Today, she is sometimes seen as a shadowy lady in Victorian dress on autumnal evenings. The last recorded sighting seems to have come from November 1971.

BROWNSWOOD PARK - Gloucester Drive

In the mid 2000's, there was a spate of paranormal happenings in this quiet suburb. The sound of ghostly children running up and down the street laughing and playing was heard on several occasions, even though nothing was seen.

A5200 DARTMOUTH PARK HILL

In Autumn 1938 Mr Worrall and his son were driving home and turned their vehicle into Dartmouth Park Hill. As they drove peacefully along with no other traffic around them, they were suddenly both horrified to find themselves facing a lorry head on which appeared out of nowhere. As his son cried out in fear the father hopelessly tried to brake and swerve, but with not enough time and nowhere to go, he knew they were about to suffer a nasty crash.

To their absolute astonishment however, instead of hitting them with the sickening crunch they were expecting, the spectral vehicle seemed to just pass straight through their car. Completely shaken, they had to pull over for a time to compose themselves.

HAMPSTEAD - East Heath Road

As the name suggests, this road runs along the east side of Hampstead Heath. If you are out enjoying the fresh air of the park though, watch out for the apparition of a smiling old man wearing a brown overcoat who starts to follow you.

He's not a peeping tom or stalker (although he might once have been). He's a ghost, and the story goes that if you turn to face him he will disappear.

HIGHGATE, Swains Lane

Swains Lane is quite heavily wooded and very steep in places, passing as it does through Highgate Cemetery. Apparently, it takes its name from pig herders who used to use it as a drover's lane.

For a time in the 1970's there was quite a furore about the possibility of a vampire on the loose around the area, when a man walking down Swains Lane was knocked to the ground by some sort of creature that had seemed to glide out at him from the walls of the cemetery. The headlights of an oncoming car seemed to scare it off. Another report of that incident claims it was a young nurse who was knocked to the ground (of course that could still have been a man, but in the context it seemed to suggest a female nurse).

Also along the same stretch of road were reported a ghostly cyclist and a gentleman in a tall top hat who would cross the road and then just disappear. Sometimes dogs are said to whimper in fear and refuse to walk up the lane. The various apparitions seemed to quieten down for a time during the 1980's, but in the 1990's and 2000's seem to have become more active again.

In 2011 some interesting photos were taken in the lane capturing a strange mist circling around, and in 2012 the North London Paranormal Investigations team caught sight of a male apparition in Victorian dress. Quite possibly well worth a visit if you are hoping to see a ghost or two?

A41 STANMORE

The original story which I found said that in October 1985 a driver went to the local police station in a distraught state. He claimed that he had been driving along the A41 when he suddenly came across a man walking his dog in the middle of the road. Finding himself unable to stop in time, to his horror both the man and the dog were thrown up over the bonnet of his car in the resulting collision.

However, when he skidded to a stop and climbed out of the vehicle, he could find no sign of either the man or the dog. He could also not see any signs of damage to his car.

Interestingly, when I asked locally about the ghost, a number of witnesses came forward to say they were sure the story was fiction. They explained that they thought that actually a local tramp who was something of a celebrity and was known as 'The Edgware Walker' was probably behind the origin of the story. He would often be seen walking the streets pushing his belongings ahead of him in an old pram or at one time, a wheelbarrow. If spoken to, he came across as well educated with a refined accent.

One witness even recalled accidentally throwing a bag of rubbish on top of him when he was rummaging around in a rubbish dumpster. The witness apologised profusely and The Walker took it in good spirits – proceeding to check through the new bag of rubbish the incident had provided!

Curiously though, none of the witnesses who spoke about him ever mentioned him having a dog. I also don't see how he could have been thrown over the bonnet of a car and then disappeared, so I'm not convinced by the logic that he is actually the apparition.

GREATER MANCHESTER

DROYLSDEN - Ashton Hill Lane

There is supposed to be the ghost of a woman wearing a dress which rustles like silk as she drifts along this lane. Sometimes she appears to be wearing quite dark clothing, and at other times very pale. There has been some speculation that it might actually be two different ghosts. There don't seem to be any records of actual sightings though, so this one is probably more likely to be urban myth.

GOLBORNE

In 1970 a motorcyclist crashed his bike when he swerved to avoid the figure of a lady wearing white who drifted out in front of him, "on the road through Golborne now bisected by the M6". The story goes that he was so worried he reported it to the local police, who told him that they'd had many such reports along the same stretch of road and not to worry - it wasn't anyone corporeal that he had seen.

There is a legend that she is seeking revenge because her lover was killed along that stretch, but other versions say she herself was killed there.

One witness contacted me to say that he remembers the tales of the White Lady from his own childhood, and that his Grandad (who was very interested in the subject) used to go out trying to find her. Sadly, his Grandad never did have any success, otherwise we might have some more evidence to add to the tale.

Another lady told me that she understood the story of the chap on his motorcycle related to a road called Rob Lane, which is indeed crossed by the M6. She also said that she had been walking her dog on a couple of occasions down a small lane close to that area, when he became spooked and would growl and shake. On one occasion he lay down flat to the floor shaking, before literally dragging her away from whatever had him freaked out.

When she asked about it on a local social media site to see if anyone had experienced anything similar, she was told that the White Lady haunted there. She was also told that several of the properties locally are haunted, possibly because there are Ley Lines crossing there. In addition, a local builder told her that he had a couple of Alsatian guard dogs he was using to protect a property he was renovating down the same lane, but his dogs were also scared of something unseen down there. Given that they were fierce guard dogs and trained to be scared of nothing, that was something quite unusual. Other locals also told her that the White Lady haunts Golborne Hollows and Keepers Woods as well.

Another witness told me about their experience close to the area, saying, "I was driving down the A580, along the stretch between the turn off for Rob Lane and the M6 South turn off. It was a Thursday in November some time around 2008 or so, and around 11.30 at night. I was on my way to collect my husband and son who had been playing in a pool match.

"I was driving along the road with no other cars around me, when all of a sudden there was a saloon type car immediately behind me, with three or four people in it. It seemed to come from nowhere, and was going so fast I was sure that it was about to crash into me, and I was absolutely terrified.

"Just before it should have hit me, it literally disappeared. I was really shaken and told everyone about it when I arrived at the club to collect my son and husband, but no-one believed me."

I can't help but wonder whether this is related to the White Lady - if either her death or her lover's death was caused in a car crash?

HYDE - A57

This haunting is said to be where the A57 and the A6017 cross, near Haughton Green, and dates back to the 1930s when an inquest was held into the death of a young man riding pillion on his cousin's motorcycle. They had been thrown from their bike, the cousin told the inquest, when a lorry had reversed into the road in front of them. Although the inquest could not find any trace of whose lorry it was, they were able to ascertain that there had been an unusually high incidence of accidents along that road, many of which seemed to be inexplicable.

A year later another incident occurred when a pedestrian was nearly hit by a large lorry that suddenly appeared in front of him, then promptly disappeared. It seems entirely possible the motorcycle accident was caused by the phantom lorry as well. I wasn't able to find any more recent occurrences, so perhaps this spate of hauntings died down permanently.

B6391 TURTON BOTTOMS

The story goes that one evening in November 1978 Mr Berry was getting ready to alight from a bus at his destination bus stop. As he stood up, he glanced out of the window and noticed a young couple waiting to get on the bus. They looked to be in their late teens or early twenties, and he noticed the girl was wearing a beige coloured raincoat while her male companion had dark hair and was wearing an anorak.

Mr Berry's attention was taken away from them when he stopped to help an old lady off the bus, and when he himself stepped to the kerb, the couple had vanished. He asked both the old lady and the bus driver – and they were both as puzzled as he, since they too had seen the couple standing there and could not explain where they had gone to.

HAMPSHIRE

ALDERSHOT - Bourley Road, towards Church Crookham

I asked locally about anybody having any paranormal experiences along Bourley Road, as the original source story I had found gave very scant detail about the ghost of a 'homeless woman' seen along here by some car drivers.

A lady wrote to me and told me about the experience her partner had on that road. It happened about 40 years ago, so it was either the late 1970's or possibly just into the 1980's.

It was a lovely summer morning with pale misty sunlight, and he had gone out training on his bicycle. It was mild and a thoroughly pleasant time to be out and about. As he approached the crossroads with Claycart Road he saw a light mist hanging in the road in front of him, and suddenly felt freezing cold. Standing in the mist ahead of him he could see a figure wearing a short army greatcoat, of the style worn by the mounted military police, and he assumed he was in fact seeing a live military policeman.

However, as he cycled closer, he realised the man was wearing knee length puttees (wrappings around the lower leg) and an old style military cap. He was staring curiously at the man, wondering why he was wearing outdated clothing, when the figure suddenly just dissolved into the mist right in front of his astonished eyes!

Although both my correspondent and the witness himself have asked around since then, they have never found anything out to explain the presence of the ghost, nor have they ever found anyone else who has seen him.

However, one other witness did come forward to tell me that he had heard of a silent WWI soldier being seen along Bourley Road.

ALDERSHOT – Alma Lane

There is a very old tale that when Wellington was successful in the Battle of Waterloo in 1815 a young runner was dispatched from Beacon Hill to give news of his victory to the officers stationed in the barracks. As he ran down Alma Lane, his heavy army boots striking the ground in a steady, heavy rhythm, he was set upon by wayside robbers and murdered. It is claimed that ever since then, the sound of his booted feet can still be heard running down the lane.

Curiously, one witness told me that he used to live in Canning road in Aldershot, which is about three miles distant from Alma Lane. He would often hear the sound of running boots on that road at a certain time of the night. It was such a frequent occurrence that he told his brother in law about it, who was sceptical until he heard it himself. They could never see any actual person to account for the noise. It seems entirely possible that there is a connection.

BRAISHFIELD – Dark Lane

Dark Lane is now a bridleway which runs out towards Eldon Road and was part of an ancient trackway to Michelmersh. It branches off from the Kings Somborne Road, past Windmill Cottages, and then across the fields to join the Eldon Road.

It is supposedly haunted by the ghost of an Edwardian woman who is eternally looking for a hoard of precious jewels and gold she hid whilst living in a building along the road. She is said to have been an eccentric old woman who lived a very miserly life, but would sometimes be seen by her servants counting gold out of small dirt covered bags when she returned from her walks.

It seems to be this gossip which has led to the belief that she secreted her wealth in hidden places around the lanes. Apparently she is rarely seen by people, but dogs will react badly to her presence, howling and whimpering in fear. Sadly, I wasn't able to find any actual sightings of her.

BRAMSHOTT

Some sources claim that Bramshott is the most haunted village in Hampshire, with paranormal occurrences of varying sorts regularly documented: and up to 17 regularly appearing spooks! I'll just mention the ones that haunt the lanes and roads around the villages, rather than the buildings, given that the theme for this book is ghosts who haunt roads.

The actor Boris Karloff (real name William Pratt) lived in Bramshott until his death in 1969. The cottage he lived in was said to be haunted by a tall dark figure. There were stories of unexplained noises in the house during the middle of the night. The ghost of the actor himself is also now said to roam the lanes in the village.

The ghost known as 'Mistress Butler' walks in the meadows alongside the river. She is supposed to have been so unhappy in life that she committed suicide by throwing herself into the river in 1745. There is also a Grey Lady ghost who haunts the well outside the inn, where she is said to have drowned centuries ago.

Yet another ghost is the figure of a young boy playing a flute. The music he plays can sometimes be heard and is apparently hauntingly beautiful in sound yet somehow slightly disturbing. There is sometimes a pale calf which is seen near the sound of the music. This sounds like a much older myth of the type relating to faerie or wood sprites: those that would whisk people away to their doom after they became spellbound by the music.

I did, however, find an account of one resident of the area who used to sometimes hear this haunting music faintly blowing on the wind when he was a child in the area. He thought it sounded like a set of woodwind pipes and heard it several times between the ages of 8 and 15. His Mum told him not to be worried by it as she had heard the same thing when she was a child in the area. Another resident also recalled hearing something similar as a boy when they used to camp out in each other's gardens at night.

There is also apparently the usual ghostly coach and horses: but this one can only be heard, not seen. One source claims that the sound of it has even been recorded on tape.

One villager recalls that his grandmother used to be terrified of the large tree in the centre of the village when she was a child herself, because she could see dead people hanging from its branches that no-one else could see.

CHALTON - Chalton Lane

In the centre of this tiny village is the very picturesque Red Lion pub which is often smothered with very pretty hanging baskets. If you leave the pub and head down the slope of Chalton Lane next to it, be careful of the ghostly horse and cart which are sometimes seen rattling its way very quickly down the road.

EAST MEON - Temple Lane

In 1977 four young lads hanging about and playing in the street saw an old lady leave a house and walk down the road. Not so unusual, except that the house was standing empty at the time because the elderly occupant had died just a few weeks prior. They watched her walk the whole way down Temple Lane, heading towards the village centre.

It seems likely this was a one off haunting, as no-one replied when I queried it.

GOSPORT - Green Lane

In November 1999 a local taxi driver was working the late shift and had just dropped a fare off. He was driving back to the taxi rank, passing down Green Lane, when a hooded black shape suddenly glided out into the road straight in front of his vehicle. His immediate reaction was to brake sharply, but he watched in horrified fascination as the hooded, slightly indistinct shape carried on its way, gradually fading into nothingness within a few short yards.

He never did drive that way at night again.

When I asked, one local recalled that they had heard about a taxi driver seeing something which spooked him down that road.

B1254 SOUTHSEA - Elm Grove

There is an account that in 2010 a car driver pulled up at the crossing to allow a pedestrian to cross the road. It was a woman who waited at the kerbside, wearing a short skirt and long boots. As she started to cross the road and the driver patiently waited and watched her, the car behind him rudely sounded its horn. Glancing in the mirror to gesture at the impatient man behind, the driver then turned to look ahead again. The woman had completely vanished.

He realised that the car behind was acting so impatient because that driver had been completely unable to see anyone waiting at the crossing and could not understand why he had stopped...

I was not able to find any other sightings of this apparition.

WATERLOOVILLE - Lovedean Lane

Lovedean Lane is supposed to harbour the ghost of a young bride dressed in a long white cloak who was killed at 'nearby Keydell' according to the source. There is a Keydell Avenue and Keydell Close near to one end of Lovedean Lane – and from the context of the source it seems likely that this tale predates the building of so many houses around this area since it talks about the farm entrance.

It seems unlikely that she still haunts since the area changed so dramatically, and I wasn't able to find anyone who knew of her.

WATERLOOVILLE - Hulbert Road

This ghost of a young girl likes to stand in the middle of the road at dusk. She was last reported in the mid 1970's, and it was thought she was the ghost of a girl who had been struck by a car and killed whilst hitchhiking along this road some years earlier.

WINCHFIELD - Bagwell Lane

Just south of Winchfield lies Bagwell Lane. It was reputed to be haunted by a lady draped in a long white dress, who would move across the road and frighten drivers. She seems to have last been reported in 1968 by a motorcyclist who thought he had hit her with his machine, but skidding to a stop and looking behind him, he saw her still drifting silently along the road...

HEREFORDSHIRE

A465 BROMYARD

There is a tale that a lady once died along this stretch of road when she grabbed at the steering wheel of the fast moving car she was a passenger in. The subsequent fight for control between her and the driver caused the car to crash and she lost her life. I'm presuming the driver must have survived, in order to explain what had happened.

Since then, the legend goes, drivers along here sometimes find that their steering wheel seems to lock as if something has grabbed hold of it and stopped it from turning.

One correspondent told me that she used to hear a lot of tales of people saying that their car steering wheel had been grabbed and pulled whilst they were descending the steep bit by Stoke Lacey. Apparently, however, there is an adverse camber on this stretch of road which can make the steering feel very strange in a car.

HERTFORDSHIRE

BALDOCK – Clothall Road

A witness told me that sometime around the year 2010 or so, she was travelling back home to Buckinghamshire after dropping her friend off for a Sunday evening flight from Stansted Airport. It was a trip she made quite frequently, as her friend lived in Europe but had family in Buckinghamshire so would fly home for the weekend several times a year.

This particular evening, as my witness followed the familiar route home, she was travelling north up the A507. The A507 Clothall Road crosses the B656 at a set of traffic lights in the town itself. As our witness waited in her car at the red light to take the straight over option, she idly glanced to her left and then her right at the junction.

As she swung her head from left to right, her thoughts suddenly caught up with what had just been in her line of vision to her left. There was a vehicle parked at the side of the road, with a person sitting in it. What had caught her attention as her brain processed the momentary image, was that the person was dressed in the oddest of attire for a modern day scene. They were wearing some kind of white ruffled shirt, with a dark colored formal style jacket over it, and something resembling a tri-cornered hat. It also struck her that the person somehow didn't look quite right, or quite real somehow.

She whipped her head back round to the left to take a better look, but the vehicle parked at the side of the road was definitely empty now and she could not see anything about it that her mind might have misinterpreted. She drove home feeling thoroughly spooked, but to this day the incident has remained in her mind as something very odd that she spotted that night.

When I looked for other witnesses for this same spot, I was told that there is a legend of a ghostly female hitchhiker who is trying to get back to Hitchin here. The tale goes that a man driving through Baldock going from east to west at the same crossroads late one night suddenly became terrifyingly aware that he had somehow 'acquired' a passenger in his car. She is described as a girl with long dark hair. For some reason he carried on driving to Hitchin with his passenger, where she inexplicably vanished. He later found out that a girl died along there whilst trying to get home to Hitchin.

This story sounds much more like urban myth. Similar versions of it are repeated elsewhere around the country but with different locations: and why on earth would you drive on willingly for another five or six miles if you had a ghostly passenger in your car! Surely you would pull over and jump out yourself as fast as you could?

It does beg the question though – why two stories of strange occurrences inside cars at the same spot? Added to that, is the fact that another witness told me about a strange experience she had whilst walking down another of the side roads (Icknield Way) leading towards that same crossroads. This happened in around 1971, and the lady, much younger then, was walking with her sister and chatting amiably about nothing in particular.

They strolled past a house that at that time was standing empty, with a very overgrown front garden and hedges giving it a slightly spooky feel. Their conversation turned to speculation as to whether the house might be haunted. No sooner had they turned to this topic, when our witness felt someone give her a very hard and purposeful shove in the middle of her back at waist level – hard enough to actually propel her forwards. Startled, she turned around to see who had assaulted her – only to find the road behind them completely empty. She has not to this day found an explanation for what happened, but says she can still vividly recall the feeling of that phantom shove.

Yet another witness told me that in 2017 her daughter was walking their dog down the alley close to this junction which leads to the High Street at about 5pm, when her dog suddenly spooked and became visibly frightened. At the same time, her daughter felt breath on her neck and a hand tap her on the shoulder - even though no-one was anywhere near her. Needlessly to say, she has refused to walk that way ever since!

Is this all one entity, I wonder, who likes to play tricks on pedestrians and passing motorists alike?

BERKHAMSTED - New Road/White Hill area

In November 1976, according to the original source story I found relating to this stretch of road, a driver was returning home at around 11pm on a fine and dry night with very little other traffic on the road to contend with.

On the road past the entrance to Berkhamsted Castle (White Hill) he came up behind a Honda 50 type moped puttering along at a much slower speed than his car had been travelling. Slowing to match its speed and maintain a safe distance behind it, he followed it up New Road towards Berkhamsted Golf course. He could quite clearly see the dark shape of the moped and rider ahead of him with its lights on.

All of a sudden, the bike and rider simply disappeared. There was suddenly nothing on the road ahead of the car driver. Puzzled - and slightly alarmed that maybe the bike had skidded over - the car driver stopped and checked all around. There were no side turnings nor gateways, nor any ditches which the bike could have turned into or fallen into.

One local told me that as a child they were told about a headless huntsman who roamed the fields not far from this spot in Dudswell.

Another witness said that further up New Road, as it opens out to fields on the left hand side, there is a circle of trees there which is supposed to be haunted and which she and her daughter feel quite nervous about walking in as there is an eerie feeling there.

Another knew of a ghostly horse and carriage said to pass along the High Street which is at the bottom end of New Road. There was also mention of a woman seen in the fields of the Common by New Road who wore a long dress, and of soldiers seen on horses whose legs were partially obscured as they were still following the original ground level. There is a World War One memorial further up the same road, and the remains of a training camp from that era. Certainly a lot of the some 10,000 soldiers who passed through there before being shipped out to the war front in Europe would have been mounted soldiers, and many would never have returned from their doom.

And finally, another witness wrote to me to tell of her father's experience on the nearby Northchurch to Berkhamsted road - back in the days before the area was as built up as it is now.

"I remember my father speaking of something he saw on the road between Northchurch and Berkhamsted long before the Durrants Estate was built, probably in the 1940s or early 1950s.

"He was walking towards Northchurch about where Durrants Road is now located, and he told us that he saw a horse drawn glass-sided hearse pulled by four horses with a horseman and coffin. The cortege then turned left into large gates which all then disappeared. My mother said he was quite shaken by what he saw and I never knew him to vary the recollection in any way. Nearly every time we walked past as youngsters he would point it out as the spot where the ghostly funeral went."

BULLS GREEN - Winding Shott / Tewin Hill

There is a wooden post called Clibbon's Post, inscribed with its name and the date Dec 28 1782, just close to the turning off Winding Shott onto Tewin Hill. It commemorates the death of a notorious highwayman of the area called Walter Clibbon and it is also considered possible that his body is buried here. There are several versions of how exactly the highwayman met his death - but they all conclude by him being shot and dying here.

In some of the stories the excited locals, pleased at ridding the countryside of this notorious thief and his villainous gang, tied either his body, or that of one of his gang, to the stirrup of a horse and jeered as it was dragged around. It is this gruesome spectacle that is still sometimes seen replaying along this lane - a shadowy horse is sometimes seen dragging something dark along the ground behind it.

BURNHAM GREEN - White Horse Lane

Curiously, geographically very close to the previous entry, is the small village of Burnham Green. Running from the pub in the village, aptly named the White Horse, down to nearby Woolmer Green is White Horse Lane. There is a legend here of a ghostly, headless white horse running down the lane.

I grew up near here, and a boyfriend and I were walking along this road one dusky evening as he told me the story - when he suddenly, and deliberately, emitted the loud screeching sound of a horse's neigh - frightening me half to death.

A witness also told me that he was driving down this road very late one winter's night in the early 1980's, with his car headlights lighting the drizzly, cold night ahead of him as he chatted to his passenger. Suddenly they both noticed a man walking along the roadside on the slightly raised up banks of the high verge there wearing only a light pair of trousers and a brightly coloured Hawaiian style shirt. They both remarked on how strange it was he should be out on such a cold damp night in such unsuitable attire - but thought no more of the incident.

Then around a year later, the witness was again driving down the same road at a similar time of night and year (he couldn't be sure of the exact dates) when he suddenly passed the same man wearing exactly the same brightly coloured unsuitable clothing! Since that second encounter, he has remained convinced that this was actually a ghost he had now twice seen.

B462 BUSHEY, WATFORD - Aldenham Road

A lady told me that as a young woman in the late 1980's she was driving home at about 1.00am in her Mini car after visiting with her boyfriend. As she was waiting at the traffic lights on the Aldenham Road, she suddenly noticed a man walking towards her car.

Worried about her vulnerability at such a late hour with not much traffic about, she turned to look at him properly to try and assess if he was any threat.

She realized that the man was wearing very rough looking clothing, and was moving towards her car in what she could only describe as, "a creepy, prowling sort of way with his rough hands held out and his eyes really staring at me". Deciding that she did in fact feel threatened, and calculating that he would reach her car long before the lights turned green, she made a quick thinking decision and immediately drove through the red traffic light in order to move away from him as fast as she could.

As she drove away to safety, she looked fearfully into her rearview mirror to see what his reaction was to being thwarted in what she was sure was his ill intent. There was no-one there.

DATCHWORTH - Hawkins Hall Lane and Rectory Lane

Rectory Lane is said to be haunted by a cart which trundles around with a heap of dead human bodies on the back - their legs dangling and swaying as the cart creaks along.

One version of the tale says it is the dead of one entire family who were sent to the Poor House when they became destitute, where they starved to death one by one and were taken for a mass burial. Another says it is a Plague cart trundling around to collect the victims of this terrible pestilence which swept the countryside in the late 1340s, killing scores of people.

On Hawkins Hill Lane there is said to be the ghost of an old woman who once lived here, but was so distraught after her husband's death that she hung herself inside her cottage. She shuffles along the road looking at first glance as if she is hunched over against the cold but a proper look tells you it is not that she is hunched - she actually has no head on her shoulders...

No-one came forward to say they had ever actually seen either of these ghosts.

B487 HEMEL HEMPSTEAD - towards Redbourn

On 19th April 2009, according to one source, a driver passing this way shortly after midnight suddenly saw a caped figure with a wide brimmed hat cross the road in front of his car. Although his lights picked it out quite clearly ahead of him, as he approached he suddenly could no longer see anything there, and nothing was picked up in his rear view mirror as he swept past.

Locals told me that their theory was that this was actually the shade of the local notorious highwaywoman The Wicked Lady, or The Grey Lady. Lady Katherine Ferrers was an aristocrat who liked to slip out at night dressed as a daring highwayman and became quite the scourge of the local coaching routes.

HINXWORTH

A witness told me of her own encounter with the supernatural, "About 18 years ago (roughly the year 2000) I had been down to the stable yard where I kept my horses and had finished the feeding and mucking out by 5.30am. It was really windy and rainy, and I left my stable yard on the edge of Hinxworth and headed towards the A1. On either side of me were open fields. As I drove along, I suddenly noticed a lady walking along the side of the road ahead of my car. She was wearing either a long coat or some sort of cloak and holding an umbrella up against the rain.

"Something seemed really weird about her being out so early where there were no houses and it rattled me sufficiently to make me lock my car doors as a precaution as I drove towards her. I watched her cross the road in front of me and pass into a field on the other side of the road. Again, this seemed really weird - as it was winter and not only were the fields ploughed, but the weather had been wet for days so they would have been virtually impossible to walk on with the deep mud formed in the furrows.

"As I passed the spot she had entered the field, I turned to look to see what on earth she was doing. There was no sign of her. She had completely disappeared in a wide open field.

My hair literally stood on end and I hurriedly drove away. Later I told my sister about what I had seen, and we used Google to try and see if we could find anything out. We did find that Hinxworth House along that road is said to be haunted, and the ghost of the lady is said to run up the road crying, especially on stormy winter nights."

ST ALBANS - Fishpool Street

If for some reason you need to walk down Fishpool Street at around 3am in the morning - be careful. You might encounter the ghost of a lady in a blue dress who is said to walk this street in great distress at around this hour.

TRING - A41 towards Cow Roast

A witness told me their own account of the ghost they once encountered here which they had never forgotten.

"I used to play Lacrosse. On this particular occasion in 1978, my team had played that day alongside the rugby pitches on Cow Lane and we had all won our matches so we stayed behind to celebrate. Afterwards, just as the sun was setting, I set off on my bicycle to ride back to Berkhamsted. As I passed the village of Cow Roast, I was aware of a large shape drifting across the field to my right. I thought to myself, speed up and you'll miss it!

"Well I didn't speed up sufficiently, so I met the strange shape and as I passed through it I felt freezing cold. Now in a blind panic I cycled as fast as I could to my nearest friend (my godmother) & when she calmed me down she got me to draw what I had seen.

"When I drew the shape, you could make out that it looked like a horse in armour with its rider. Later I was told this was probably the ghost of a soldier (or knight) on his way to Berkhamsted Castle."

Interestingly another witness said they too had once come across a cold misty patch in Cow Lane that frightened them so much they ran away.

A1170 WARE - Ware High Street

In 1998 a lady driver was approaching the roundabout on the High Street just next to The Waterside Inn, when she was suddenly 'cut up' by a very old fashioned car driven by an older gentleman, which she hadn't seen until the very last moment when it was right upon her.

She braked sharply to avoid the collision – only to see the car disappear right in front of her eyes and as quickly as it had arrived.

WHITWELL - Codicote to Whitwell road

Legend says that there is the ghostly sound of an axe chopping wood, and then a tree falling, which can be heard on Christmas Eve on the lane from Codicote to Whitwell in Hertfordshire. The sound is supposed to repeat all through the night. Some sources cite the lane as being Bendish Lane in Whitwell (which is definitely not the lane towards Codicote).

Certainly, there used to be a pub in the village called The Woodman which was apparently named after this ancient ghost story. There is also a tale that two real life woodsmen were frightened half to death when their colleagues dressed up in white sheets complete with clanking chains and leapt out on them where they were working one night in the woods along Bendish Lane in the middle of the 19th Century. This tale suggests that the original ghost tale is therefore much older than the 1800's – since the pranksters were using knowledge of that tale to scare their poor mates. The men apparently never did figure out they had been pranked but spoke for the rest of their lives about the night they encountered the ghost of the woodsman.

When I asked about any recent experiences around these lanes, I got a wealth of replies that were really quite amazing for such a small village. Several witnesses explained that there is a picturesque walk from the village of Whitwell which goes alongside the River Mimram and then the church, and eventually up to St Paul's Walden through the Bowes Lyon Estate; a path which is known locally as The Bury. Although beautiful during the day, it was described to me as very eerie to walk at night.

Astonishingly, it is meant to be haunted by a lady frying fish – aptly called The Spratt Lady. Her name was Betty Deacon in life and she used to buy fish at the market on a Friday, and then fry them up for sale outside her cottage near Bury Farm.

There is also a headless horseman who rides through the village to mark the death of anyone in the houses, and the ghost of a soldier haunting The Bull pub in the village itself, as well as a Screaming Lady down by the small lake formed by the Mimram!

One witness had a friend who used to recount the tale from around the early 2000's of how he and his mates were walking the path leading to Water Hall Farm when they saw the shadowy outline of a man walking ahead of them wearing a long cloak – who suddenly vanished as they watched. The friend said he had later been told that other people had seen the same figure along that spot, and although he and his friends who were there that day were all quite big burly lads, they remained quite freaked out by what they had seen for some time.

ISLE OF WIGHT

A6054 LOCKS GREEN – Whitehouse Lane Crossroads

This stretch of rural road is supposedly haunted by a World War II dispatch rider on a motorcycle. A few drivers are said to have reported having to swerve to avoid hitting him.

B3330 NETTLESTONE – Eddington Road

There is an account that a ghostly Lady in White haunts this road. She is said to appear suddenly in front of cars at night, who drive through her misty form much to the horror of the poor drivers. When I asked for any witnesses, one came forward who explained that he had seen a different figure along there.

One night years ago, he was making his way home to St Helens at about 3am in the morning on foot. As he was climbing the sty from the footpath close to St Helen's Church, he saw a tall figure of a man leaning against the wall of the church. The figure seemed to be wearing a cloak with a tall hat on its head, and leaning on a walking stick. He also recounted that one of his friends had once seen the same figure when driving past the church late at night.

On another occasion as he passed the church on a moonlit snowy night, he heard the faint sound of singing coming from inside.

KENT

BEARSTED - Road leading to Pilgrim's Way

The original source story I found says that there is the ghost of a man wearing a large hat riding a horse who haunts the lane connecting Bearsted Way and the Pilgrims Way. He apparently looks perfectly solid and normal right up until the moment he and his steed just disappear.

Locals from the area were able to pinpoint for me that the road in question is actually Hockers Lane, leading up to the Pilgrims Way at Detling Hill. One witness told me that whenever she tried to ride her own horse near Pilgrims Way it would always spook for no particular reason that she could determine in the exact same spot.

There is also a video on YouTube of the image of a ghost captured in the background when a father was videoing his wife and daughter riding their horses at nearby Cobham Manor riding school in the 1980's. It looks like the very still form of a man in the bushes staring at them as they ride their horses. Look for it under the title 'Ghost Captured - Cobham Manor, Kent, UK The Pilgrim's Way' if you're interested.

Just a little further along the Pilgrim's way in Burham there is also said to be a spectral coach and horses. I can't help but wonder if these hauntings are all connected - a highwayman and his victims perhaps?

A25 BOROUGH GREEN

I discovered whilst researching that the spelling of this village is vital - and not to be mixed up with the spelling of Burrough Green in Cambridgeshire. You'll find that some published accounts of this entity seem to do just that, causing much confusion if like me you try to look up the location for the haunting on a map.

Some reports of this haunting describe a man seen as a white shape – others describe just a misty white object seen moving along the pathways.

I spoke to one lady who explained that her son is a chef who works late hours but who does not drive, so for a while it fell to her to go and pick him up from work late at night. About 18 months ago she was driving from Borough Green towards Sevenoaks, when a tall man dressed in black stepped out into the road from one of the lay-bys along there straight in front of her car.

She slammed her brakes on so hard, it made her pet dog fall off the passenger seat where he had been happily sitting. The man, on the other hand, had completely disappeared.

She also knew that one of her work colleagues had seen an apparition near The Crown Point pub, but her colleague described the ghost as looking like a lollipop lady in a white coat and with a smiling face.

Then less than twelve months ago, my correspondent again saw an apparition on the road, not far from that same pub. This time he was a soldier wearing a long grey coat with two rows of buttons down the front – but he was floating several feet above the ground!

One local historian was able to tell me that at nearby Oldbury Hill there is supposedly the ghost of a hanged man. The legend is that he robbed and murdered a fellow traveller by cutting his throat, but was himself pursued by the local villagers and brought back to face justice. His body was 'hung in chains', otherwise known as a gibbeting, and left to rot. One of the local fields is still named Gibbet Field.

There is also a Roman soldier who still marches along the old roads – but he is only seen from the shins upwards because the ground level has changed since Roman times. To the East of Bearsted, where the A25 passes through St Marys Platt, there is the ghost of a peddler who still walks his old route.

Another local resident pointed out that he has walked his dog in these local woods and fields for many years – often in the dark hours when the days are short. He has never encountered anything supernatural – not even in the days when he used to work the fields, including in Gibbet Field.

BRENZETT – King Street

Brenzett is a very small rural village in Kent, and King Street is a small lane which runs from there to the nearby village of Brooklands.

During my research one witness said that this lonely stretch of lane is haunted by the ghost of a man walking a dog. She saw him in the late 1990's, and then again in 2016. He was walking down the middle of the road with his faithful companion (even in death) trotting along beside him. Both times that she saw him it was winter, around 7pm in the evening, close to the small level crossing there.

CHARING – Pett Lane

There is one account of a man driving home along this lane one evening with his mother in the car, when they spotted a man wearing a mackintosh walking his dog. The driver slowed his car and then stopped to let the man and dog cross, but to the astonishment of both him and his Mum, the man and his furry friend passed straight through the side of the car, briefly illuminating the inside before vanishing without trace.

I was not able to find any other accounts along this road.

A299 CHILTON

It took me quite a while to work out which bit of road this sighting relates to, because the road names have changed since the sighting was last reported.
It seems that there is the ghost of a monk – or possibly someone wearing an army greatcoat, according to one witness – who stands in the middle of the road and then vanishes as cars approach him. He is supposed to be in the vicinity of the railway where the modern day A299 and A256 cross.

CRANBROOK – the lanes around the village.

The original story which I had on my radar for this book was as follows; In September 2011 a driver and his passenger were said to be driving along the road towards Marden, when to their horror a cloaked figure jumped down from the trees in front of their car before leaping spectacularly over the vehicle.

They could even hear the 'whooshing' noise the cloak the entity was wearing made as it was dragged over the roof of their car. They reported that the figure was too tall for the driver to see the head, but they definitely thought the rest of the entity was humanoid.

However, when I researched the sighting I came up with a number of locals who knew that there was a tale of a man who haunts one particular road, which is the B2085 Glassenbury Road and which runs past The Peacock. One witness also knew of several people who had seen the ghost of a lady wearing a black nightdress standing in the roadway near to The Peacock pub.

Another witness explained that there was a ghost of a lady who haunted the lanes just a little further south of here, between their farm and The Great House in Gill's Green, which is now a gastric pub/restaurant in the village but used to be known as the Duke of Wellington.

The main A229 which links all these sightings is itself said to be haunted by both a Black Shuck type entity and also the ghost of a jilted bride. Apparently, she discovered on her wedding day that her fiancé was also sleeping with her sister behind her back – is she, I wonder, the woman dressed in black seen so close to here? The Black Shuck in this version is said to have the body of a dog and the head of a man.

Another witness came forward to say, "I work as a gardener and one February morning in 2012, I was working on a hedge when the weather was a bit foggy. I was working beside a lane, where the hedge formed the boundary. I became aware of a person walking past and since she was looking my way I said 'good morning' to her".

The lady didn't reply but the gardener carried on climbing his ladder to cut the hedge, then glanced around thinking something slightly odd about her had struck him, only to realise she had completely disappeared.

Even from his vantage point he couldn't see her anywhere. He said, "I then became numb with fear as I thought back to how oddly she was dressed – she was pale and wearing what I think was Edwardian clothes".

Although still working in the same general area to this day, he has never seen her since.

EAST MALLING

If you find yourself driving through Barming Woods, between East Malling and East Barming, just keep a careful eye out and be ready to break sharply. This ghost of a galloping horseman is sometimes seen and sometimes heard as he charges through the trees, crossing the road and on at least one occasion appearing to charge towards a car.

The last time it seems to have been recorded was in 1971.

GRAFTY GREEN - Headcorn Road

There is a legend that a coach and horses travelling along this stretch of road overturned, killing all the passengers and the coachmen. Their bodies were taken to the local pub, The Kings Head.

On misty nights it is said that the sound of the coach crashing and the passengers and horses screaming can still faintly be heard. Unfortunately, I could not find anyone who had ever actually heard this.

HERNE BAY - Thornden Wood Road

In 1986 a motorcyclist riding along the road late one night suddenly had the horrible experience of all of the lights cutting out on her machine, leaving her careening dangerously along in the dark.

Reacting swiftly, she tried to apply the brakes, but even as she did so the bike's engine sputtered and died and she discovered the brakes were not responding either. Being an experienced biker, she managed to keep the bike upright as she tried to coast it to a safe stop. As she wrestled with her machine, she suddenly saw the misty outline of a human figure crossing the road ahead of her, accompanied by the sound of barking dogs.

As soon as the apparition and its accompanying soundtrack vanished, she found she was able to bump start the motorbike and coax it back into life.

B2169 HOOK GREEN – leading to Bell's Yew Green

One source claims that this lane is haunted by an older style dark-coloured limousine, which disappears as cars approach it. There are also reports further down the same road of a white-coloured limousine being seen. I could not however find any reports of anyone ever actually seeing either car. Further down the same road, closer to Frant, there are claims of an old style bus which also vanishes if cars approach.

Is this road subject to 'Stone Tape Theory' style hauntings or timeslips, possibly? The Stone Tape Theory postulates that certain types of background stone or ground can act like a giant recording device, which under certain circumstances will trigger to play back what it has recorded: thus the casual observer caught up in a playback sequence might see something which happened years ago unfolding in front of their eyes before fading away again.

Alternatively a timeslip would also perhaps give the observer a momentary glimpse into the past – hence seeing all these older vehicles on the same stretch of road?

Or you never know, maybe someone around there has a stable of vintage vehicles they like to take a little spin out in every now and then?

LYDD – Jury's Gap Road, the last bend before entering Lydd

Around 1998, very late one evening, a driver travelling along Jury's Gap spotted a young man walking in the road. The driver slammed on his brakes and the man in the road jumped to the side, seeming to land down in a roadside ditch.

The driver stopped to make sure the man was okay, but to his consternation found that the man was nowhere to be seen, and even though he searched up and down the side of the road he could find no trace of the young man he had tried to avoid.

B2160 MATFIELD - towards MAIDSTONE

I found an account that on 11 December 2009 at around half past six in the morning, a driver was on his way into work. Suddenly, two tall figures darted out in front of his car forcing him to brake hard to avoid them. He needn't have worried though, as their almost immediate vanishing act showed that they were not as corporeal as he had at first supposed.

Another account stated that the writer's sister and then boyfriend had been driving home through Matfield in 1964 when they suddenly came across a man in a top hat and a lady wearing a full skirted dress walking in the centre of the road.

MEOPHAM - Steele's Lane

The original story tells of a young French girl working in one of the large houses in the area as a maid, who fell in love with a soldier. Sadly, her love remained unrequited and she was so distraught that she hanged herself. She now haunts this road, wearing a burnt orange coloured dress which rustles as she walks since it is made of silk.

Interestingly, one witness contacted me to explain that his Great Grandfather had seen her. He says that she is known as the Orange Lady, and is the ghost of one Mademoiselle Pinard, who fell in love with a British soldier named

Bennett during the Napoleonic Wars. She followed him home to England – only to discover that he was married! Unsurprisingly she was not made welcome by the locals (especially by the soldier's wife!) and she was so distressed by her lover's perfidiousness that she hanged herself in Steel's Lane.

His Great Grandfather was reported as saying "...she came past me, I turned round, and there she was....gone!"

He was also able to tell me that there is a headless monk that walks from Meopham Church to the George pub who has been seen on a few occasions, and that Meopham Windmill is said to be haunted by the old miller Mr Bennett who hanged himself in there.

A259 OLD ROMNEY / NEW ROMNEY

In the late 1990's a driver reported driving his car through a phantom man along this stretch of road, who had stepped out onto the road in front of him. The driver stopped to look for the figure, but could find nothing.

I also found a record of three completely separate witnesses in 2018 who had been driving along the road and seen car headlights coming up behind them, as if a car was rushing up to overtake. On all three occasions, the lights suddenly disappeared and there was no car there.

A258 OXNEY BOTTOM – Deal Road

The accounts of this ghost span at least a couple of decades with occasional sightings documented and the usual 'lots of people have seen it' claims.

The ghost in question is that of a Grey Lady who drifts across the road in front of oncoming traffic. She was seen in

1973 by two ghost hunters, who caught a fleeting glimpse of her sad-seeming face.

She was also recorded as being sighted in 1999 by the passengers on a coach whose driver braked sharply as she drifted across the road in front of their vehicle. At least one account describes her as an old woman, who shuffles along the road. Several of the accounts describe the road as either having a sharp S bend, or having tortuous twists and turns but the A259 as it is today is a relatively straight stretch of road. These accounts must therefore date back to before any road improvements were made.

RUSTHALL - Broomhill Road

There is said to be the ghost of a man wearing a grey suit standing by the roadside here, his presence denoting the location where a cottage once stood.

SANDHURST - Bodiam Road

Just on the outskirts of the village of Sandhurst along the Bodiam Road there are two ponds which are known as Chapel Pond and Brick House Pond. There have been two suicides by drowning here - one of a man in 1870, and another of a woman in 1950.

On Christmas Eve in 1973 two young lads called Henry and Brian were walking along Bodiam road when they saw a man standing in the hedge next to Brick House Pond. He seemed to be smiling at them in a slightly creepy way, and then followed them for a few yards before just vanishing.

A21 SEVENOAKS - Gracious Lane

There are two curious phenomena sometimes reported along this stretch of road. Occasionally, drivers have said that the road ahead of them suddenly disappeared and a different road, curving away to their right, appeared ahead of them in its stead, just before they rather unsurprisingly crashed their cars.

It has also been reported that a car driver will sometimes pull up sharply, thinking he has just mown down an old lady with white hair, who is seen wearing a beige coloured coat. As he does so, there is inevitably a driver performing the same action on the other carriageway - also believing he had just run into the same woman.

I have not been able to find any actual witnesses for either type of report.

A262 SISSINGHURST CASTLE - Biddenham Road

When I was asking about Cranbrook, another witness came forward to say, "I'm definitely a sceptic when it comes to these things but I did have one weird encounter in the autumn last year coming past Sissinghurst castle on the main road towards Biddenden."

This would have been in the autumn of 2017. He described how he was driving down the A262 during the middle of the day, just past where there is a gateway entrance into the woods, when he noticed a lady walking towards him on the side of the lane. She was walking on the correct side of the road for a pedestrian where there is no footpath (i.e. on the side facing the on-coming traffic).

He described her as a blonde haired lady, perhaps in her mid-thirties, who was dressed very smartly, looking like she could maybe work in a bank or some similar profession. He checked his rearview mirror to make sure no motorbikes were coming up behind him, before edging his car into the middle of the road in order to give her a safe leeway. Although it took but a moment to glance in his mirror, when he looked forward again, the lady had completely disappeared.

He was utterly bewildered by this sighting, since on that stretch of the road there is simply nowhere she could have turned off and out of sight: she would have had to clamber up the bank to get off the road. He is still at a loss to explain what it was he saw that day. Possibly the same lady ghost seems to be making an appearance in the next encounter too.

Just a very short distance (probably around a mile or so) south west of the Sissinghurst castle sighting, a motorist witnessed the ghost of a blonde haired lady in 1999. This driver was travelling along the A229 at Hartley when he suddenly had to swerve to avoid a blonde haired lady wearing very neat and tidy business type clothing standing in the middle of the road. Even as the car swerved, the apparition vanished.

There have apparently been other reports of a blonde haired lady along this same stretch of road. I can't help but speculate whether this is all the same ghost – Edwardian clothing tended to be very "prim and proper" in appearance – and you might use that same phrasing to describe clothing suitable to wear in a bank or business setting. Our brains tend to categorize memories instantly into something familiar, to help us with our memory recall, like a mental 'filing system' if you like. So one person seeing neat ladies clothing style might think 'banker' where another might think
'Edwardian'. It's very interesting that blonde hair features in both descriptions.

A28 TENTERDEN - Silver Hill

This is another report of the type of ghost who is apparently hit by a car but when the driver gets out there is nothing to be seen.

This one occurred in 1997 and it was the semi-transparent figure of a man wearing dark clothing who stepped out in front of an oncoming car. Although the lady driver thought she might have hit him and stopped to check, there was no sign of him nor any damage to har car.

UPPER DARTFORD - Heath Lane

There is a legend that this lane is haunted by the ghost of a soldier on horseback from the time of the English Civil War. Unfortunately I was not able to find anyone who had ever seen him.

WYE - White Hill

Just to the north of the village of Wye there is a road called White Hill, which travels from the wide valley floor up the gentle slopes of the hill. The source story says that a man called Keith Scales was travelling on his way to work early one morning in January 2000, when he saw a woman standing in the middle of the road. She was blonde haired and wearing a brown coloured coat - and eerily just smiled at him as he braked as hard as he could, but still seemed to hit her.

He was sure he had hit her, as he felt the thump, but when he stopped the car and tried to find the lady, there was no sign of her. It seems that this is the one and only time this ghost has made an appearance.

LANCASHIRE

ACCRINGTON - Black Abbey Street

This town centre street is haunted by the ghost of Ursula, said to be a nobleman's daughter who fell in love with one of the monks in the Abbey the street was named after. Her father got wind of their secret trysts and plans to marry and captured the monk. He chained the poor man to a wall and then set him on fire where he died an agonising death. Ursula ran to try and save him from the flames, but was engulfed herself, and both died.

Her ghost is said to scream if you try to approach her.

ASHWORTH VALLEY - Heywood / Rochdale Road

There is a report that on 30 July 2008 at around 10pm at night, a black animal (either a dog or a large cat) was seen running across this road followed by a woman in her thirties. The animal disappeared into a wall, and the woman vanished as a car braked hard to avoid hitting her.

One correspondent was able to tell me that they had walked up that road on many occasions, and had never seen or sensed anything. Another person, who is sensitive to the world of the paranormal, wrote to me and said that he was able to sense a female presence in the area.

A675 BOLTON - Belmont Road

This stretch of road seems to have quite an active paranormal history. At the area where the road crosses over the Gale Brook, just past the junction with Scout Road, there is said to be the ghost of a highwayman who was hanged near here. Some accounts I found said he was unjustly hanged, but either way his spirit staggers along this stretch of the road, clutching at his own throat and with his eyes bulging, as if he can't quite believe he died that way.

Closer to the Bolton end of the road, there is also supposed to be the ghost of a Viking, who only haunts on 20th December each year (which is the Winter Solstice Eve). He is said to look like he is drunk and celebrating - sometimes holding an earthenware jug.

In January 2015 the local newspaper ran an article about a video of a ghost on the road, supposedly captured using a mobile phone by the passenger inside a car. You can watch the video yourself online as several national papers also picked it up.

Personally, I would make the following observations about it: it doesn't look like a roadway to me - it looks like an unmade up track. The engine sound is not an ordinary car, but more like either a jeep or quad bike type sound. The person videoing is speaking in a foreign language - the articles usually say Arabic - which obviously makes it difficult to judge what is being said unless you happen to speak the language, and also difficult to judge what makes it get reported as Belmont Road when it looks more like someone driving off road... and therefore could be anywhere. And lastly - it really does look like someone wearing an elaborate costume (although the movement of the figure is quite creepy at times) and therefore a fake video: but see what you think. I was not able to find anyone who had actually seen any of the ghosts.

FLEETWOOD - Chatsworth Avenue

In March 1964, according to one source, two workers left their homes and started to make their way to their employment on the late night shift at the docks, independently of one another. One was in his car, the other was on a moped.

As the car driver approached his car to get in it, he noticed a shadow of something stooped over next to him, but thought nothing of it and just assumed it was being cast by the lamppost or whatever. He got into his car and started to reverse it out of the parking bay. However, the stooped shadow seemed to actually approach the car as the car moved – and he realised it was moving independently as a shadowy figure. Terrified, he sped off in his car and arrived at work very shaken up.

Unbeknownst to him, his colleague was also setting off and driving up Chatsworth Avenue on his moped. He saw the same tall, stooped, shadow figure make its way down the road ahead of him – and as he watched it, trying to work out what he was seeing, it suddenly disappeared into thin air. When I asked locally, a couple of people remembered the occurrence and one knew one of the people involved, which tends to lend some credence to the original account. Nobody had seen anything along there since that I could find, however.

A565 FORMBY – towards Ince Blundell

One account I found claimed that the stretch of road between Formby and Ince Blundell was haunted by a lady wearing a green coat. Curiously, just slightly further down the same stretch of road, but on the other side of Ince Blundell where Cross Barn Lane and the A565 meet, there is the ghost of a Grey Lady – or possibly a nun.

Even more curiously, Ince Blundell (which incidentally has some of my favourite street names in the country!) also has a Lady Green Lane which meets the same A565. I think it is very likely this is all connected. When I asked locally, I got a wealth of responses: many people were well aware of the stories and had heard them since childhood. Some had heard of a white lady, others of ghostly nuns. Some tales were of the ghosts dancing in the woods, but a lot were about them appearing on the road and causing people to swerve. One even knew of a door which stood completely on its own in the middle of the woods.

One witness explained that in the late 1970's her father in law had seen what he thought was a white deer run out in front of him near the Roundhouse (a round building in Ince Woods), but when he looked there was nothing in the rearview mirror. When later he told his own mother (who lived in Formby) about what he had seen she replied. "Oh that will be the white nun".

Another witness told me about a strange incident that happened to her and her husband in 1999. They were driving back to Formby from a weekend away in the wee small hours of Monday morning. They were driving through Ince Woods on the main road when they saw a man standing in the road waving at them just after the round house on the left, and before the house on the right.

Feeling a bit concerned as it was so late, and as there have been tales about robbers pretending to flag down cars for help, they decided not to stop but drove around and on past him – looking in their rear view mirror for any signs of trouble as they did. As soon as they passed him the man disappeared completely from their mirrors in the space of a split second. As my witness said, "It still gives us the shivers to think of it! I always wondered if it was just someone walking home but the fact that they completely disappeared so soon as we passed has always struck us as very odd!"

Another witness, who was keen to remain anonymous, told me that in late September 1984 they were cycling through the woods along the road at 9pm, as they did every night. On this particular night, they saw an elderly lady walking in the road close to the Round House. Concerned that she might need help, walking along there alone in the dark, they stopped to offer assistance. As they got within touching distance of the old woman, she literally evaporated in front of their eyes.

Another correspondent told me that there used to be a convent along here and that the building is now used as a nursing home. As a child, she was told the story that one of the nuns was crossing the road when she was hit and killed by a car.

Another lady told me that her uncle and his friend were once driving through these woods when ahead of them, a skeleton suddenly pushed a coffin across the road! They were so shocked by such a macabre and bizarre sight, that he swerved the car too violently, causing it to go into a barrel roll and flip over onto its roof into the field next to the road. Both he and his passenger were quite seriously injured and had to spend some time in hospital – but they both agreed on what they had seen which made them flip the car. She says that her uncle still talks about it now, even years later, as he has never been able to make any sense of what they saw that night.

FRECKLETON – Kirkham Road

There have apparently been several reports of a lady seen along this road wearing a floaty, flimsy dress and noticeably minus her head. One version described the dress as 'petrol coloured'. There doesn't seem to be any knowledge about who this ghost is or why she haunts here, although there are accounts of the pub on the corner of this road being haunted too.

NEWTON LE WILLOWS – Hermitage Green Lane

Just to the south of Newton Le Willows runs Hermitage Green Lane. The legend is that Highlanders were caught by Cromwellian troops here during the English Civil War in

August 1648, and were hanged from surrounding trees. Since then, in the summer months, the sound of running feet can often be heard in the area. One account says that in January 1990 the sound of drumming was heard moving down the lane.

According to historical records on 19th August 1648 the Royalist army was moving south, trying to escape from the Cromwell army who had defeated them at the Battle of Preston a couple of days earlier. There are three contemporary accounts of the battle that took place 'just north of St Oswald's Church' where the Scottish foot soldiers were separated from the main Royalist Cavalry who had already crossed the river ahead of them.

The Scots were forced to stand and fight to the bitter end when surrounded. Around a thousand of them died that day, and the cries of, "Mercy, Mercy!" from the survivors could be heard for some considerable distance according to the records written just after the battle. The description 'just north of' in the contemporaneous accounts could very easily refer to the current day site of Hermitage Lane, which is less than a mile north of St Oswald's Church. I did speak with a local Paranormal research group and they had not heard of any reports along this area.

STUMP CROSS - Horns Lane

Just outside Goosnargh is the tiny hamlet of Stump Cross, and from there runs Horns Lane, which runs past Horns Reservoir.

On 15th November 2007 it was reported that several people had seen a lady standing in the middle of the road wearing a long dark coloured cloak. When vehicles approached, she would disappear. I could not find any other accounts of anyone seeing her so it remains as an odd curiosity why this ghost seems to have made this one day the focal point of her appearances.

LEICESTERSHIRE

BROUGHTON ASTLEY

Broughton Astley is either a large village or small town, depending on which source you want to quote, but either way it seems to have its fair share of haunted roads. There is one report that on 11 August 2014, at around half past ten at night, two people driving along the B581 Broughton Way had to brake sharply as a hooded grey figure stepped out and crossed the road in front of their car. Having reached the other side it just vanished next to a gateway, leaving the witnesses understandably shaken and puzzled by what they had just seen.

At the junction of nearby Cosby Road and Main Street stands The Bull pub. Several witnesses report seeing a policeman standing on the pavement outside the pub. They say it is obvious he is not of this world not just because of the outdated uniform he wears, but because when he is seen there is also a strong feeling of a heavily charged atmosphere.

One witness saw him in 1996 and at the same time as he saw the ghost, he saw another man walking the other way up the road towards it with a small dog. The animal took fright at the apparition and ran off.

CHARLEY - Abbey Road, by Mount St Bernard's Abbey

Charley is a civil parish in Leicestershire, wherein stands the picturesque Mount St Bernards Abbey, which is still home to the Trappist monks. Passing slightly to the south of the Abbey is Abbey Road, and it was here in autumn 1987 that a passenger in a car driving along in the direction of Shepshed noticed a figure walking towards the car on the grass verge.

Mildly curious at first, as the figure was wearing a long cloak with the hood up, the passenger was terrified when the figure suddenly looked up at the approaching car – revealing that there was no face underneath the hood. At the same moment, the figure stepped out onto the road straight into the path of the car.

The passenger screamed at the driver to stop, only to find that the poor driver was shocked rigid at his passenger suddenly screaming – since he had not seen the figure at all.

The Abbey itself is reported to be haunted by a monk, and one researcher in 2012 caught a light anomaly and three EVPs (Electronic Voice Phenomenon) on tape there which you can find online and listen to.

B667 EVINGTON - Shady Lane

Possibly the most aptly named road on which to encounter a ghost, Shady Lane runs past the Arboretum on the very outskirts of Leicester City.

Curiously, various reports I found said that it was either the figure of a man who steps out in front of cars along here, then vanishes with no trace – or the figure of a nun.

KNIPTON

There is a report that in 1994 witnesses in a car saw a figure wearing a long coat thumbing a lift at the t-junction on the road from Belvoir castle. The driver had no intention of stopping to pick him up as something seemed 'off'.

As the car approached, however, the figure stepped out into the road – making the driver brake hard. Even as the car screeched to a halt, the figure simply vanished.

No-one locally was able to tell me anything more about the apparition, and the exact location is hard to pinpoint as there is more than one route from the castle to Knipton.

MARKET BOSWORTH

There is a local legend that the ghost of a soldier who was decapitated in the Battle of Bosworth Field wanders the roads and lanes near the battle site looking for his missing head. When I asked for any information, I was told by Katy [pseudonym] that she had heard of the '9pm Horseman'. She explained that she had been told that if you were to drive down the straight road which passes the entrance to the battlefield at 9pm precisely, then the ghost of a horse and rider will be seen crossing the road ahead of you.

Katy had also heard of the ghost of Luigi, an Italian man who was a prisoner of war from the Second World War. In life he used to ride his bike with a squeaky wheel around the lanes and apparently still does even after his death.

Although Katy has never seen the figure herself, her partner did once when they were out walking together. They were passing the mirror pond in Bosworth Park, when her partner said to her to wait a moment, as there was a chap on an old fashioned bike coming towards them that they would need to make room for. This puzzled our witness, because although her partner was insistent she had just seen him, our witness saw nothing, and no bicycle came past them.

Another witness told me that when she goes out walking in the area there is one particular tree that her dog flat refuses to walk past - and she has been told by a fellow dog walker that the lane itself is haunted.

LINCOLNSHIRE

ALKBOROUGH - West Halton Lane, near the cricket ground

In the late 1970's a man was cycling home late one evening down West Halton Lane, when a small dog or puppy crossed in front of him just as he passed the cricket club making him brake hard on his bicycle.

It's quite a lonely stretch of road with only a very few houses along it, but he barely had time to wonder if he should try to catch the puppy and see where it had come from, when it vanished right in front of his eyes – only half a meter away from him.

I wasn't able to find anyone else who had seen this apparition.

A52 FRISKNEY

One autumn morning in the early 1990's, a family driving along the A52 just outside Friskney passed a lady walking along the roadside who was dressed in Victorian style clothing and had curly hair under a wide hat. They were so surprised they turned around and drove past her again, noting this time that her face seemed to be glowing a faint green colour. They didn't turn around again but went a different way.

It's difficult really to say whether this was a ghost as it could have just been someone wearing a particular fashion statement and certain types of makeup can appear greenish in the wrong light. I wasn't able to find any other accounts of her.

A16 GRIMSBY -towards Louth

When I was asking about other areas in Lincolnshire, one witness wrote in to tell me his own tale. Many years ago, probably around 1968, he was riding down the A16 travelling from Grimsby towards Louth with his girlfriend riding pillion on his motorbike. They were on their way home from work and it was about 6pm in the evening but already dark. At a certain point along the road there is a set of bends which he has always known as 'Cordeaux Corners'.

As he put the motorbike into the bends, he found himself having to take evasive action to avoid hitting an old lady who was walking in the middle of the road, apparently oblivious to the motorbike and the sound of its engine.

Both he and his girlfriend saw her and were concerned enough to worry that she might not be so fortunate when the next vehicle came along, so he turned his machine around and they went back to see if they could escort her to safety. There was absolutely no sign of her anywhere. He says that even today, he thinks of her when he goes round those bends and still feels a little creeped out by what happened all those years ago.

KELSTERN

During the First and Second World Wars, there was an airbase at Kelstern. Today there are just fields and some vague remains of old structures visible, as it was completely disbanded and returned to agricultural use after 1965. There are numerous accounts from over the years of people still hearing the noise of the aircraft circling to land - especially on foggy nights.

Several people have encountered an airman carrying his kit and trying to hitch a lift and others have seen him standing close to the lonely war memorial that now occupies the site. There are accounts spanning from 1983 through to 1995 at least. There is also a very interesting online sound file of an investigation and research into the site complete with Spirit Box results if you search for 'Haunted Airfield - RAF Kelstern'.

(A spirit box is used by some paranormal researchers - it is a device which scans rapidly across the radio waves, never settling on one output so that it produces a lot of white noise. The theory is that you can ask questions and voices can be heard responding. In my opinion, they are usually just giving out random words which people try really hard to ascribe some meaning to - but every once in a while I have seen one used where the words it comes out with are just so specific to the location that it does make one wonder..)

A52 LEVERTON - towards Wrangle

There is a report that one person who regularly cycled this route around 2002 often encountered a strange big dog trotting along the road. He really only began to think of it as supernatural after he had seen it several times. Another witness heard it howling in the field and then spotted two red eyes in the dark. He was convinced he had encountered a Black Shuck.

When I tried to track this report down, I found an identical description of a fellow who regularly cycled the route but it was dated 'towards the end of the 19th Century' - which is the late 1890's. This report said the dog was usually seen skirting a long deep pond near the road and would then trot off down a lane. I suspect this is an unfortunate instance of someone repeating an earlier tale and not understanding that 'late 19th century' does *not* refer to the late 1990's...

B1190 LINCOLN - Doddington Road

There is an account of a lady who was out walking her dogs one night down Doddington Road in Lincoln when she noticed just ahead of her a woman dressed in Victorian clothing. Surprised, she glanced down at her dogs for a split second and then back up to take a good look at the lady, only to find she had disappeared.

LOUTH – Between roundabout at London Road and the A157

One source lists the account of a couple who were returning home from their holiday in 2004, when they saw a man cycling down the middle of this stretch of road just outside Louth. He caught their eye partly because of the fact that he was in the middle of the road, but also because he was wearing Victorian clothing and riding an old fashioned bicycle. As they drove towards him, he vanished right in front of their astonished eyes. Another source gave the same occurrence as June 2006.

When I asked for any other sightings, a witness came forward to tell me about his own encounter with the supernatural on the stretch of road from Kenwick to the Manby roundabout (possibly the B1200). It was in 1976 and about 11pm at night, when he was driving home in his first ever car. At a point on the road where there was thick hedge on one side and woods on the other, a horse and rider suddenly galloped across the road in front of him causing him to hit his brakes a bit sharpish.

He was certain no corporeal horse and rider could have crossed just there, so went back in daylight to double check. He was able to confirm that there was no gap or anything that a real horse could have passed through. As he says, the encounter, "fair frit me".

NORTH HYKEHAM - Mill Lane

I found one account where a gentleman described driving home towards North Hykeham along Mill Lane one sunny, warm day in Spring 1999.

As he went to turn into Kings Meadow estate, he suddenly noticed a man walking in the opposite direction along the lane. The man was wearing what looked like clothing from the 1920's and was wrapped in a warm jacket with its collar up. The figure seemed to be leaning slightly forward as if he was walking into a cold wind. Sadly the witness didn't stop to take a closer look.

A15 RUSKINGTON

Sometimes referred to as 'The Ruskington Horror' this ghost has been seen a great number of times, according to numerous sources. It caused a stir on the 'This Morning' T.V show in 1998 when a caller rang in to describe his own encounter with the entity and two more viewers then rang in with their own accounts much to the excitement of the show presenters. The original caller had encountered it that year, 1998, and the other two in 1984 and 1997 respectively.

The first caller first noticed something white at the side of the road. It was around 1am and he was driving south towards Sleaford, so that the turning for Ruskington was on his left hand side. As he approached the white object it suddenly seemed to move right up against his car windscreen - and now it looked like an olive skinned, pock marked face of a man, with his arm raised.

It was on the car for around 40 seconds or so and then just sort of slithered or faded into obscurity out of view down the side of the car. He described it as looking sort of fluorescent - like a picture of a man with the flash too bright. He was terribly shaken by his encounter.

One witness wrote to me and said he believed it more likely that the driver had seen his own face illuminated by the dashboard lights and projected onto the windscreen. Another said that in the version he had heard, the figure stands with its arm out as if trying to ask for a lift.

In 1984 a lorry driver saw a man in white standing at the side of the road at about 9pm in the evening with his hand up - everything about the figure was white so he was sure it was not a real person.

In 1997 a lady was a passenger in the car her husband was driving when she saw the dark figure of a man dash out into the road in front of their car. Although she called out a warning and her husband braked, the figure disappeared and her husband had seen nothing.

Other accounts say that in November 2013 a driver saw a man in a dark, possibly leather, jacket standing at the side of the road who inexplicably disappeared as soon as he was noticed, and another account from 1960 says it was seen by a school coach driver. Other accounts have apparently also come forward over the years.

Various witnesses told me that they had heard different accounts of who exactly this man was - from a motorcyclist who tried to warn people of the bends, to a priest from the nearby village ravaged by The Black Death in centuries gone by.

One gentleman told me that he was driving along there with a friend once, when both he and the car in front stopped to let something go across the road. It was 1am in the morning and as they stopped they momentarily saw that it was some sort of horse and carriage before it disappeared. The figures were faint, as if not quite solid.

One witness wrote to me with his personal account, "Around October 1999 I passed my driving test, and bought myself a little Mini from Kirkby la Thorpe near Sleaford. It had no Tax or MOT so I took it home at night on the back roads to Ruskington where I used to live.

"I went through Evedon, which is a desolate back road. My parents were following me in their car in case anything went wrong all the way home. To me, the journey was uneventful, but when we arrived home my Mother jumped out of their car and said to me, 'you wont believe this, but I saw you drive through a ghost near Evedon!' She had seen a guy walking on the side of the road and I never saw him!"

He went on to tell me how a few days later, with his car now legal and checked out for soundness, he visited a friend and afterwards drove down the same road.

He wrote, "I was going round a bend and something jumped out in front of me! I automatically braked and swerved and ended up in a ditch! I got out of the car and nothing was there! I went to my friend's house and he managed to pull me out of the ditch [using his vehicle] and luckily the car was fixable, after about a month or so I was back on the road".

Then again, on Christmas Eve of the same year, he had allowed his friend to drive the mini on the way home, and the friend took the route down the same fateful stretch of road.

Our witness explained, "I had a terrible feeling. I didn't want to go down there but never said a word. We were driving and suddenly my mini engine cut out and we pulled over wondering what the hell just happened! My friend tried starting the car up again but there was nothing, it wasn't turning over or anything. We sat there a minute and then my friend said 'can you smell that burning?' I couldn't smell anything, but he was dead serious and said 'we need to get out NOW!' and with that he jumped out of the car and ran up the road! I naturally panicked and started to fumble with my seatbelt, the car started to fill with smoke and I managed to get out and scramble up the road. It was like a scene out of a film as my poor car went up in flames."

The fire service later told him that the fire had been caused when a tin of chemical sealant left in the boot of his car had overturned and had hit the battery, causing sparking and eventually a fire. Not surprisingly, he was now a little wary of driving down this particular piece of road and tended to avoid it for the next couple of years.

However, some years later a girl he was chatting to one night persuaded him to take her out and show her where it all happened, so against his better judgment they set off together in his car.

He said, "I went down the road again, but I was scared and not ashamed to admit it."

As they reached the spot where the fire had been, his car radio, which was turned off, suddenly switched itself on. There was the sound of white noise coming through it, which you get when no radio station is tuned in. It scared him so badly that, "I will be honest I dropped it down a gear and raced off to never return for nearly 20 years!"

He finally plucked up the courage in August 2018 when he and a friend decided to go ghost hunting, and used an App on his phone which gave a spirit box. They thought they heard a voice come through the noise as they passed the fateful spot, but they were unable to tell what it said.

My husband and I drove down the road on 23.07.18, but unfortunately saw nothing. It does seem feasible however that this is a particularly active haunting.

MERSEYSIDE

BROMBOROUGH – Poulton Road, Poulton Hall Road and Dibbinsdale Road

There is an old tale that a young girl left Poulton Hall intending to go and join a nunnery. She set off walking but was attacked by a thug where the road crosses the Dibbinsdale Brook, who raped her, murdered her, and then threw her body into the water, leaving her poor ghost to haunt the site of her demise.

Another version of the story says that a nun was walking from Birkenhead Priory to St. Werburgh's Abbey in Chester and stopped to spend the night in a manor house near the bridge. However, the lord of the manor was not as gentlemanly as he had at first seemed, and when she refused his sexual advances he kept her prisoner and starved her to death. In still another version, he lost his temper when she refused him and murdered her by beheading her with a single swing of his sword.

Whoever she was, and however she died, ever since then her shade has haunted the roads around this area. Apparently in 1970 a driver saw her standing in the middle of the road, but when he looked fully at her she vanished.

Another version says that in 1970, a woman on her way back from Clatterbridge Hospital saw a girl apparently waiting for a lift by the side of the road, but as the woman approached, the girl vanished. A few years later another man driving along Poulton Road stopped to offer a lift to a woman 'wearing a long dark coat', but as he opened his door she vanished.

There is also said to be the ghost of a Quaker on Kingswood Road near here.

A5038 LIVERPOOL - Lime Street

The accounts I could find all say the sightings on Lime Street of a tall entity with no visible legs and a silently moving mouth go back 'hundreds of years' - but none of those experiences or sources are actually cited as far as I could see..

LIVERPOOL, FAZAKERLEY - Higher Lane

This haunting is supposed to be a semitransparent or 'smoky' figure which has been appearing in front of cars for about six decades and causing accidents: although no actual events other than being seen by a policeman once in February 2006 are cited.

I did however find one particularly creepy account which described it as looking like an oily patch oozing along the road which then morphed into the figure of a man.

LIVERPOOL Maryland Street

The ghost of a beautiful petite woman wearing a Regency-style bonnet walks down Maryland Street in the company of a small girl ghost. Today, the city centre street is pedestrianised, with stone benches all along it, so that should at least give the ghost hunter somewhere to sit whilst they wait to see if any apparitions appear.

LIVERPOOL - Queensway Tunnel to Birkenhead

There is a local story that in the 1960's a young lady who was riding pillion on a motorbike was killed when she fell off it as it rode through the tunnel. Since then, the story goes, her ghost has been seen in the tunnel trying to hitch a lift.

There is also supposed to be an old style police car sometimes seen in there, as well as a gold coloured futuristic looking car, leading some to believe the tunnel is subject to momentary time slips (although why it should repeatedly pick on the same two moments in time is unclear).

One witness did say he had heard a story of a young girl who gets into a taxi on one side of the tunnel and has disappeared by the time the taxi reaches the other side. Curiously, another witness said that he had been told, by staff and police working in the tunnel, that there was a ghost of a man on the Birkenhead side of the tunnel who would sometimes hitch a ride but then disappear from the car part way through the tunnel.

NORFOLK

A47 ACLE

It seems that this particular stretch of road is very active with paranormal occurrences. Some drivers are reported to have seen a ghostly horse and cart along this stretch and to have braked sharply at the sight of it. Apparently, it has also been reported that other drivers feel the bizarre urge to suddenly brake hard here, even though nothing visible accounts for their sudden odd behaviour.

The origin of the tale seems to be a legend that a drover using the old droving lane which crossed here was killed by a highwayman, who left his body beside the lane having taken his money, but had no interest in the man's horse or cart. After waiting a while, the faithful horse decided it might as well make its own way back to its stable. It plodded off down the familiar route pulling the cart all the way home on its own and thus inadvertently became the harbinger of bad news as the waiting family realised something bad must have happened for the horse to have made its own way home.

When I asked locally, one witness had heard stories of drivers seeing a horse and carriage here and having to swerve to avoid hitting it. Another explained that when he was a child, in perhaps 1976 or thereabouts, his friend's father had an experience on this stretch of road and was left very shaken up by it. He had been travelling home from an evening event, when he suddenly had the horrible sight of what looked like a Roman soldier pass through his car – but only visible from the shins upwards.

Later in life, in around 1985 or so, the same witness was now a grown man and was working on erecting some new farm buildings next to the road. They were digging out for the footings of the new building when they dug up small

Roman coins which were handed in to the museum. He describes how finding evidence of Roman presence close to where his friend's father had seen the ghost of a Roman gave him goosebumps.

A148 BALE - crossroads

One source gives the account of a driver on this stretch of road one afternoon in December 2010 just after sundown, who was forced to brake sharply when a cyclist pulled out in front of their car at the crossroads. The cyclist promptly disappeared.

BLAKENEY - Little Lane

This lane, despite the fact that it lives up to its name by only being quite a short stretch of road, has the dubious distinction of allegedly being haunted by both the ubiquitous ghostly carriage and a Black Shuck.

Unfortunately, no-one came forward with any accounts of having actually seen either.

A1067 FAKENHAM - towards Norwich

In 2006 a report was given by a driver returning home from a trip to the cinema. He said he had seen what he thought looked remarkably like a black wolf calmly eating the carcass of some animal at the side of the road. He described the creature as around three feet tall at its shoulders, with black matted-looking fur and yellow eyes.

One local told me that there had been quite a few rumors over the years of various animals escaping from the nearby Wildlife Park. Black Shuck, or carelessly owned zoo animal?

GORLESTON - Suffield Road and High Street

In 2006 according to one source a lady reported that she had twice seen a strange looking, dog-like creature but with long legs - the first time on Suffield Road. When she saw it again shortly afterwards running down the High Street, it ran out of her sight and she has not encountered it since.

Although I asked locally for any other experiences, no-one came forward with any corroborating information. This and the previous location are some fifty miles apart, which casts some doubt on whether the two sightings in one year were likely to be one creature.

A12 / A47 HOPTON

Until fairly recently, the main road which ran past the small coastal town of Hopton was the A12 - now renamed the A47. In November 1981 a gentleman called Andrew Cutajar was driving towards Great Yarmouth on a dark, wet, and miserable evening. As he passed Hopton he noticed a white mist in the road ahead. As he drove closer, he realised he could make out a figure of a man with long straggly hair, heavy laced up boots and wearing either a long coat or cape.

He was standing in the middle of the road, causing Mr Cutajar to brake so sharply that his car slid on the wet road surface and its momentum carried it straight through the figure - which promptly disappeared. I was only able to find this one account.

B1354 HORSTEAD - Norwich Road bridge over River Bure

I've included this entry out of curiosity. I actually came across this evidence when researching for my previous book, The Almanac of British Ghosts, which details ghosts who only haunt on certain dates of the year. This bridge over the River Bure was of interest to me for that book because supposedly, on 19th May each year, the ghost of

Anne Boleyn's father, Sir Thomas Boleyn, rides across this and a number of other bridges in Norfolk trying to get back to Blickling Hall before the cock crows - in penance for bringing his daughter to the attention of the King which ultimately led to her death at such a young age.

Curiously though, two witnesses have told me that the story they had heard as children growing up locally was that the bridge is haunted by a Black Shuck - and one of them had heard that the dog was heading towards Blickling Hall. This could be a fascinating example of an ancient tale transmuting over time.

A11 NORWICH - slip road towards London

In 2006 early one winter's morning, a driver and passenger pulled up next to a set of temporary traffic lights on this slip road, waiting for them to change to green.

Also waiting at the lights was a vintage 1930's style car, whose driver was warmly bundled in goggles and hat. They glanced at the car, mildly interested in seeing such a lovely old vintage vehicle in use in winter. As they drove off when the lights turned to green, they suddenly realised that the old car had disappeared...

REEDHAM

There is a legend that on August 21st every year, you can see the ghost of 'Old Man Bern' running for his life as he is pursued by Vikings down to the waters' edge, where he makes his escape. The most commonly given version of this story is that Bern was a huntsman to King Edmund, but became insanely jealous when the King struck up a friendship with the Viking Chief, Ragnar Lothbrok, and preferred to go hunting with him instead.

Bern seized his chance whilst he and Ragnar were alone one night on a hunt, with only Ragnar's hunting hound as a witness. He killed the Viking and professed to know nothing as to what might have occurred when the body was discovered. However, the faithful hound was determined to take revenge on his master's killer. Every evening he would sneak into the Great Hall as everyone gathered for the evening meal and sink his teeth into Bern, until eventually the hapless man was forced to confess his heinous crime. As punishment some versions say he was cast adrift in a boat, others that he was chased and escaped in a boat.

Either way, the sons of Ragnar Lothbrok were understandably peeved at the treatment of their father and attacked the settlement at Reedham, killing all who lived there including the King.

Historically speaking, this gets a little confused though. There was a King Edmund, who was killed by Viking raiders in around 869 a.d. The earliest English account comes from around 100 years after the events, and it names the Vikings involved as Ragnar's sons, Ivar and Ubbi. An account from 300 years after the event names three sons of Ragnar – Ivar, Ubba and Beorn – or Bern.

It is not until nearly 400 years after the event that the tales first start to describe Bern as the King's huntsman rather than as one of the Vikings.

In truth then, the ghost of Bern, if ever seen, could either be a murderous huntsman escaping after killing a Viking Chief, or a murderous Viking escaping after killing the King! That there is paranormal activity in general around Reedham is likely, as I found several accounts of haunted buildings and houses when researching as well as a UFO sighting in 2016 but no accounts of anyone actually seeing Old Man Bern, whoever he was.

SHELFANGER - Wash Lane

There is a story that at some point during the 1990's, a ten year old girl was completely terrified when the apparition of what looked like a man on fire suddenly ran out in front of their car. There is no additional detail on the story that I could find, and I was unable to get any corroboration.

A11 THETFORD

This next story is really quite bizarre when you try to break it down. It is listed as the ghost of a Gamekeeper. The claim is that on 20th November.2006 a man was driving on his way to pick someone up at around midnight and was on the dual carriageway part of the A11.

He suddenly saw the apparition of a man actually on his car bonnet, who is described as wearing 'a light thorn coloured suit with a thin red pinstripe', and had dark hair. The figure was said to be smiling. The driver is supposed to have briefly glanced at his passenger (presumably to see if they were reacting to the apparition) who turned out to have fallen asleep, and when he glanced back ahead the apparition had vanished.

I can't see what about the apparition made someone make the connection of 'gamekeeper' - why on earth would a gamekeeper be wearing a pinstripe suit? And what exactly is 'thorn coloured'? And honestly, if an apparition suddenly appeared on the bonnet of my car whilst I was driving, I wouldn't be noticing what colour pinstripes there were on its suit, wondering what job it did in life, or calmly turning to see what my passenger thought - I'd be too busy screaming my head off and frantically braking.

It would be really interesting if anyone else had come forward with any corroboration.

A1075 THETFORD – towards Wretham

This is not strictly a ghost sighting by any general definition, but I have included it out of interest. There is a level crossing along this road, and in June 1986 and then again over ten years later in December 2007 there were sightings of a long haired, greyish white creature – possibly with black patches in its fur.

It ran on four legs, had small ears with a long snout, and large eyes. One of the brave drivers who saw it in 1986 drove backwards and forwards three times to get a proper look at it and on the third time past it rose up on its hind legs. This had the effect of making it seem around 6' tall and more humanoid in appearance.

NORTHAMPTONSHIRE

BOZEAT - Dungee Corner

Just slightly to the west of Bozeat is an area called Dungee Corner, which is supposedly haunted by a headless horseman. Although several locals had heard of the horseman, no-one had actually seen it. Curiously, there are also accounts of Roman soldiers being seen along the same stretch of road, and in 1985 there is an account of a strange mist which enveloped a car and stalled it on nearby Slade Road.

A couple of people did come forward independently of one another to tell me that although they themselves had never seen anything, their dogs were very nervous walking along The Slade (a trackway) and would cling close to their owners and display clear signs of anxiousness. One said that the area always felt very uncomfortable to them too. I took my dogs for a walk along there one bright winter's day to test the theory, but they were completely unbothered.

COLD ASHBY - East bound from Long Buckby towards Cold Ashby

There is an account that in 1999 a man returning home one stormy night after his night shift saw an old woman walking along the road towards him. She was bent over as if she had a bad back and held a shawl close to her head. Her clothing looked old fashioned 'as if it was from the eighteenth century'. As with so many of these types of encounters, the driver is said to have looked in his rear view mirror only to realise she had disappeared, then driven back to look for her but there was no sign of her anywhere.

The difficulty with this account is that it is at least 6.5 miles between Long Buckby and Cold Ashby - and not by direct road. In fact, there are at least seven different roads that could potentially fit the bill of being 'between Long Buckby and Cold Ashby' - making any sort of attempt to corroborate the account impossible. Furthermore, if the clothing was '18th century' then it was from some period in the 1700's. Just how many people, unless they happen to be clothing historians, could pinpoint the century of dress? Why not just instead describe what she was wearing as that would have more meaning to the majority of people reading the account. When that kind of reporting - deliberately appearing detailed but actually unnecessarily vague - is used, it always makes me very sceptical as to the origin of the story.

A4500 ECTON - where it crosses Wellingborough Road and Ecton Lane

Next to this crossroads is The World's End pub, parts of which date back to the 1600's and the time of the English Civil War. There used to be a gallows near this crossroads (as there did at hundreds of crossroads around Britain), and the site is said to be haunted by the ghost of a nun with a grinning skull instead of a face. Although I asked locally, no-one came forward who had encountered anything here.

Curiously though, I found an account which said that the road between Ecton and Mears Ashby was haunted by a grey woman, and the road between Ecton and Earls Barton by a headless woman - which does rather tend to suggest that there is something around here - in female form - which has sparked all these old tales.

HARRINGTON - Road leading to Lamport

There is supposed to be a World War II style car full of military personnel which still drives this lane heading towards RAF Harrington (now a military museum). When seen, it slowly fades from view as it travels.

One local told me that there had been all sorts of strange sightings around this area over the years, but declined to elaborate further. Conversely another said she had lived here most of her life and had never heard of or seen anything.

B672 HARRINGWORTH – under the Seaton Viaduct bridge

The Seaton Viaduct – also known as the Harringworth Viaduct and the Welland Viaduct – is a truly stunning piece of architecture and well worth a visit if you happen to be in the area. And if you do go you might see a ghost too.

One report says that after midnight on 12 April 2007, a driver was travelling home towards Seaton. As he passed under the viaduct he saw a woman wearing what he took to be white clothing standing under one of the arches of the viaduct next to a gate.

He thought it was very peculiar that a woman should be out there alone at such a late hour and slowed down wondering if he should offer help. However, she was completely motionless and ignored him as he passed her, so he thought better of stopping, just glancing in his rearview mirror to see if she went to walk on. She had completely vanished.

IRCHESTER – Farndish Road

According to one source, a chap and his mother were walking their pet dog along this stretch of road, one summer's evening in 1992 at 9.45pm. As they walked a car drove past them quite slowly and then seemed to just disappear into thin air. The account says they ran back to their own car and attempted to follow where the car had gone to try and explain what they thought they had just seen. (Presumably to see if there was a side turning or something). They could not see anything but as they turned the car around to go back, for a moment there were car headlights behind them which also promptly disappeared.

I was not able to find any corroborating evidence for the haunting.

A508 LAMPORT - Harborough Road

Just outside of Lamport on the A508 Harborough Road, there is what used to be a level crossing over the now disused railway - it's a nice walking path now. Although you might not want to go for a walk along there after dusk, in case you see the ghost of the monk that haunts just here, holding a lantern. Several drivers are said to have reported seeing him, as well as a couple out walking.

I can't help but wonder if it's actually the ghost of someone wearing a long coat, rather than a monk, because someone carrying a lamp near an old railway line tends to make me think more of signalmen than monks.

A5213 NORTHAMPTON - Kettering Road

There is a source which says that in summer 2010 when driving back in broad daylight from a day's shopping a driver had to brake sharply when a tall figure stepped suddenly off the kerb in front of both him and a car coming in the other direction. The other car also reacted - but the figure vanished just as it reached the opposite kerb.

Curiously, the source says this occurred on the Kettering Road 'between Bailiff Street and Spinney Hill' - but that makes no sense as there is more than one road between those two destinations. I was not able to find anyone who could shed any further light on this haunting.

RAUNDS

One witness wrote to me to say that around 40 years ago she was in a car with her Nan and Grandad on a road between Raunds and Rushden. She cannot now be sure which road exactly it was, but she recalled looking back at the dark lane behind them at one point and seeing a young girl wearing a long white dress float eerily across the road behind the car. She recalls that the figure seemed to glow slightly, even though there was no light source nearby which could have been lighting her up.

A6003 RUSHTON - Between the 'Mount' burial hill and Barford Bridge

The original source I found said that in the 1980's, a ghostly monk was seen several times drifting across the road here, sometimes seemingly carrying something in his arms. Also, some people were said to have reported glancing in their rear view mirrors when driving along this stretch of road only to see a man's face looking back at them from the back seat of their own car! One source said that it was a police sergeant who was one of the ones who reported seeing the face in the back of his car in 1984.

Supposedly the monk was connected to a long vanished chapel in the old village of Barford, which had a single monk who used to live in it. His ghost is also often seen in the back of cars driving along the tiny lane leading to Geddington. When I asked for any local experiences, one witness told me that when he was a child and was being driven to school along that stretch of road, his mother would tell him they had to be careful going under the bridge as a ghost might appear in the back of their car. It's surprising the poor kid ever wanted to go to school!

One witness explained that she and her husband moved to the village around ten years ago (2008 or so), and knew nothing of the local legends at that time. They had been living in the village for about a year, and were going out this particular evening in early November to a bonfire party. They set off around 7pm to drive to their friend's home a couple of miles away where the party was being held. The husband was driving, and they were chatting amiably about nothing in particular as they drove under the bridge, and passed the turning where the lorry park was.

Suddenly, at the part of the road bounded on each side by thick hedges, they were astonished to see a 'thing' step out of the hedge and into the full beam of their headlights. The creature was distinctly humanoid in shape and crossed the narrow country road in front of their car, stopping briefly as the husband braked sharply to avoid a collision. It slowly and calmly turned its head to gaze at the car for a moment, then equally slowly turned its head away again, resuming its lope across the lane and disappearing into the hedge.

The witness described it as around 8 feet tall, completely naked and hairless with pale skin and with weirdly elongated arms and legs. Even its face seemed to be longer than a human face. The whole encounter lasted a matter of seconds, but to this day the witness shudders at the memory of how it slowly turned its head to look at them, swivelling it round and then back again in a way that seemed almost robotic.

Shaken up, they carried on to their destination where they discussed their sighting with their friends. The following day the witness asked her neighbours if they could shed any light on what she and her husband had seen. They then told her about the ghostly monk which haunts that same stretch of road. But as she says, "That wasn't a monk we saw!"

She explains that even now her husband doesn't like talking about it because he can find no explanation for what they encountered that night, particularly since a daylight visit to the same stretch of road a few days later made it abundantly clear that the hedges along there are simply too thick for anything bigger than a rabbit to step through, let alone something 8 feet tall.

Another witness explained that the burial mounds mentioned in the original report used to be in their field at Keeper's Lodge. He remembers the mound being excavated in the late 1970's and the skeletons exhumed before the site was compulsorily purchased in 1982 to make way for the dual carriageway. He recalls as a child playing in the holes left behind by the exhumed skeletons.

Another witness explained that she once lived at Storefield Cottages for six years. She remembered that when the digging for the dual carriageway section began, there was a Roman burial ground unearthed. They had numerous ghostly sounds in their garden, and sometimes in their kitchen too. They would hear footsteps when no-one living was there, even though the kitchen had a cork tiled floor so footsteps should not have been easily audible.

SALCEY FOREST - Forest Road

Salcey Forest covers a huge area of around 160 hectares, close to the village of Hartwell. It is actually the fragmented remains of a medieval Royal hunting forest and when you walk in it you quickly leave the sights and sounds of the modern world behind. Even the hum of the nearby M1 motorway is quickly lost in the trees. It can feel slightly spooky even on the brightest of days (as well as very beautiful and well worth a visit) but at night, you might just hear the sounds of a coach and horses careening wildly and out of control through the trees.

There are also recent reports of the figure of a monk seen walking the area, and possibly even a phantom cyclist.

NORTHUMBERLAND

A696 BELSAY

There is a report that two men, Rob Davies and Chris Felton, managed to film a figure who looked like an RAF pilot standing on the roadside here late one night. He was holding his arm out in the way someone might do if they were hitchhiking. They turned the car around to get another look at him and maybe offer him a lift, since they were travelling at speed when they first saw him and had no time to slow down or stop, but he had completely vanished.

He was holding some sort of bag, and yet he was two miles north of the village on quite a lonely stretch of road. You can watch the video online and see what you think.

B6309 BLACK HEDDON

There is a bridge just south of Black Heddon which a lady ghost called Silky haunts. The legend is that she was both beautiful and spiteful when alive in the 1700's and now causes road traffic accidents. Before there were cars, she was said to jump on the backs of horses being ridden across the bridge – scaring them so badly they threw their riders and bolted. Curiously the actual village is said to have another female ghost, who drifts sadly around the lanes after she was trampled to death by the carriage horses. They are generally said to be different ghosts – but you can't help but wonder.

The earliest written account of Silky comes from 1841, in M.A.Richardson's 'The Local Historian's Table Book of Remarkable Occurrences'. In these older versions, Silky gets up to all sorts of mischief and is much more like a sprite or Brownie. I could not find any accounts which suggested there is still paranormal activity here.

B6306 BLANCHLAND – Park Bank

The ghost of Dorothy Forster haunts this tiny village road, and also the local pub called the Lord Crewe Arms. Dorothy Forster played an active role in some parts of the Jacobite uprising in 1715, riding to London to rescue her brother and then smuggle him safely to France. It is said that her ghost still waits forlornly for him to return home.

There are possibly also the ghosts of the monks from the Abbey here, who wore white habits which gave the village its name. One report says one was seen as recently as the late 1990's by an American tourist.

A1 BUCKTON

There is an old story that a woman called Grizelda once dressed as a highwayman and held up the stagecoach on the old North Road here, which she knew was bringing with it the execution order condemning her friend who was the real highwayman. Her ghost still enacts this ride at the end of every month and one report claims she was last seen in 1987.

A1058 NORTH SHIELDS – towards Willington

This road is supposedly haunted by a grey lady ghost with nothing but grey shadows where her eyes should be. The story goes that she murdered someone and tried to confess her sin to a local monk. He refused to hear her confession, thus condemning her soul to hell (assuming it wasn't already for the sin of committing murder in the first place!) Distraught, she committed suicide. The monk felt so guilty for his part in this sorry tale, he also took his own life shortly afterwards.

One correspondent recalled reading about a female ghost wandering down Burn Close near here.

NOTTINGHAMSHIRE

CALVERTON

The haunting of Old Hall Close apparently started in the 1960's when an old house was demolished to make way for the Miner's Welfare building, which in turn has also since been demolished. The close is now a cluster of stylish, mostly detached, modern homes.

The ghost of an old lady stands at the side of the road here, and sometimes materialises in the back of cars driving past the close. Drivers spot her face in their rear view mirror, but when they turn around in shock no-one is there. I found an account of someone in the late 1990's who had experienced something similar except it was the face of a man in the back of her car and on nearby Georges Lane, which is literally around the corner.

The street which runs past Old Hall Close is Main street, and this also sports two ghosts of its own. Apparently a man wearing a tweed suit is sometimes seen here, and also a woman in white waits patiently at the bus stop on some quiet nights.

A6075 EDWINSTOWE - Ollerton Road

One account tells of a ghostly cyclist that can sometimes be encountered along this stretch of road - appearing directly in front of cars before just as quickly disappearing.

NOTTINGHAM - Stone Bridge Road

This road seems to be haunted by sounds - rather than actual visual apparitions. There is supposed to be the sound of a factory siren which sometimes goes off in the dead of night even though the building it once belonged to is long gone. And sometimes a woman can be heard screaming in the early hours of the morning even though there is no corporeal person in distress.

WATNALL – Main Road

In 1964 a motorcyclist narrowly missed a woman who crossed the road in front of him close to where the Royal Oak pub stands. Angry at her inattention, he turned to shout at her – and only then realised she was actually floating rather than walking.

OXFORDSHIRE

ASTON TIRROLD

I struggled to find any true source information about the phenomena related to this particular village. Such sources as I could find must have been prior to the county boundary change in 1974, since they list the village as being in Berkshire, when it is actually now in Oxfordshire. All I could find were unsatisfying statements that, "sometimes unaccountable lights are seen floating around the village, or other times seen as long flashing trails of light between Lydds and Blewburton Hill or on Mile Furlong lighting up the trees at Lollington".

I can't even find where Mile Furlong (it sounds like it might be an old field name maybe?) or Lollington are. The same accounts usually mention the phantom coach and horses which gallops madly along Turnpike Road: but I can't find that in the locale either. If anyone can shed any light on the origin of these elusive statements and on whether there are still any phenomena in the area - I'd love to hear from you.

A4095 BAMPTON - towards Clanfield

There is supposedly a figure who can occasionally be seen along this stretch of road - and sometimes it appears to be naked! I also found an account from the middle of the 1800's which claimed that the crossroads along this road was haunted by the ghosts of suicides who had been buried there.

A local also told me that there used to be a gallows on this same crossroads (the one leading to Black Bourton), so it would not be surprising if that produced a ghost or two.

BURFORD

Burford is a wonderfully attractive small town in the Cotswolds, with many of the buildings made from stone. The lanes around it are perhaps less attractive though as they are said to be haunted by a strange black mist which moves against the wind and which animals are terrified by. Local witnesses also told me that there is an Old Grey Lady ghost which is associated with the mist and one recalled actually seeing it in his youth.

Others told me about the ghost of Old Black Stockings on the road towards Minster Lovell. They are what the name suggests – the sight of some floating black stockings that seem to get caught up on cars. One witness said that her Nan had seen them in the 1950's. Children of that era were apparently warned that if they were naughty 'Old Black Stockings will come to get you'.

In the same area, one witness told me that she had been riding her horse across the fields when she was about 12 years old, around 1987, and had seen the apparition of a man in old fashioned clothing hanging from one of the trees in the field. Her pony was so terrified by the sight, it bolted. The pony she had at the time was a docile creature called 'Fudge', and very safe to ride in normal circumstances.

Another witness told me that years ago she was told that the ghost of a lady was often seen on the road between Burford and Taynton, and that her appearance would cause drivers to swerve off the road by the bridge.

Another lady wrote to me to explain that for many years she worked as a community nurse, based in Moreton in the Marsh in neighbouring Gloucestershire. In 2008 she was driving her rounds as normal, but because of a road closure found herself taking a slightly different route than she usually did, down the B4425 near Burford.

She told me, "Driving along a straight stretch of road with no other traffic I saw a large horse and rider standing in the road more like a statue than anything real and then they were gone. My first response when I saw them was to think to myself what an incredibly big horse it was.

"I only glanced away from them for a split second, and when I looked back they had vanished. As I drove past where they had been there was no gate or gap in the hedge they could have gone through. The horse was huge, and the rider was wearing a coat that went out behind him over the horse's rump."

It was a fine clear morning at approximately 8am in early summer, so the light was good. There are fields and hedges on either side of the road and although there was very little traffic, she was driving along reasonably slowly as often there are deer in the road around this area. Although she has driven the road since, she has never encountered whatever it was again.

DENCHWORTH

Unfortunately the actual location of this sighting is not given in the only report I found, but I have included it in the hope someone else might come forward.

In January 2006 at about 9 o'clock in the evening a couple were driving into Denchworth. Suddenly a panicked looking horse galloped from a side road straight out in front of their car. The driver, thinking and reacting very quickly, immediately slammed on his brakes and turned the headlights down to sidelights so as not to startle the poor horse even further. After a few seconds he turned the headlights up again - only to see the horse galloping away in front of the car before vanishing right in front of their astonished eyes.

EAST HANNEY - Brookside

This stretch of road is said to be haunted by a chap wearing an overcoat and cap. He darts out in front of cars close to the bridge and the mill, only to vanish at the last moment. The cars can't be going very fast at this point as this is a small urban road with a sharp bend as it crosses the river.

When I asked whether anyone local had seen him, I got some very interesting replies. One gentleman recalled his parents saying how they had been for a drink at the local pub one evening (The Plough at West Hanney) and a chap came in who was very shaken and quickly downed two shots. When asked what was wrong, he said he had just had a chat with the ghost of Bert - forgetting for a moment that Bert had died a few weeks earlier.

One witness recalled that his late parents had seen the ghost of a woman wearing black at Dandridge's Mill, sometime in the 1940's. Another said he had been told it was the ghost of a woman in white, who was searching for her child who had drowned there. Yet another had been told the lady ghost would only be seen at New Year, when she would appear to run down Brookside and then jump into the leat by the mill.

I also found an account that described her as a little old lady wearing a white skirt and white bonnet, who would scurry along the road lifting up her long skirts as if to keep them clear of mud. She seems to climb the metal railing of the bridge and then disappears. She was possibly last sighted by two Home Guards on duty during WWII. And finally, another witness had heard of a ghostly horse and carriage which would trundle up nearby road Crown Meadow.

B4031 HEMPTON

You might be wary if you choose to cycle through this tiny village near Deddington. Apparently it hosts an entity which, though unseen, likes to try and push cyclists off their bikes as they pass by. The earliest source I found for it was dated 1954 and suggested it would push people off their bikes and spook horses - so it might be an even older tale than just the last few decades.

There is also supposed to be the sound of a horse galloping through the village often heard late at night.

A4329 LITTLE MILTON -Rofford Lane

Just south of Little Milton is Rofford Lane. One source says that in 2006 a man was driving home towards the village along this lane when he saw a cyclist ahead of him, who was there one moment and literally gone the next. Puzzled, he stopped to check the cyclist hadn't fallen, but could find no trace of him. Nine years later, in 2015, he was travelling the same route but now with his son in the car. This time, they both witnessed the exact same occurrence.

There is also an account from 2000 of the ghost of a tall lady wearing old fashioned dark coloured clothing seen along the same stretch of road.

SHROPSHIRE

ASTLEY ABBOTS – Stanley Lane

In the early 1980's Mr Owen was returning home at about 10 pm to Little Severn Hall on Stanley Lane, not far from Astley Abbots. A short distance from his home he suddenly saw a small slim woman, in old fashioned country working clothes, wearing a long skirt and with a shawl pulled up over her head cross the road in front of his car and promptly disappear.

He was later told the story of the ghost of Hannah Phillips. She was a young woman who lived on the other side of the Severn River, but was due to get married at Astley Church. Apparently, there was a spot here where the river could be forded and she was on her way back home when she slipped and fell into deeper water, where sadly she drowned.

There has also been a ghostly gentleman wearing a suit with a waistcoat and bowler hat seen along the same stretch of road. One witness said that a work colleague of his was in the back of a friend's van on a summer evening when he needed to answer the call of nature. The driver stopped in a gateway somewhere around this area, and the colleague stood looking across the field as he relieved himself. He suddenly saw what looked like a small ball of mist moving across the field towards him and watched it for a moment with curiosity.

As he watched he realised it was speeding up and starting to look vaguely human as it got closer. He dived into the back of the van and screamed at the driver to go. As they pulled away with the van doors still flapping open the mist came through the gate and stopped, floating above the middle of the road.

BOMERE HEATH - Baschurch Road

In winter 2005, one story tells us, a couple driving along this lane saw an elderly lady wearing grey clothing with a headscarf run across the road ahead of them. The scene was weird, as the figure looked somehow 'wispy', and her clothes appeared to be moving more slowly than the rest of the apparition. When the couple compared notes they also realised that one of them had seen the apparition cross from left to right, whilst the other had seen it cross from right to left.

I was unable to find anyone else who had experienced anything along here.

B4373 BRIDGNORTH - High Street

In the early 1970's two policemen having a crafty smoke in the wee small hours of the morning saw the apparition of the woman in black said to haunt this road. They were sheltered in the lee of a building close to the Swan Inn, when they heard footsteps approaching. Given the lateness of the hour, they both looked up to see who it was. At first there was nothing to be seen, but then suddenly the figure of a woman wearing a long dark cape came into view just a few feet away from them. She glided along the street, then turned out of sight down Cartway, an old narrow lane.

I have quite a dose of scepticism about this tale, as it goes on to say she was seen on three consecutive nights by the same policemen, and gives theories that she was actually a doppelganger of someone living in the town at the time. That sounds far-fetched to say the least to me, but what also strikes me as odd is the name of the pub. Unless one of the pubs on the High Street has changed their name over the years, then the nearest Swan Inn is a couple of miles south of Bridgnorth...

BRIDGNORTH - Moat Street

The same source for Bridgnorth also gives us the sighting on Moat Street in 1984. A girl was waiting in her mother's car whilst her mother popped in to pick up fish and chips one dark evening.
Suddenly the leaves lying in the lane started to whirl about as if the wind had picked up, causing the girl to look up. She saw a tall man with a ghastly white face and wearing a dark cloak standing in front of the car. As she watched he seemed to flicker and disappear, then reappear with a young girl standing beside him looking up at him. The encounter left the girl in quite a state of shock.

I wasn't able to find any corroboration for either of these Bridgnorth tales.

CHATWALL

Some years ago, in 1965, there were reports of a ghostly cavalier soldier on horseback seen in the lanes around this tiny hamlet.

HORSEHAY - Jiggers Bank

This really is a curious set of tales. I found one source that claims there is a friendly spirit of some sort who lives on this strangely named road. It claims that many years ago, before the advent of motorised transport, a tinker was struggling to pull his hand held cart up the incline. A figure in dark clothing suddenly appeared at the back of the cart and started pushing, helping him reach the flatter area. When he turned to thank his benefactor, the figure had disappeared.

Then, once cars were in use, a young lady was driving along the road when her car suddenly developed problems near the top of the hill. She opened the bonnet and tried to see why her car had stalled and would not start again. Seeing nothing obvious amiss, she climbed back in the car and decided to wait for another vehicle to pass and offer help. She had left the bonnet up as an indicator that she needed help and suddenly through the crack below it she could see that someone was leaning over and fiddling with the engine. Before she had a chance to get out of the car, the engine suddenly started, much to her relief.

The relief didn't last long, for when she got out to thank her benefactor there was no-one there.

Conversely, another source tells us that in 1954 a postman doing his rounds in the very early morning suddenly encountered a strange mist across the road at the top of Jiggers Bank. As he drove into it, he suddenly saw the face of a man looming towards the van, whose engine promptly died when he slammed his brakes on. Although the figure disappeared the van refused to restart, so he had to walk and get help.

LOGGERHEADS - The Rudge

There is a source story that says that there is a shadow figure sometimes seen on this old lane and that in 2003 someone walking down it felt a heavy weight settle briefly on his back! Local witnesses were able to tell me that the Rudge lies just off the Eccleshall Road, and it is so called because there was an old house along there called Rudge Hall. At least one was aware that it was known to be haunted.

Mention was made of the ghost of a little boy who haunts the woods and the lane. Some knew the ghost as 'Red Socks'. The story they were told by the nuns who then lived in the nunnery was that he was accidentally shot, and the hosiery he wore was red, hence the name.

There were also several people who knew of a small church near Broughton Hall not far from there, where you could see the ghost of a crying lady sitting on the steps outside at night. One witness had seen her twice during her own childhood years and another was aware that she was sometimes seen crossing the road there. One witness had seen some very strange things happening at his friend's house in nearby Ashley, and said the whole area is very active in a paranormal sense.

LONGNOR

Although only a small village, Longnor boasts a very famous ghost - the White Lady of Longnor Bridge. She wears her long white wedding gown and haunts the area around the bridge where she threw herself to her death by drowning in the Cound Brook after being jilted on her wedding day. She was last seen in August 1975 in broad daylight, as far as I could find in any records.

LUDLOW - Corve Street

There was originally a priory along this street housing the Grey Friars. Although the monks themselves don't seem to make any appearances, it is alleged that dogs are very reluctant to walk along this street and will often react badly here.

In 1971, according to one source, a nurse walking along the street suddenly saw a gentleman walking ahead of her who was wearing old fashioned white britches and a frock coat. As she watched, he suddenly disappeared right in front of her.

A458 MUCH WENLOCK

This ghost is said to haunt a crossroads 'two miles southeast of the town'. From the description, it looks like the most likely spot to fit is the crossroads to Atterley. However, I came across a site survey by Occult Investigations performed in October 2018 which suggests it is actually the crossroads closer to Much Wenlock which is the B4376 turn to Broseley.

They stated that, "Mary Way's Ghost appears as that of a Headless Woman, holding her severed head in her hands, and wearing a shimmering long dress. Mary's severed head has been known to scream. Legend says that Mary Way was murdered on the site, and that her Ghost is trapped there forever, until her soul can find peace. Despite research, at the time of publication, I have been unable to locate any further details of Mary's back story: either when, how or why she was killed."

Nevertheless, the story seems to persist that her appearance causes car crashes here.

A442 TELFORD - Between Telford and Bridgnorth

There is an account that in March 2009 at about 8pm one evening, two people travelling in a car along the A442 halfway between Telford and Bridgnorth suddenly spotted a dark shape at the side of the road. They thought it looked like a person wearing either a long coat or cloak. They both watched it for a moment, thinking it was a real person who was about to step out into the road, when the figure simply vanished. By the description it seems likely they were roughly in the Sutton Maddock area.

When I tried to find any local corroboration, I was told that there is also a tale of a ghostly coach and horses which travels this road, but another witness thought that apparition was more likely to be along the much older road that runs alongside the River Severn.

One gentleman explained that for his working career he travelled the A442 between the two towns every day from early morning to late at night depending on his working hours any given day, and in 35 years of travelling he never encountered anything paranormal.

SOMERSET

For ease of reference, I have covered Bristol within this section, even though I am aware parts of it lie within Gloucestershire, and it has its own county boundaries of the City of Bristol.

A38 BARROW GURNEY – Near the junction with the B3130 Barrow Street

This is the classic roadside haunting of a lady in white who seems to step into the road forcing cars to brake sharply to avoid hitting her. On some occasions drivers have been sure they did collide with her – only to stop and find nothing there.

Unfortunately I wasn't able to find any actual sightings of her. But as a curious side note, there is a deserted psychiatric hospital site in Barrow Gurney which is also haunted... might there be a connection?

A372 BRIDGEWATER – towards Weston Zoyland

This alleged haunting has a very sad tale attached to it, and I would be very interested to hear whether anyone has actually heard the sounds that are supposedly reported.

Apparently, on 6th July every year, one can hear the defeated soldiers of the army of the Duke of Monmouth singing as they marched away from defeat at the battle of Sedgemoor in 1685, trying to keep up their morale.

B3219 BRISTOL – Clifton Suspension Bridge

This beautiful bridge has many tales of ghostly encounters associated with it. It is said that car drivers can sometimes see dark shadow figures near the bridge's parapets, and that these are the ghosts of those unfortunate souls who have chosen to commit suicide by throwing themselves over the edge. On average, 8 people a year used to die this way off the bridge, although since 1998 this has halved to around four people per year as new safety barriers were installed.

Curiously, it is reported that one 22 year old threw herself off the bridge in 1885 but was saved because her voluminous skirts billowed out and acted like a makeshift parachute, pushing her fall off course and slowing her somewhat, so that she landed in bushes at the side and survived. She went on to live to a ripe old age.

Even the designer of the bridge, Isambard Kingdom Brunel, is said to haunt the site, possibly because he didn't quite finish it before he died. In actual fact the bridge's final design, although based on Mr Brunel's plan, is by William Henry Barlow and John Hawkshaw, so really it could be either of them who remain to admire their handiwork.

One witness came forward to say that one November night in 1964 she was travelling from Bristol towards Pill. She was quite close to the suspension bridge, when she suddenly saw the apparition of a man on a white horse ride across the road from right to left in front of her, and disappear through the fence at the side of the road. She was very shaken up by the incident, but continued on her journey.

Bizarrely, she saw the same figure a few months later in January 1965 and after that sighting she talked about it a bit more as she was sure, having seen it twice, that it was no optical illusion or trick of her mind. She said that an old lady she spoke to at that time told her that she too had seen the same apparition on several occasions.

B4467 BRISTOL - Pembroke Road

Most sources who describe the ghost on Pembroke Road seem to get quite carried away with their descriptions. They usually describe the ghost as being that of one Jenkins Protheroe, a notorious highwayman. Some give the date of his death as 1793, and some the date 1873. Many go on to say that he was a hideous looking dwarf with unusually long arms, who would wait at the side of the road pretending to be injured. Whenever anyone stopped to help him, he would leap up and rob them. His ghost is said to haunt the road because this is the site where he was gibbeted.

The actual historical version is that one Jenkin William Prothero was tried for murder and sentenced on 26th March 1783 to execution by hanging on 31st March 1783, and then for his body to be gibbeted, or hung in chains, on Durdham Down. This slight gap between sentencing and execution was very likely to allow time for the gibbet cage to be constructed. These were iron contraptions which fitted the corpse in hoops and which were then hung in prominent locations to serve as a warning to others. The idea was that the corpse would swing there in its cage, gradually rotting away and filling all who saw it with horror and revulsion. The purpose of the cage was to keep the rotting corpse intact for as long as possible: and indeed some gibbets are known to have been left standing with their gruesome contents for decades.

Curiously, with Jenkin Prothero, there is historical record that after a period of time the locals petitioned for the gibbet to be moved, claiming that the sight and stench of it was turning people away from visiting the nearby hot springs and the businesses associated with them were suffering.

I was unable to find any actual sightings of Jenkin, but at least one local came forward to say he had heard the tale of the gibbet at the top of Pembroke Road, but not of the ghost supposedly associated with it.

BRISTOL - Willsbridge Hill

Whilst I was asking about Bristol, one witness told me that she had heard of a ghost that crosses the road here, close to the pub. She explained that the tale is that it can only be seen from the knees up, because since the time that the person was alive, the level of the road has risen - but the ghost still walks along the old level. It's not clear exactly where she meant.

Interestingly, there is also a story of a girl called Betty who either killed herself or was murdered by poisoning and drowning at the Mill here.

BROCKLEY - Brockley Combe Road

Brockley Combe Road crosses the ancient woodland southeast of Brockley. Although it is fabulously pretty during the day time and in Autumn especially, you might be a little more wary driving it at night. There are said to be numerous ghosts, not least of which is the phantom horseman who can be seen riding on moonless nights. A coach with four horses careens down the road sometimes, terrifying oncoming car drivers. It is supposed to have been seen on at least three occasions.

There is also a strange 'bounding' ghost which runs in great leaping strides ahead of people walking along this road, only to disappear.

Then there is the ghost of an old woman who seems to be terrified. She is thought to be the spirit of one Dinah Swan, an elderly lady who was literally frightened to death in 1833 when a gang of would-be robbers broke into her house. The last recorded sighting of her seems to be from around 1940 and that is perhaps just as well as she is said also to be a harbinger of ill fortune.

The ghost of the evil churchman John Hibbetson also haunts here. In 1776 whilst alive he diligently nursed the local squire James Stevens back to health after a fall. So grateful for the pastor's gentle care was the squire, that he changed his will to include him. The good pastor thought it would be a great idea to receive his just rewards earlier than they would otherwise be due, by murdering his benefactor.

Another ghost is thought to be the spirit of a young girl who committed suicide here, and also there is the ghost of a man who is just sometimes seen silently standing under the trees. Definitely worth having your camera and your EVP recorder with you if you visit!

A39 CANNINGTON

A car driver was heading west out of Cannington along this road in November 2016, and had not yet got as far as the Apple Tree Hotel. He saw the outline of a misty white horse cross the road in front of his car and jump the hedge on the opposite side. As the form was not solid it was very clear he was not seeing a real horse.

One witness contacted me to say that they had heard of this ghost, but in the version she had heard the ghost was that of a headless horseman.

B3114 CHEW VALLEY LAKE

This forlorn ghost was seen a number of times in the late 1990's. Thought to be the ghost of Catherine Brown, who drowned in the late 1800's, she has been seen wearing Victorian style dress, with her hair loose and flowing (and sometimes appearing wet) walking along the road, or drifting across it. Each time, it's been clear from her not-quite-solid appearance that she is a ghost.

I could not find any more recent sightings of her but I did find a report that in 2017 a small (and rather skinny looking) alligator was captured in the lake!

A30 CREWKERNE – towards Chard

This eight mile stretch of road is said to be haunted by the sounds of a battle between revenue men and local smugglers, which fade away into the gasp of someone dying and taking their final breath.

A396 CUTCOMBE – towards Timberscombe

This picturesque, winding hillside road is haunted by a phantom coach and headless horses which careen out of control down the hill. As with many an old myth, it is retold with the modern twist of cars swerving to avoid it, but there are no actual accounts of that happening that I could find.

A30 EAST CHINNOCK

The A30 forms the High Street for this pretty village, and is said to be haunted by the sound of galloping hooves.

A39 KNOWLE

A gentleman told me that in the 1970's he was told by a customer of his that her son, who at the time was courting a young lady who lived at Woolavington, was driving home down the hill near the Knowle Inn on his motorbike, when suddenly he noticed a lady wearing a long flowing grey dress running down the road ahead of him.

She kept looking over her shoulder as she ran, and he swerved his bike out into the road to avoid hitting her. As he did so, 'something damp' swiped into him, and he was knocked off his bike. The woman had suddenly disappeared.

He never went that way home again.

NUNNEY - Frome Road

This road boasts an often cited report of a hitchhiker, wearing a flannel shirt (or in some versions a sports jacket), trying to catch a lift and seen several times in the 1970's. In some reports, he is said to suddenly materialise in the backseat of passing cars. The sightings of him tend to range all along this older stretch of road, but also sometimes out on the newer A361 at Nunney Catch. When I asked for local experiences, I got some very interesting results.

One witness told me that about 40 years ago they were driving home from the pub in Nunney towards Frome, on a particularly foggy and unpleasant night. They suddenly saw a young man walking in the fog, and thinking how dangerous that could be, they stopped to offer assistance.

He said he was looking for somewhere to stay, so they offered to drop him off at Frome police station. When they arrived, they pulled up in the car and he stepped out. They turned to watch him go into the police station, but he had completely vanished. They were so puzzled they got out of the car and checked but he was nowhere to be seen and the policeman at the desk inside confirmed no-one had come in.

Another witness explained, "Hi Ruth, I am a builder and was working on the Police Station in Frome in the 1970s. I was told by a police officer who was working on the desk one night that a man came in very distressed saying he had picked up a hitchhiker on the Nunney to Frome road, but after traveling a short distance the man disappeared." I wonder if this was the same occasion of the above account, but seen from the other point of view, or whether it is a totally separate occurrence.

I also got a message from a gentleman who knew a man who had picked up a hitchhiker in the early 1970's on the Critchill Road. His passenger, who looked like an airman, only spoke to ask him to turn the heater on as he was very cold. After a couple of miles of quietly driving, the driver turned to chat - only to find the seat next to him empty. The driver went straight to the police station on Oakfield Road and reported it, but was frightened half to death by his experience. Another correspondent remembered this same occurrence, and remembered the local community association organising a search to try and find the ghost.

Another witness told me that her mother had often seen this same ghost walking from the quarry by Holwell towards the pub. Yet another came forward to say, "My dad used to live at Nunney Catch and was walking along the road from Frome to Nunney before it became a bypass - probably around 40 years ago. He was walking home from visiting his girlfriend - later to become his wife and my mother. He was aware of an old man walking behind him but he felt uneasy and felt something wasn't right so picked up pace. When he looked behind the old man had also picked up pace so my dad began to run and so did the old man. At that moment a car came along and flashed his headlights and the old man disappeared."

Certainly not all the ghosts seen along that stretch of road were authentic, as one man explained that he used to work with a chap who used to go out at night with a mate of his to Critchill, and attach a sheet to a long piece of rope. They would then hook the rope into the trees stretching above the road, and when a car came along they would haul on the rope in such a way as to make the white shape of the sheet float quickly up into the trees. Apparently it fooled a lot of people and fuelled the stories of the ghost until they were caught out.

Several other witnesses mentioned the cycle track from Frome to Radstock, and how uncomfortable the part of it close to the bridge with trees hanging overhead can feel. There are high banks there which give an enclosed feeling, and small rocks sometimes tumble down as if someone is moving on the banks near you.

Another local remembered that there used to be an old 'tramp' as they were once known, called Harry, who used to frequently walk the area and wondered whether he had sometimes been mistaken for a ghost. And another said that he had found tales from as far back as the 1930's that lorry drivers were nervous of this stretch of road because of the 'mischievous spirit along it.

A few years ago, one lady's brother and sister were out in the car travelling home from a night out. The brother was driving, and at one point he glanced in his rearview mirror and to his absolute horror saw a man wearing a light brown raincoat sitting in the back seat. It was obvious that he was not a solid, corporeal person, so to try and keep his sister calm he said nothing until they got home and he hurriedly got her out of the car. They turned to look in time to see the entity step out of the car and disappear. Not surprisingly, they hightailed it into the house, very shaken up.

Another man told me, "My late wife once said that when she was a child, in the 1960's, she and her friends used to play in the ruins of a house in the field at the top of Nunney Road, near to where the schools are now. The foundations can still be seen– just! On one occasion, she was standing at the top of the stairs, throwing stones and stuff down, with other kids, and this man appeared at the bottom of the stairs, who appeared to be glaring at them, then disappeared. She maintained there was no way a man could have gotten into the house at that point, and they all ran like hell, never to play there again."

A lady also wrote to me to say, "I used to go to a yoga class every Wednesday evening at the sports centre in Frome that finished at 9:30pm. I would always drive home along the Nunney road and every week during this journey I had an intense eerie feeling that if I dared to look in my mirror I would see someone sitting behind me. I used to try and ignore it but found it quite terrifying, I always felt it was a dark haired man in a red checked shirt. The feeling was always very intense until I reached the village and it only seemed to happen heading back but never going.

"A few years later I was looking up some information about Nolton Church and stumbled across a ghost hunters website where I discovered the story of the hitchhiker who apparently got knocked off his bike by a motorist whilst cycling to Critchill from Nunney who had apparently sworn revenge on drivers for his death. It sent chills down my spine when I read it and to be honest even the thought of that journey now makes me feel very uneasy."

And finally, a lady wrote to say, "My daughter and I have both seen a young boy sitting by a tree at the top part of Nunney road at the top of the hill. He was watching us as we approached in the car and was still there as we drove past. He was wearing old fashioned breeches and a white collarless shirt. His hair was dark and messy, partially swept over the front of his face. I have heard that there are three Quakers buried in unmarked graves on the Hill down Nunney Road. One of my friends told me that their father had tried to pick up someone who was hitchhiking on that road when it was raining. He stopped to ask where the person lived, but they had just disappeared."

This is clearly a very paranormally active area – and difficult to say whether it is a ghost in the traditional sense, or some sort of mischievous entity.

A39 ST AUDRIES - towards Holford

This four mile stretch of road is supposed to be frequented by a Black Shuck, although I wasn't able to find anyone who had recently sighted it. And curiously, there is also a legend that a coffin is sometimes seen just lying in the road along here, as well as a strange misty shape that crosses the road.

THORNBURY - Kington Lane

There is a fascinating report from October 18th 1995 at nearly midnight, when Brian Taylor was travelling along this road with a passenger in his car. He was forced to brake sharply when a strange mist, about five feet in height, suddenly appeared on the road in front of the car. It was quite a defined shape, giving it some appearance of solidity, which is what caused him to brake.

Whatever it was seemed to react to the presence of the car, as it moved quickly away from the car, and passed through a solid stone wall into the field beyond. Mr Taylor was quite certain that it did not go over the wall - it went through it. In the field beyond was a herd of cows who suddenly went ballistic - bellowing and seeming to chase after something only they could see.

A39 STREET - towards Walton and on to Loxley Wood

There is a tale that along this road there can sometimes be seen the ghost of the highwayman named Pocock, who still rides his frantically galloping horse. It has been said that although the apparition is seen to be clearly galloping, it actually doesn't have any forward movement - as if it were held in one spot. One witness recalled being told of the ghostly highwayman along there when she was much younger.

A correspondent told me that the story actually relates to a robber called either Jan Swayne or Jan Willcox, who became known as Pocock. He lived in Morelynch and was dragged from his bed by the militia to be taken to Bridgewater for trial for his crimes. However, he persuaded his captors to uncuff him by betting them that he could take just three leaps to escape them.

They knew that no-one could jump very far, and laughingly agreed to take the bet, thinking they would easily chase after him and overpower him anyway. Wily Jan made two big jumps, and on the third threw himself to lay across the back of one of the horses, which ran off into nearby Loxley Woods and relative safety, carrying him slumped across its back.

Apparently this tale is also mixed up with that of another robber who was rumoured to live in the grotto at Chilton Priory. This is why sometimes the tale is told that he died in a cave of his wounds.

My correspondent told me that around 1986 his girlfriend and he were returning from a night out at the Pipers Inn and were driving towards Street at about 11 pm when they saw a strange figure in a gateway along that stretch of the A39. They both saw a small man, about 5'5" tall standing by the gate, who looked like he was wrapped head to toe in slightly shimmering bubble wrap!

They were so astonished at the strange sight that they drove on until they could turn the car around, and went back to have another look. The strangely attired man was still there. This time they could see that he was actually hunched over, so could have been taller than they originally thought, and was slowly moving forward. They turned the car around again, but this time when they reached the spot he had disappeared.

When they told their families about their strange encounter, his Uncle said that there used to be a Hobo (another word for a tramp) known as Whistler who walked the roads from Swindon down to Truro and back twice a year, and he would often shelter under the bridge close to where they had seen the figure. His Uncle had last seen him in 1947, when Whistler would have been around 50 years old or so, and that although he died in hospital some years later, there was a small headstone either for him under the bridge, or possibly for another Hobo who was hit and killed by a car along the same stretch.

There is yet another reference for the same stretch of road of two ghostly cars seen, one in 1981 and one in 1982.

A38 TAUNTON - towards Wellington

This report comes from 1973 and at the time the writer claimed it was just one of many regarding this particular ghost.

Mrs Taylor was driving down the road one evening when she suddenly saw a man standing smack dab in the middle of the road. He was wearing a long grey overcoat of some sort and seemed to be looking at the ground, perhaps as if he had dropped something. In other reports I found the lady is suddenly called Mrs Swithenbank. Whatever her name was, it is claimed that she swerved in order to avoid him, nearly causing herself a close encounter with the ditch at the side of the road, but when she looked back to give him a piece of her mind, he had vanished.

There is another, far more fanciful report about the same ghost purporting to date back to the 1950's, when a lorry driver supposedly picked him up several times over the course of a year on wet and gloomy nights. Finally, on one such occasion he refused to stop for the man, whereupon the figure in the grey overcoat jumped out in front of his lorry, almost causing a crash, before promptly disappearing.

In other reports, the area was wrongly listed as 'near Teignmouth' and this can cause confusion. This is compounded by the fact that the hotel along the road is now called The World's End and used to be called The Heatherton Grange Hotel. One correspondent told me that he used to live in Heatherton Park House, and although he never heard them himself, the story was that you could hear the sound of horses and carriages rumbling through the archway entrance.

Many other people told me they had heard of the hitchhiking ghost in the grey raincoat, and that he tended to haunt on rainy days, carrying a torch or a lantern. Some had heard that he was supposed to actually get into cars and then disappear. One thought he might have actually seen it around 2012, but wasn't entirely sure if it wasn't just a product of wet roads and tired eyes.

One lady recalled that her father used to say that the ghost was that of a hitchhiker who had been clipped by a car and killed and that ever since if you happened to drive past The World's End on a rainy night, there was a possibility you would see his face in the rear view mirror of your car. Still others had heard he was likely to be seen a few hundred yards further down the road, near The Blackbirds pub.

One correspondent had heard that it was actually the ghost of an old tramp who used to frequent this road before his death.

Another witness told me of her experience one night in 2005 on this stretch of the A38, close to the Willowbrook Garden Centre. It was rainy and dark, but she suddenly saw a dark human shaped figure cross the road ahead of her going from right to left. She realised it was not a real living breathing human, because as she got closer she realised that the whole shape was a deep black in colour, but covered in tiny sparkling prisms of light.

One witness, who is sensitive to such things, told me that she had seen the ghost once. It was a very rainy Friday night, and he was standing in the middle of the road at the crossroads by The World's End wearing what looked like an old fashioned oilskin coat and carrying a lantern, which he was holding at shoulder height to peer at the cars as they passed him. She could see him quite clearly, but realised that the other cars on the road were not reacting to him, which made her sure he was actually an apparition.

She said that according to a gentleman who spoke to her on the subject, there are also some Roman soldiers who march in the field next to the pub itself. She had also seen a different ghost outside The Blackbirds pub a little further down the road, which is interesting as it suggests more than one haunt along this road. She also said that not far away, at the junction with the M5 motorway (junction 26) there is the ghost of a young girl wearing 1960's era clothing.

Even further south along the A38, where it passes the Beambridge Inn, there is the ghost of a lady wearing a long beige coloured mackintosh style coat and walking two large Greyhound dogs. She has occasionally been known to step out in front of cars, causing them to swerve.

A little further down the A38 is an area curiously called White Ball, and one witness told me that this stretch is haunted by a soldier in a World War II uniform, who can be seen walking up the hill in foggy weather. Others had heard of him, and had a vague recollection that he was somehow connected to the nearby railway tunnel.

If you are travelling the A38, especially on a wet night, keep your eyes peeled and your dashboard camera running!

B3170 TAUNTON – Shoreditch Road

There is very little detail given on this ghost, but supposedly there is a man sometimes seen along this road riding a nervous looking horse which prances about.

STAFFORDSHIRE

BOBBINGTON - Six Ashes Road / Tom Lane towards Wombourne

In summer 2009 two people travelling in a car along this stretch of road one evening saw a figure dressed like a monk run across the road in front of them and disappear into an open field next to the road.

CLAYTON - Aynsley Avenue

According to one source, a man was walking his dog early one bright summer's morning in August 2009, when a horse pulling an old fashioned cart suddenly appeared in front of him as if out of nowhere. The dog walker was so shocked, he stood frozen to the spot, unsure of what he was seeing or how to react.

The cart was being driven by a weather-beaten man, and seemed perfectly solid and real: right up until the moment it simply vanished.

FAZELEY, TAMWORTH

This account says that a young man who had been for a night out in Fazeley with friends was driving home alone, leaving Fazeley to head back to Birmingham. The account doesn't specify, but it seems possible his route was the A4091. It was a wet and windy night in March 1972, and as he drove out of the built up area and into the more rural part of the road, he spotted a tall man walking along heading in the same direction he was.

He noticed that the man had a scarf wrapped closely about his head and neck to ward off the inclement weather, and was wearing a long greatcoat and boots underneath. Realising that the man was probably a soldier, he decided to offer a lift. However, as he went to pull up his car next to the man to ask, the figure seemed to shimmer slightly and then fragmented away into nothing.

One witness told me that she had heard of the ghosts of little girls near there, and of a headless horseman that rode through the deer park. Another had heard of a ghostly highwayman who rides the old road from Weeford. Unfortunately, nobody knew anything of the ghostly soldier.

GREAT HAYWOOD – Rugeley Road

Since the late 1940's it has been claimed that the ghost of a man on an old style bicycle has been seen cycling down this road. He is the ghost of an engineer who drowned at the nearby pumping station. I could not find any recent sightings of him.

M6 TOLL near LICHFIELD

In 2005 a lady was driving her husband and child home along this (then) brand new stretch of road.

She pulled the car up and stopped because she could see something moving across the carriageway and assumed at first that it was an escaped herd of animals.

However, as she got a closer look she realised that they were actually shadowy figures of what she took to be Roman soldiers, who were walking along with only the upper halves of their bodies visible above the tarmac – as if they were actually walking on a surface hidden below the new layer of road.

A460 RUGELEY – towards Hednesford

There have supposedly been numerous reports between the 1980's and 2001 of this rather disturbing ghost, who materialises on the back seats of vehicles passing along this road. He is only visible if the driver happens to actually turn and look at the back seat. He cannot be seen in the car's rear view mirror.

A witness told me that in early summer 2018 she got in her car to drive the ten miles or so to her boyfriend's house in Walsall Wood at about 11.30pm at night. She says that for some reason she can't explain, as soon as she got into the car she began to feel that something was slightly 'off' but could not put her finger on what, especially as it was a journey she usually made two or three times a week. As she drove toward Slitting Mill Road on the first part of her journey, she describes herself feeling a surge of dread and worry, which quickly changed into a feeling of deep depression. This was in complete contrast to her normal sunny disposition.

She found herself feeling strangely 'zoned out' as she put it, and although this stretch of road has a 60 mph limit, and even at night she would normally travel at least 40 mph along it, she found herself slowly driving along at 30 mph feeling in a bit of a 'fog', as if driving faster was just beyond her capability.

She explained, "As you enter Fair Oak along the Slitting Mill Rd, there is a short stretch of houses on both sides of the road and as it was so late there were no lights on and I hadn't passed another car since I had started my journey from Etching Hill.

"I remember feeling this buildup of emotions, but then suddenly they vanished and it felt like a weight had been lifted and the second this happened I saw a figure on the right hand side of the road."

The strange thing is, this is a perfectly straight piece of road and as it was late with little traffic she was using the car's high beam headlights. This meant she should in theory have seen the figure much earlier – from further back down the road.

The figure was male and stood upright in a military type fashion with a straight back. Our witness recalled seeing a rich red colour jacket which went down to the knee with long white socks or tights underneath. There was also rich golden embroidery on the upper half of the jacket and a large sash which went across his chest, and he had something standing up next to him. Thinking back now she thinks it might have been a large gun, but she didn't really register that at the time. As she passed him she felt that he perhaps needed help, so she stopped the car, watching him in her mirrors. She could clearly see the red lights of her brakes reflecting off him. Her windows were open, and there was no sound (unusual in itself, as she would normally play music in the car). She was only about 30 feet away from him, so just as he went to step out into the road she glanced down to put the car into reverse to go back and see if he needed help. When she looked up again a mere moment later he was gone. She put the car into drive and sped off.

She says that for her, the most confusing thing is not just what she saw, but her own actions that night. As she says, she is only a young girl, and would never normally contemplate stopping to help someone whilst on her own late at night. But something about that whole journey was not 'right' – from the strange emotions she was experiencing, to the weird way she was driving sluggishly, to her strange impulse to stop and help him and the way all the feelings of depression lifted the moment she saw him. She has since looked online for identification of the type of clothing he was wearing, and it was typical clothing for an officer's uniform circa 1780.

She was also able to tell me that on several occasions, whilst driving down the A460 a little further on, both she and her friend have seen two or three shadowy figures standing together at the side of the road, on the side closest to the train tracks.

One witness told me about a ghostly train seen on the line between Rugeley and Hednesford, close to Marquis Drive.

SUFFOLK

BARHAM - Church Lane, outside Barham Hall.

This story dates back to the early years of the 1900's, before World War I broke out. A couple of men were walking back home from their day's labour, when they were suddenly threatened by a huge rough coated dog with bright yellow eyes.

One of them tried to shoo it off by hitting out at it with his stick, but to their astonishment the dog disappeared by walking straight through the adjoining roadside wall. In other versions of the tale, his stick passes straight through the dog, alerting them that they were dealing with an apparition.

One witness who was born in the village told me that she used to live at Barham Hall thirty years or so ago, and remembered being told then that the entrance to The Slade was haunted by a dog with yellow eyes. (The Slade is a leafy bridle path which runs alongside the hall, away from the road itself at right angles.)

Another longtime resident who used to live close by had heard that there was the ghost of a boy who was knocked over on the lane here. At certain times of the year, his ghost would be seen again. She was also aware that there was a dog which haunted The Slade, and that there is an old war bunker not far from the church.

She had also heard that there used to be a ghostly horse and carriage which would pass the church before disappearing.

Some local witnesses with family dating back generations had never heard the stories at all, but did know of a legend that there was a plague victims burial ground behind the church somewhere.

A146 BARNBY - Bindmans Gate

One lady told me that when she was young, her grandfather used to tell them about the 'Old Shuck' who roamed the fields near the Barnby Bends. He told his grandchildren that anyone who saw the dog was likely to suffer some sort of ill fortune shortly afterwards. Her grandfather was born in 1904 in a cottage close to where the modern day Bindmans Gate service station stands.

B1062 BECCLES - Road past the War Memorial

There is a legend that the sound of chains rattling can be heard on this piece of road. It will sometimes happen when the church bells are rung. Apparently, the sound is caused by the ghost of an erstwhile highwayman who frequented this road and who was caught and sentenced to hang for his crimes. Afterwards, his body was gibbeted in chains - hence the noise.

One local was able to tell me that she had also heard of a Black Shuck haunting along here.

BENTLEY - Bentley Road towards Brantham

Dodnash Priory used to stand close to here, marked now by just a single stone. The priory was founded in around 1128 a.d. and was in use until around 1545 a.d. There is a story that a ghostly monk now haunts this part of the lane, and one local told me that there is also a legend that hair will grow out of the marker stone in certain conditions. Several recalled old stories from their younger years about animal sacrifices taking place at the site of the old priory on the marker stone.

When I asked if anyone had seen a ghost along this stretch of road I got back rather more than I bargained for.

Apparently, along this road there is a small red brick bridge where the road crosses the Stutton Brook which seems also to be known as Samford Brook. This bridge is close to the site of the old priory.

My first witness asked me whether I meant the stretch of road with the old red bridge at the bottom of the hill by Dodnash. She explained that she and a friend were busy one day in around 1978 'bunking off' or 'skiving' from school. (Not attending when one was supposed to – but going off somewhere more fun for the day).

They had leant their bicycles up against the parapet of the bridge, and were hiding out underneath it playing around in the stream the way kids do. As they played they suddenly, and very clearly, heard someone messing about with their bikes up above. Fearing theft, they jumped up and scrambled back out onto the road, only to find no sign of anyone there. However, on one of the bikes, the pedal was slowly spinning around as if someone had just that moment taken their foot off it.

Curiously, another witness wrote to me to tell me that around 1982 he used to cycle from Brantham to Capel St Mary to see his girlfriend. At the time, he was a young 15 yr old lad with a racing bike. He would wear an old World War II rucksack with a tape recorder in it as he rode so that he could listen to music since the journey would normally take around 40 minutes.

On this particular night he was making the return journey and came to the top of Dodnash Hill. He remembered that the sky was quite clear and the moon was shining. An owl was hooting nearby and his bicycle chain decided to ruin the perfectly tranquil moment by coming off its sprocket.

He used the momentum of the hill to free wheel the bike and slip the chain back into place, but it did it twice more and seemed reluctant to catch and stay in place.

At this point he was reaching the bottom of the hill where the bridge is. Suddenly, his rucksack was violently snatched from his back and fell into the road behind him. He jumped off the bike and ran back to where it lay in the road, fearing for his beloved tape recorder. He was astonished to find that the straps of the rucksack were still perfectly intact and there was no reason why it should have come off his back the way it did.

At that moment, he noticed something white moving over the field next to the road. He mounted his bike and raced home as fast as he could, never once daring to look back. When he got home his mother asked him what was wrong and told him he looked like he had seen a ghost.

He avoided that route for months afterwards, even though it meant going around the much longer way through Tattingstone. When he finally plucked up the courage to return to the usual route, he did notice that there was a grey horse in the field next to the road, which was picked out by the moonlight. This could conceivably have been the thing he saw moving. He still never found an explanation though for what happened to his rucksack - how it managed to be yanked from his back without breaking the straps and without breaking his tape recorder. And perhaps more importantly, who or what did the yanking..

He did recall a myth which said that if you ran around the stone six times whilst swearing then the devil would come and get you.

Curiously, another witness then told me that when he was at school, this bridge was always named 'Devil's Bridge'. Another agreed, and said he had heard a story of a motorcyclist who went across it once and had his head pulled back when he went over it - as if something had briefly but forcibly grabbed at his crash helmet. When he got home, there were inexplicable scratches on his crash helmet.

Another witness remembered being told that a headless monk could sometimes be seen walking along the brook here.

One gentleman, Anthony Goodluck, explained that he and a paranormal investigation group once conducted an investigation along here, and on three separate occasions they had balls of light come up to them and seem to go through them. They also saw three misty figures running straight towards them in the path through the woods, and heard the sound of a horse galloping.

He told me that he and his fellow investigator had walked through Dodnash Woods at around 10.30 at night in autumn one year. After climbing over the stile from the wood they walked down the field and scrambled over the stile leading into the water meadow at the bottom, which is where they stood quietly for a moment whilst he scanned the area with night vision binoculars.

He explained, "this is when I noticed several balls of light coming towards us from the hedgerow to the right. I told my friend what I was looking at and he naturally wanted to see so I handed him the night vision binoculars - which is when I realised I could still see them even with the naked eye!"

This meant of course, that the balls were actually emitting light rather than it being the night vision goggles which made them seem to glow. The two men were stunned and watched as the balls came closer and closer. There were about ten in total with the biggest being about the size of a tennis ball and the others in various smaller sizes.

Anthony explained, "The large one stopped about 6 feet from us and just hung still in the air. Hearing my friend laugh I turned and saw one go straight through him – and yet strangely neither of us felt scared or apprehensive, but quite the opposite – we felt warm and could not stop smiling."

The balls of light moved around and through them for a few minutes then slowly retreated back the way they had come and the two men decided to call it a night for their investigation. Anthony could not offer any explanation for what happened to them that night, but said it felt beautiful.

The only odd thing was that although they had both a camera and a video camera with them, neither of these would work.

B1074 BLUNDESTON – Flixton Road

There is an account that on 20 September 2009 at around half past nine at night, two people driving home spotted a small monk-like figure gliding across the road ahead of them. It was glowing slightly, and the clothing seemed to be made of roughly woven cloth.

They only caught a brief look at it as it passed through the headlight beam from their car. I wasn't able to find anyone else who had encountered this apparition.

A1065 BRANDON – heading towards Lakenheath

In 2011 one early morning, a lady was driving away from Brandon towards Lakenheath and happened to glance in her rear view mirror. To her horror she saw a young lad, maybe fourteen years of age or so, sitting in the back seat of her car. She was so shocked she looked forward for a moment as the surprise registered itself, then glanced back again only to see there was no-one there.

A similar thing is said to have happened to a man driving along the same stretch in 2014. When I asked whether anyone had experienced anything along here, one person told me that she had heard as a child that Dick Turpin and his band of robbers were supposed to haunt this stretch of road, having frequented it in real life.

Another told me that he had not heard of any ghosts along that particular stretch of road, but he was aware that there was a phantom coach and horses which was supposed to be seen around the railway crossing near Feltwell.

Branching off from the A1065 is Wangford Road, and one lady told me that she and her friend had once seen a ghost near the traffic lights there. Another correspondent explained that there is supposed to be the ghost of a monk close to here.

One witness wrote to tell me that when she was about six years old, she was travelling along that stretch of road in a car with her Mum driving and her two siblings in the car with her. She remembered that it would have been a Saturday night, and that it was late in the evening and pitch dark.

Suddenly, as they were driving, their Mum instructed them to lock the car doors. (The car did not have central locking, and doors were locked by pushing the pin down). They looked to see what had alarmed their mother, and all of them saw a man walking along the road with something reflective on his clothing. Even as they watched, the man just vanished.

Her mother was panicked by his sudden disappearance – as she had glanced back at that moment to check the children had obeyed her instruction to lock the door. She assumed that she had either hit him, or come so close to him that she had caused him to fall into the ditch. She stopped the car and the children remained inside while she searched for him - but could find nothing. She then returned to the car and telephoned for the police from her mobile and explained what had happened. They waited there for maybe 25 minutes until a police car arrived. The policeman searched around using a large torch, and even searched in the field, but there was absolutely nothing to be found.

Our witness recalls the policeman then telling her mother not to worry - there was no evidence of damage on her car and no suggestion anyone had been injured, and that in fact they had received other calls along this same stretch of road about a phantom hitchhiker!

BUNGAY - Ditchingham Dam

In the early 1970's, a man driving along this road in the late evening suddenly saw a coach pulled by four horses heading straight towards his car. He was just starting to panic about taking evasive action, when the coach itself swung away from him and sort of floated into the side of the road, narrowly avoiding a collision before disappearing.

Although no-one had seen the phantom coach when I asked locally, there was mention made that the same area is also haunted by marching Roman Soldiers.

BURGH - Whitefoot Lane

Although there don't seem to be any recent sightings of this ghost, it piqued my curiosity because supposedly the lane is actually named after the ghost. When seen, it is noticeable particularly for its pale white feet as it walks along...

CHELMONDISTON

When I was asking about other roads in Suffolk and their ghosts, I was told by one man that he works as a mobile patrol and response security guard. He had once been going towards the church in Chelmondiston just as the sun was setting, when he encountered what he now thinks must have been a Black Shuck. It made him think he was going mad at the time, but has since come across other strange things with the odd hours he keeps, so tries not to think about it too deeply.

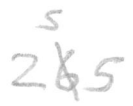

CORTON - Tramps Alley

The ghost of a tall woman wearing a long white robe has been seen for many years in the grounds of the old house which stood here before the sea caused its erosion and demolition, and since then, she haunts the lane known as Tramps Alley. The last recorded sighting was in 1974, by a couple out walking their dog one evening.

When I asked locally, it was explained that Tramps Alley is a narrow lane leading from the main road down to the beach, virtually opposite the pitch and putt golf course. It still has a reputation for being haunted even today.

B1077 DEBENHAM

It is unclear from the original account just where exactly this encounter took place, but it was roughly two miles outside of the village on the B1077, although in which direction the report doesn't say. A van driver called Arthur was finishing his day's run at about 6.15pm on a January evening in 1973 and was heading back to the depot. Suddenly, he saw a man standing at the side of the road ahead of him who caught his attention because of his odd dress. He was wearing a tall hat, and loose trousers tucked into high boots, with a cloak.

Arthur slowed down a little, intending to drive carefully past him, but found that he didn't seem to be getting any closer to the figure. Just as Arthur figured out that this didn't make any sense, the man suddenly swerved into the path of the van, which seemed to just travel through him. Shocked, Arthur got out and looked all around with his torch, but could not find anything to suggest a collision had occurred.

However, when he started his van back up and switched its lights back on, there was the figure running alongside the ditch. Thoroughly spooked by now, Arthur sped off, finally managing to outrun whatever it was when he got to about 35 mph. I wasn't able to find any other encounters with this entity.

B1070 HADLEIGH - towards Layham

There is a tale that the grave of one Mary Miller, who committed suicide, is alongside this road and that her sad spirit can be seen walking along here. When I asked locally, some witnesses remembered there used to be a house along this stretch of road which was reputedly haunted. Strange noises could sometimes be heard coming from it, and local children were afraid of it.

One witness remembered that many years ago there were tales of a few near-crashes from cars who had tried to avoid hitting a woman seen walking down the road dressed in a nightgown. Another witness remembered that the tale was of 'Mad Mary' who committed suicide.

A47 HOPTON - Junction between Jay Lane and Rackham's Corner

There is supposed to be a phantom cyclist along this stretch of road seen once in 1988 in the winter, and again in August 2001. On that second occasion, the driver was sure they had hit the cyclist, and so they phoned the police, who came out but could find nothing. The road was the A12 until it was renamed, so several published records show it as happening on the A12, if you are trying to research it yourself. I was not able to find any recent sightings of this phantom.

There is also mention of a man often seen standing in the road along here, wearing a brown suit. Some reports say he is 'leering', others say he has his mouth open as if screaming.

MARTLESHAM HEATH

As the A12 passes through Martlesham Heath, it also passes the main Police building on Portal Road. There are supposedly numerous reports of the sightings of ghostly soldiers around this area from the days when there was a World War II airfield close by.

When I asked for any information locally, one lady wrote in to say that she has worked at the Police Headquarters for 34 years and had heard numerous stories of the grounds being haunted by an airman.

She explained, "It's an eerie place at night and you often get the feeling of not being alone. The old guys who used to work on reception overnight reported seeing him on a night shift when they were doing their rounds."

Another witness reported that he had heard that the airman will even appear during daylight hours. Another man told me that his mother used to work as a cleaner there many years ago, and she had related a strange tale to him.

She told him that on one of her early morning shifts, she saw a man wandering around the building wearing an old fashioned pilot's uniform, and he asked her if she had seen his plane and seemed somewhat confused. She told him that no, she hadn't, and he turned away and walked off. She thought she had better follow him as it occurred to her he shouldn't be on the premises, but as she went to do that, he just disappeared.

One gentleman got in touch with me and told me in person about the experience he had very close to here, on Bell Lane. He explained that when he was a teenager in 1981, a group of his friends and he used to meet at the Village Hall in the evenings to hang out together. This particular October evening our witness left the hall at around 11.00pm and was driving down Bell Lane towards Ipswich, when he saw what he presumed to be either a bicycle or moped headlight coming towards him down the lane.

He slowed down, thinking they would need to let each other pass, but as he came round a slight bend there was suddenly no sight of the light any more. Puzzled, but not unduly bothered, he carried on driving and turned onto Foxhall Road at the crossroads.

He suddenly had an overwhelmingly strong feeling that someone was actually sitting in the backseat of his car. He was immediately absolutely terrified, too scared to even look and see – so he just pressed his foot on the accelerator and raced towards the streetlights and house he could see ahead of him.

Just before he got to the 'safety' of the lit up streets, his car engine and electrics all suddenly died. He was too terrified to stop and get out of the car to try and investigate the issue, but fortunately the road is on enough of a downward slope there that he just let its forward momentum and gravity take over, and used that to 'bump start' the engine. His car had never done anything like this before, and never repeated it after that night.

As soon as the engine restarted, the weird terror he was feeling and the sensation of someone being with him lifted, and he was able to drive the rest of the way home shaken, but in a much calmer frame of mind. When he got home, his Dad remarked to him that he was as white as a sheet. He is in his fifties now, but says he still remembers that night as vividly as if it were last week – because he has no explanation for what happened.

Strangely, some years later he himself had an accident at exactly the same spot whilst riding a motorcycle.

A1088 NORTON

The story is that in 1989 and preceding years, the spectacle of a motorcycle crashing was often seen along this stretch of road. When anyone witnessing it rushed to help, suddenly there was no sign of any bike or rider. I was also told that there is the ghost of a horse pulling a carriage along Church Lane, a lady in Victorian clothing who walks in the streets of the village, and also the ghost of a man riding a bicycle along the A1088.

To make you even more afraid of venturing out at night in this otherwise peaceful village, there is a headless man who floats in the fields behind the church, and a ghostly child in Prospect Road (who was apparently killed when hit by a horse and cart).

PETTISTREE – The St

Whilst quite conceivably being in the running to win any competition for most strangely named street, this rural village also boasts a headless horseman, seen at least twice since the 1990's, trotting down the main street in the early hours of the morning.

POLSTEAD – Near the village green (Heath Road and Rockalls Road)

At about 4.00pm one summer's afternoon in the 1990's, so the story goes, a Mrs Hackford was driving in her car when she suddenly saw a horse and carriage carrying an old lady and two men, all wearing Victorian era clothing, go past her travelling in the opposite direction. She glanced behind her to watch it go (assuming no doubt it was some deliberate dress up for an event or something) - only to find the whole thing had completely disappeared.

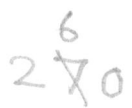

When I asked locally, some had not heard of the haunting at all, even people who had lived in the village their whole lives. Conversely, one witness had heard of a phantom coach with headless horses, but thought that was supposed to come down the hill by the church. (Polstead Hill - which leads to the village green, so quite possibly related). Another had heard it would be seen around Christmas time near the Rectory.

Curiously, another remembered hearing about it in the late 1970's when he was in primary school - but it was a headless horseman who rode down Polstead Hill and into the pond. This sparked other people to say that it was the coach which drove into the pond, and still others to remember that the pond itself is said to be haunted by a woman in white, who is also seen walking along Mill Street but only when it is raining. Only one person remembered that there was also a ghostly monk near the Rectory.

B1078 POTSFORD WOOD

There was a murder near here in 1698, when a father and son were hacked brutally to death by a man wielding an axe, and then their bodies hog tied and hoisted up to a beam to deliberately display what had been done. There is even some speculation that they might not have been dead when they were hoisted up.

Jonah Snell was sentenced to death for their murder and afterwards his body was gibbeted here for over forty years. There is still a plaque marking the spot on a remaining piece of the gibbet post. The rumours of his restless and evil spirit haunting the woods have persisted over the intervening years. In the 1980's, supposedly a lorry driver stopped to relieve himself and walked a short distance into the woods in broad daylight. Seeing the plaque, he stopped to read it, when someone tapped him on the shoulder and he turned around to see someone in a black hood and with a skeletal face next to him.

In 1997 a couple followed some lights they saw in the woods, and heard the clanking of chains. They saw a formless black shape hovering in the trees and quickly left. Paranormal investigators have also visited the site and recorded EVPs there.

SNAPE - between Snape and Sternfield

This tiny rural lane running between these two villages is reported to have harboured a grey, humanoid shape which was seen in December 1974 by a couple driving towards Sternfield. It was in the middle of the road when they first saw it, but quickly moved out of sight by vanishing through the hedge.

TUDDENHAM - Fynn Lane

One bright mid-morning on 23 June 2011, according to one source, a woman walking her dogs along Fynn Lane noticed a cyclist approaching from behind her. He looked perfectly modern and ordinary except that when she stepped to one side and politely held the dogs on a close lead to let him through - he had vanished.

SURREY

A25 BETCHWORTH - towards Dorking

This tale dates back to 1924. A driver was taking passengers to Dorking, and was on the stretch of the A25 between Betchworth and his destination. Suddenly, in his headlights, there appeared a large shire horse galloping straight towards the car. He immediately brought his vehicle to a swift stop and the horse galloped past, avoiding the collision he had thought might be inevitable. Given the year and the fact that horses were still in common use then, it could just have been a runaway horse - except that as it passed the car he realised that its form was sort of fading away and becoming translucent.

When I asked, several people who had lived in the area for most of their lives said they had never heard of a haunting along this stretch of road. The nearest they knew of was a headless horseman in nearby North Holmwood. One person, however, remembered that there had been several sightings over the years of a horseman on the Dorking bypass back in the late 1950s and early 1960's, but did not think that anything had been reported since then.

Several thought the horseman actually haunted the road close to Betchworth Golf Club, although the golf course does in places skirt next to the A25. One person remembered a gentleman many years ago who lived up Stubbs Hill coming home with his hair on end claiming he had just encountered the horseman. Several more came forward who remembered being told the tale when they were younger of the horseman.

One witness explained that her brother had actually seen the horseman when he was walking back after escorting his girlfriend home. He was close to the bridge near the castle gardens.

A person who used to live in Chart Lane South told me that they recalled standing at the gate in their front garden listening to the sound of horses hooves go past, even though there was nothing to be seen. She explained that it had scared the living daylights out of her.

And finally, a man wrote to say that as children they used to camp out in the woods at night around Dorking and sometimes would hear galloping hooves, even though there were no horses in the nearby fields.

CHALDON - Roffe's Lane

This lane is said to be haunted by sound, rather than by anything visual. Sometimes, the sound of a galloping horse rings down the lane and will even pass by any witness and carry on into the distance, but always with nothing to be seen to explain the noise.

The last account I could find for it though was from 1975, so it is perhaps no longer an active haunting.

DUNSFOLD - Church Road

The backstory behind this ghostly tale is the age old one of unrequited love, but with a bitter twist. The story goes that one of the monks who lived near here fell in love with one of the nuns from a neighbouring convent, whom he would see sometimes as they went about their respective duties.

She, however, took her vows rather more seriously than he apparently did and refused to acknowledge him or give him any encouragement. He fell into a fit of jealous pique to be thus rebuffed, and to get his petty revenge he stole something of value and then hid it amongst the nun's possessions. It would be nice to think that he only meant her to get into some slight trouble, but in those days theft was taken rather more seriously than it is today, and she was convicted of the crime and sentenced to hang.

When the poor innocent woman went to her fate, the monk was so ashamed of his deed that he committed suicide. Since then, it is said, his forlorn ghost has been seen a few times and one lady in 1978 said her dog was very reluctant to walk down that lane for no apparent reason.

The story was known locally when I asked about it, and one gentleman told how he and a group of friends had created a prank based on the tale. Three of them conspired against their fourth friend, with one of the trio hiring and dressing up in a monk's costume. The other two arranged to meet their friend for a drink, and walked together up the lane.

It was a clear night with some low hanging mist and a full moon. To add to the ambience, as they walked up the lane, an owl flew hooting out of one of the trees. As they rounded the slight corner, they were met with the eerie sight of the monk, bald head slightly bowed, standing motionless in the road. Their poor friend was so terrified he turned and legged it back to the pub. After they let him in on their joke, he was so unhappy with them he refused to come out with them again for a while.

One witness told me that the history he had read showed that the haunting happens on 24th November each year, but this is in the Rectory itself and reenacts the monk murdering the nun, which is an entirely different version of the story.

Curiously, the Mill House is also supposed to be haunted by a monk. There is a legend in the village that a secret tunnel runs between the rectory and the mill (the old rectory, not the modern day one) and secreted in it there are rumoured to be hidden treasures from the church.

A246 EFFINGHAM

In the wee small hours of the morning in May 2015, a motorcyclist was riding his bike home when he came upon a pair of red tail lights ahead of him in the road. He assumed that he would catch up with whatever vehicle it was and would then need to overtake it, but for a few moments it seemed that the other vehicles must be matching the speed of the bike, since he did not seem to be getting any closer.

Suddenly, the lights ahead of him veered off to one side and the biker heard loud crashing sounds before the lights extinguished. Fearing the worst, he rode to the spot closest to where he had last seen the lights, killed his bike engine and, having dismounted, searched desperately for the stricken vehicle.

There was nothing to be found and everything was eerily quiet.

A325 FARNHAM - West Street

This urban street is said to be haunted by the ghost of an old lady, (in some accounts, an old man) who on winter nights is sometimes seen limping along the road at quite a good turn of speed, before disappearing into a house. Sometimes, instead of the old lady, it is a black dog who is seen running and limping into the house. It is noticeable that in whichever form, the ghost only appears on wet nights in winter.

One witness told me that in the 1980's her partner was the shop manager in one of the shops along Lion and Lamb Way, which runs parallel with West Street. On one particular night he was called to the shop by the police because the front had been ram raided, leaving the shop unprotected. He therefore had to stay on the premises for the rest of the night, until workmen could be contacted in the morning to come and make it secure. Once the police left, he tried to settle down for his wait, but kept feeling uneasy as if someone were watching him, making the hairs on the back of his neck stand up.

Worrying that the thieves might have returned, he went out into the street to look up and down and see if anyone was about. As he glanced around, he suddenly noticed a reflection in the window of the nearby Jeweller's shop of someone standing there. He whipped around to see who it was but no-one was there. He looked back at the window and the reflection had gone.

He returned to his own shop but could not settle and kept looking out on the street. One of the times he did so he saw a misty shape go through the wall of the Jeweller's shop. When the early morning cleaner arrived and he told her about his horrible experiences during the night, she told him she too had often seen the same misty shape.

B365 HERSHAM - Seven Hills Road

In 1966 a cyclist riding along Seven Hills Road reported passing through the form of an old lady which stepped out in front of him. Other reports say that often the form is just that of a strange, white mist which seems to cross the road where it bends, and some say it is a lady wearing a grey coat.

I could not find any current sightings of the ghost. One person told me that Seven Hills Road is actually in Walton, but the maps all classify it as Hersham.

A lady also told me that Burwood Road, which branches off from Seven Hills Road, is haunted by a woman in black whom she saw a few years ago in the 1990's. The apparition walked along wearing Victorian style clothing and then just vanished. Another gentleman had also heard of the same ghost and was also sure she had recently been sighted.

A23 HORLEY - Bonehurst Road

In March 2007 at about nine o'clock one evening, a driver reported that he had to brake hard to avoid hitting an elderly man who had stepped out in front of his vehicle. The man was wearing a flat cap, tweed jacket and bright blue trousers.

Even as the car skidded to a stop, the apparition of the man had completely disappeared. One witness did say she had also seen him, but declined to say any more.

A3 MILFORD

At around eight o'clock on November evening in 2010, an off duty police officer driving home from his shift had to brake hard and swerve to avoid what he thought was an oncoming motorcycle. As the car stopped, and the bike should have passed him, the officer noticed that although the light went past, there was no motorcycle attached to it as he had thought, just…nothing. Completely confused he looked into his rear view mirror – and the road behind was completely empty.

I was not able to find anyone else who had experienced anything along here.

A324 PIRBRIGHT

In 1995 or thereabouts, a man driving in a convertible car towards Pirbright with the roof down saw an old fashioned double decker bus driving along the road towards him from the opposite direction. However, what struck him as odd and convinced him he was seeing an apparition, was that there was no sound coming from the bus, no smell of exhaust, and no wind turbulence caused as they passed one another. Normally, since he was in an open topped car, he was very aware of sounds and smells as he drove.

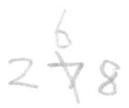

I have not been able to find anyone else who has seen this phantom bus.

A31 TONGHAM

This stretch of road is said to be haunted by a horse and carriage with dimly lit lamps attached to it. It crosses the road even though there is no side road for it to be using. Presumably it is following the path of a long since lost side road or driveway.

There is also said to be the ghost of a long haired woman in a white dress who stands at the side of the road. There don't seem to be any recent accounts of either of these apparitions.

SUSSEX

A27 ARUNDEL

There is a report that a woman wearing what looked like a pale brown raincoat was seen standing at the side of the road. She appeared to be glowing slightly as if lit from within, and was also grinning wildly Her appearance was supposedly strange enough that the police were called. They did not find anything.

I'm always a little sceptical of such vague reports. For me a host of questions always spring to mind: what year was this, did the person see the woman disappear or did they have to leave to go and phone the police, and why would they phone the police in the first place? Looking a bit strange and grinning seems a poor reason to call out the authorities!

When I asked for any local knowledge about the haunting a lady told me that years ago, probably around 2006 or so and during the winter, she was driving towards the roundabout on the A27 from the direction of HMP Ford, after 9pm at night.

She had a passenger in the car with her and they both saw someone cross the road ahead of them. They thought the figure was male, and he crossed the road from right to left, but promptly disappeared. Both she and her passenger were left feeling very unsettled and confused by what they had just witnessed.

A23 BOLNEY - near the Queens Head public house

This ghost is listed as being on the A23 at Bolney, near The Queens Head pub. This description of the location took a little bit of tracking down and dates the story as older than first glance suggests.

The Queens Head pub closed down 18 years ago. It stood on the London Road, which would have been the old A23 before the new bypass was built, and was opposite the entrance to Ryecroft Road.

The story is that the ghost of a woman in a grey dress stepped out in front of a car, which when swerving to try not to hit her crashed off the road. I was not able to find anyone who had actually encountered this ghost.

BRIGHTLING PARK - Kent Lane

In 1976 a man walking down Kent Lane one evening saw a woman walking ahead of him. She was dressed completely in black, and seemed to be gliding rather than walking, which made him stop in his tracks. He watched her warily and actually saw her disappear when she turned towards the verge at the side of the lane. Although he was actually brave enough to go and check the spot, there was nowhere she could have gone and nothing to be seen.

She was seen again later in the same year by another man, and he described her attire as Edwardian widow's costume.

There is supposed to have been a cottage at the spot where she disappeared, long since demolished even in the 1970's, and the tale was that she was the ghost of Barbara Allen, who drowned in the well in the cottage garden in suspicious circumstances.

BRIGHTON - Nile Street

Nile Street in Brighton was pedestrianised in 1989, so if you happen to be walking along it one dark evening, watch out for its ghostly resident. You might see the hooded figure of a monk who still silently walks here, even though the chapel he belonged to was destroyed in 1514.

BUCKBARN CROSSROADS - A272 / A24 road junction

There are several accounts spanning at least two decades from the late 1940's to the late 1960's of a ghost being seen at this location. He is said to be the figure of an old man wearing ragged looking clothing, who sits on a stone at the side of the road. He has been known to suddenly step out in front of vehicles. In 1947, when a passing motorcyclist was subjected to this prank by the ghost, it almost caused him to fall off his motorbike in shock.

Apparently, since the road was updated and made into a wider carriageway, this ragged looking old ghost has been seen less and less. When I asked if anyone had actually seen him recently, one lady explained that before the road was widened, it was a dangerous crossroads with a lot of crashes. There were also tales, she said, of a ghostly coach and horses there which would pull out in front of vehicles.

Another lady told me that when she and her husband were driving along the A272 coming from Cowfold and heading towards the crossroads, they suddenly saw a dark shadow cross the road ahead of their car, causing them to brake sharply and look to see if they had hit something. When they spoke of it with local friends, they were told many others had seen the same thing there. Perhaps this is the same ghost, but now diminished to a dark shape?

Further to the east along the A272 near Ansty, she explained that there used to be The Ansty Cross pub, where many people saw the figure of a man hanging from a tree. Very curiously, the tree itself was also part of the spectral vision as any living tree at the spot had long since disappeared.

My witness had once joined a paranormal investigation group conducting an investigation on the site. During their visit they captured several EVPs with their equipment, including a voice saying, "hung".

BUXTED – Nan Tuck's Lane

There are several versions of the life – and death – of Nan Tuck. She was said to be a witch by some, or just a village girl accused of witchcraft by others. Whatever the truth about who or what she was, most versions say that a mob of vengeful villagers chased after her down this lane, and that they either caught her and lynched her, or that she escaped into the nearby forest, only to later take her own life when she realised she could never go home. Since then, it is claimed her ghost can be seen still fleeing from her tormentors, just as she did in life.

Several local people claim to have seen a figure down there in recent years, and some people say that dogs are nervous about walking down the lane.

One lady in particular told me that in summer 2018 she walked her dog along there at dusk one evening. He is a very calm and laid back Labrador who generally never bothers to bark at anything or anyone. However, as they walked the lane he suddenly swung round to face the woods and started barking and growling. He kept it up for about five minutes, fixated on something only he could sense or see. In the end his owner had to literally drag him away.

A259 CHICHESTER

This stretch of road on either side of the roundabout with Drayton Lane seems to be quite actively haunted. There are sightings reported from 2003 to 2014, some of a shadowy figure stepping in front of a car and others of a more definite figure of a man dressed in black.

One lady told me that in about 2008 or so, she had just gone over the roundabout and was heading away from Chichester on the way home one night, when she was sure that for a moment she saw someone riding a bicycle pull straight out in front of her car.

As fast as the thought crossed her mind that she was going to hit them, there was suddenly no-one there. She even pulled her car into the layby and looked back to make sure, but there was definitely no sign of anyone. She felt very shaken up afterwards and has never forgotten it to this day.

Another lady told me that exactly the same thing had happened to her daughter when driving that same stretch. This second sighting was in approximately 2013.

Then yet another lady wrote in with another sighting, only this time the cyclist appeared to be on the wrong side of the road aiming straight for her. She desperately swerved her car to avoid a collision only to suddenly find there was no-one there.

Curiously, another lady told me that she lives about a mile from this spot and had a very odd experience at their address. About 18 months ago (sometime in 2017) she had a phone call late one evening from her next door neighbour to come out and look at what was in the yard between their two detached properties.

She said that there, twirling and swirling about at quite a speed, just a few feet above their heads, was a cloud-like object, the like of which she has never before seen. She has absolutely no idea what it could have been, even though she and her neighbours watched it in astonishment for several minutes.

We discussed the possibility of a dust-devil, or ball lightning, but she was very sure that it didn't fit any of those categories.

B2141 CHILGROVE

A lady wrote to me to tell me of the strange experience she and her husband had one night on the road from Chilgrove towards Petersfield. Her husband plays in a band and on this particular night they were returning home from a gig, sometime close to midnight. Shortly before they reached Petersfield on this quiet back road, they came across a road traffic accident.

There were police cars, an ambulance and the fire service all in attendance, with flashing blue lights, and the passengers from the crashed car walking about with the policemen. Our witnesses waited in their car for a few moments, expecting to be given instructions to pass through, but were completely ignored. Eventually, they wound down their car window and asked a policeman if they could pass safely. Again, they were completely ignored.

Eventually, they gave up and turned their car around and found another way home. Chatting about how strange it was that no-one would acknowledge their presence, they realised that actually, even more strangely, there had been *complete silence* at the scene even when they wound their window down. They are still not sure today what it was they witnessed that night.

CROWBOROUGH - Walshes Road

In 1969 Roy Blackman was walking along this lane with two friends when they saw a local rag'n'bone man driving his horse and cart along the lane, whom they were familiar with.

(Rag'n'bone men were old fashioned refuse collectors, who used to scour the streets for items that could be salvaged or sold or recycled. They would often ring a hand held bell to signal their presence as they drove their horse slowly along the streets, and as a child I remember rushing out excitedly every time I heard the bell to see the horse of the one which frequented where I grew up. Sometimes, he would stop and let me pet the horse).

The difficulty in this particular instance was that the rag'n'bone man had in fact died four days earlier. His spirit was seen again making its usual rounds in 1977.

When I asked around, one lady told me that there used to be an old farm along that road and as children they would dare each other to go into a disused old building there, which had a dusty old piano in it quietly rotting away in a corner. A group of them were playing there one day, when a single loud note suddenly sounded from the decrepit old instrument. They never ran away so fast from something as they did that day.

Another local said she would not walk down Walshes Road alone as it has a distinctly eerie feel about it and a third agreed that when she used to go down it to attend riding lessons at the Orchid stables, they always found it felt very spooky and unpleasant.

Curiously, two people had heard the tale of a haunted 'bag of soot' which was supposed to chase people down Walshes Road. I wonder if this is somehow an urban myth, a corruption from the original sighting of the rag'n'bone man – as they often used to carry soot or coal as well? One other had also heard of a headless horseman said to ride down nearby Tollwood Road.

CROWBOROUGH – Alice Bright Lane

Not far away from Walshes Road there is Alice Bright Lane. A young woman was found drowned in the stream along here in the early 1900's, and it is she whose ghost is said to run along the lane in stormy weather. The area was called Alice Bright not in honour of the young woman (as that wasn't her name), but after a house which stood here of that name but sometimes spelled 'Allice'. It was originally called Izzard's Farm.

Several local people told me that they found the lane spooky to walk down, and that there is a care home on the lane which is also haunted. Sadly, no-one seems to have actually seen the ghost of the drowned girl.

B2169 FRANT – Bayham Road

A number of reports were made of this ghostly limousine, which was usually seen parked on the side of the road. Cars coming up behind it would have to swerve to go around it, as the road is reasonably narrow, but as they did so it would simply vanish.

The last time it was reported seems to have been in 1978.

A23 HANDCROSS – towards Crawley

There is a tale here of a lady who stands at the side of the road as if hitchhiking, but when drivers slow down to offer help, she disappears. There are also sometimes reports of a male figure seen along here. Several witnesses had heard of the story and one was sure she had seen the ghost around 30 years ago, on a summer's evening at about 11pm at night.

This witness told me that the figure of a woman was standing on what used to be the very old stone bridge on the old A23 at the turn off for Slaugham. The woman suddenly crossed the road as our witness approached, forcing her to stop the car to avoid hitting the lady.

When the car screeched to a stop, the driver realised she could no longer see the pedestrian anywhere. Nor had she hit her - there was no impact or sound of collision. Over the years, she said, she has tried to persuade herself it must just have been a trick of the light, but deep down she knows that what she saw was not 'right'.

At least one other witness knew of someone who had seen her and one lady told me that when she was driving with her young son in the car once, he saw her even though she couldn't see anyone. Some had heard that there was also the ghost of a lady in a red cape.

Another witness had heard of ghostly horses pulling a carriage along this same stretch of road which had crashed here many years ago, and possibly also a highwayman who was hanged for his crimes close by: some described him as the headless horseman.

The victims of the coach crash were taken to the nearby Red Lion pub, and the highwayman was hanged at the crossroads in front of it.

There is also supposed to be a ghost who walks along High Beeches Lane, just east of this stretch of the A23.

A259 ICKLESHAM

At the junction with Laurel Lane, there is said to be the ghost of a World War I soldier who appears wounded and can be seen standing at the side of the road. He was last seen in 1978 as far as I could find out.

A21 JOHNS CROSS - towards Vinehall Street

There is said by one source to be the ghost of a scruffy looking man who can sometimes be seen crossing the road here before disappearing when he is half way across. The last sighting was possibly in 1983.

A286 MIDHURST

In 1999 a man driving into Midhurst along this stretch of road saw the figure of a man step out into the road in front of him. Even as the driver instinctively slowed his car down to allow the man to cross, his initial puzzlement as to where the man had suddenly appeared from just increased as he realised that not only was the man wearing baggy trousers, a waistcoat, and a Quaker style hat – but he was also slightly transparent!

Now completely astonished, the driver watched the figure drift across the road in front of him and then slowly fade from view. When I asked for any other witnesses a lady told me that her mother, who is now in her eighties, once saw a figure along this stretch of road.

It was about 25 years ago, probably 1993, and she and her husband had just driven out of Midhurst and were driving towards Fernhurst. It was about 4.30pm, and they were starting on their long drive back to Yorkshire.

My correspondent asked her mother to write it down to give to me and she wrote, "After going through Fernhurst, up Friday's Hill and along a straight bit of road, in misty conditions, I saw an apparition of a man from the past. He was dressed in a knee length tan/brown coat with a wide brimmed hat carrying a pole over one shoulder with a bag at the end. He had shoulder length wavy hair. My husband, who was driving, didn't see him. The man was walking on the opposite side of the road travelling away from us."

She went on to explain that they had talked with their friends after it happened, and were told that they knew of someone else who had also seen the figure – with the same description – and they had refused to ever drive that stretch of road again!

A21 ROBERTSBRIDGE – Battle Road

In 1974, a policeman followed a cyclist for a short distance along this road, debating whether he should pull him over and tell him he had no lights on, or whether the cyclist would realise it for himself.

As they got level with the turning for Poppinghole Lane, the policeman decided he had better stop the cyclist before he came to grief, and pulled his car around in front of him to make him stop.

When he got out of the car, mere seconds later, the cyclist had completely vanished.

B2100 WADHURST – Bestbeech Hill area

Part of the Bestbeech Hill area is known as Beggar's Bush, around where Buckhurst Lane meets the B2100. In the 1960's, there was a report that the ghost of an old man wearing a long coat and carrying a sack over his shoulder was seen. One version claims he is the ghost of a poacher killed by the gamekeeper in years gone by, and other versions say he is the ghost of an old beggar who died along here.

When I asked locally, several people said that despite living in the area for years themselves, they had never heard of such a story. Only one had heard the old tale and said that the figure was supposed to appear at dusk whenever the fruit is ripe, which could be taken to mean in early autumn.

Another had heard that a house at the bottom of Buckhurst Lane was haunted.

A2270 WILLINGDON - roundabout with Kings Drive

This ghost of a lady in grey has often been seen in the late afternoon, when she looks as if she is about to cross the road, causing drivers to pause. Her attire is said to date from the 1920's, and it is assumed she was killed in a car crash near here.

She was seen in 1976 by the same driver on two separate occasions – both times he felt he was in danger of running her over but she was suddenly no longer there.

Kings Drive crosses the roundabout and becomes Upper Kings Drive and then a little further on the road becomes Coopers Hill. One lady told me that a few years ago she was driving up Coopers Hill at about 7pm when something on the corner of the road caught her eye.

She slowed her car down to take a proper look, thinking it was maybe an animal like a cat or dog about to bolt across the road. What she actually saw was a large, black, formless shadow which crossed the road in front of her car and then just disappeared. She had her two daughters in the car with her so she kept deliberately quiet, not wanting to frighten them, but then one of them said, "What was that thing that just crossed the road, Mum?" She could not give her daughter any rational explanation for what they had just seen.

WARWICKSHIRE

A428 - the ghostly lorry.

Whilst researching for this book, I came across this fascinating set of different records for the ghost lorry on the A428.

One source says the lorry can be seen outside Brandon on the A428, where it crashes off the road at speed. Another says you are likely to meet it coming towards you head close to Church Lawford, but it disappears before hitting you. Another version has it haunting the nearby A45, especially some years ago before it was widened. It is said to be a 1930's style lorry here. Curiously though, another source reports the phantom lorry as having been *seen* in the 1930's.

It is also listed as frequenting Knightlow Hill near Ryton on Dunsmore, where in 1952 a policeman attended a scene where two cars had skidded and hit each other. The policeman set out warning flares a little way up the road to try and stop other cars from joining in the pile up, but as he did so he heard the sound of an approaching lorry. Looking up, he saw the lorry heading towards him at speed and showing no signs of slowing down or heeding his flares.

Frantically he tried to flag it down but even as he did, he realised the lorry was actually transparent and that he could see right through it. Lowering his arms, he watched in terrified fascination as it drove straight through the wrecked cars without wavering at all, then promptly disappeared completely a short way past the accident.

A local historian told me that there is a story that a lorry crashed near Knightlow hill in the winter of 1926, setting the vehicle itself on fire and killing the driver. (This would explain why the phantom lorry was seen in the 1930's, and would make it a slightly earlier make of vehicle)

Sadly I have not been able to find any recent sightings of this well-travelled spectral vehicle, as it would be an interesting sight on today's roads.

A3400 ATHERSTONE ON STOUR – towards Alderminster

There is a legend that this area is haunted by a farmer who was killed when riding his horse recklessly at full gallop and as a result hit a low tree branch at speed which unseated him from the saddle and killed him. The same ghost is also said to haunt the nearby B4086.

BEDWORTH – Bellairs Avenue and Bedworth Lane

In June 1996 according to one source, a man walking down Bellairs Avenue with his brother saw a nun walking towards them in the middle of the road. Surprised at the sight, he commented about her to his brother. Imagine his astonishment when his brother replied that he could not see a figure at all! I was not able to find any other sightings of this ghost.

Just outside of Bedworth, near Rabbit Lane Woods on Bedworth Lane, there is said to be the ghost of a lady who committed suicide. She can be seen standing at the side of the road wearing a long white gown and sometimes covering her face with her hands. According to one source, she was seen in 2005 and again twice in 2012.

A4141 CHADWICK END

I found an account that in the 1960's a police car driving along this road late at night saw a small group of nuns walking along the edge of the road. The policeman turned his car around, planning to find out where they were going, if they were OK, and at the same time have a chat with them about the wisdom of walking along a busy road in the dark dressed all in black.

They had disappeared.

COVENTRY - Coat of Arms Bridge Road

There is a local legend that this strangely (but aptly, since the bridge over it bears a coat of arms) named road is haunted by a young girl who runs out in front of cars and then promptly disappears.

I could not find any records at all of actual sightings, and no-one responded to my requests - so there has to be some doubt about the validity of this tale.

A426 DUNCHURCH - towards Kites Hardwick.

Many years ago, one witness told me, she had been driving to work on an early shift at a nearby school. As she happens to be personally known to me, I am as certain as I can be that she is sure of what she saw that day.

She drove through Dunchurch, and was heading along the A426 towards Kites Hardwick, quite close to Draycote Water. It was still pitch dark and was very foggy, making the drive quite difficult. She was alone in the car and there were no other vehicles on the road at that early time.

Suddenly, on the verge on the left hand side of the road, she saw what she can only describe as a small chap with an aboriginal-type face. His appearance immediately made her think of archetypical dwarves from old tales. He had curly orange coloured hair, and was grinning straight at her as she glanced at him. She looked briefly ahead and then back to look at him again - but he had vanished.

She travelled that same route for 8 years in total, from 1989 to 1997, but only saw him that one time. She has no rational explanation for what she saw that foggy early morning.

A4177 HATTON

In September 1982 a couple passing by in a car saw a figure standing beside this stretch of road who resembled a Cavalier from the English Civil War period.

Apparently completely unrelated, but interesting for its proximity, on nearby Dark Lane in October 2007 a driver saw a ghost car, light in colour, travelling on the wrong side of the road close to the bridge. He slowed down to allow space for them to pass each other, but the oncoming car suddenly vanished. It was midafternoon and therefore in broad daylight.

A5 HINCKLEY

There have apparently been reports about this phantom highwayman since at least 1926, when he was seen wearing a jacket with bright crimson sleeves. He was seen again in 1927 riding his horse, and again in 1979, when he was more of a shimmering outline.

The earlier tales claim him to be the ghost of Dick Turpin, but since there was a set of children's comics published in the 1920's all about him, which depicted him wearing a crimson sleeved jacket, this may be viewed with a certain amount of skepticism.

There was, however, a long since vanished medieval village along this stretch of road called Stretton Baskerville, so the idea that a common or garden *local* highwayman, rather than the celebrity Dick Turpin, could have roamed these roads is not of itself far-fetched.

A435 KINGS COUGHTON

This stretch of road is said to be haunted by a lady wearing a pale coloured raincoat. She was seen in the late 1990's by a couple driving along who saw her step out onto the road and then just vanish.

There is also supposed to be a figure seen pushing a bicycle as well as a phantom coach and horses. I was not able to find any corroborating sightings of any of these apparitions.

RYTON ON DUNSMORE - Old Ryton Bridge

The Editor of Ryton on Dunsmore Magazine shared the following account with me, "On 2nd May 1734 Thomas Wildey allegedly murdered his aunt and her daughter, who owned a pub in Coventry. He was found guilty and subsequently hanged and then his body gibbeted as a warning to others. Eventually, what was left of his remains were taken down and scattered in a nearby sandpit.

"In 1793, sand from the same pit was used in bedding and jointing for the Old Ryton Bridge stonework. Since then, the bridge has had strange sights and noises occurring over the years, normally in May and in the dead of night. A strange patchy mist hangs over the area and lights seem to flitter nearby."

Apparently many Toll Keepers left their post over the years frightened by the strange happenings by the bridge, and it was assumed Thomas' spirit was angry as he was wrongly accused and convicted.

WESTWOOD HEATH

I came across an account that said a young lady was leaving her friend's house in the early hours of the morning to drive home one night in 1986. As she set off, she suddenly saw the figure of a man on horseback standing beneath a street lamp. He was wearing a wide brimmed hat which was pulled down low in such a way as to cast complete shadow over his face.

She was so surprised that she stopped the car to get a better look at him, but he had simply disappeared.

WHITACRE HEATH - Halloughton Grange

Halloughton Grange is a narrow rural lane just outside the village of Whitacre Heath. It is quite a short stretch of mostly tree-lined road. There are said to be numerous accounts, dating from the 1930s right through to the most recent sighting in 2010, of a nurse wearing an old fashioned uniform with a cape standing at the side of the road.

Sometimes, she has stepped out in front of cars, causing them to have near accidents. Apparently she once frightened a cyclist half to death when she stepped in front of his cycle, forcing him to ride straight through her!

WILTSHIRE

A365 ATWORTH

The original source story I found said that in winter 1944, a driver passing along this lane had to brake hard when a horse and rider emerged from a hedge on one side of the road and crossed in front of him. Both rider and horse then disappeared into a wall on the other side of the road - confirming that what he had seen was not of this world.

When I asked locally about the tale, a witness told me that she remembered her primary school headmaster (who lived in Devizes) saying that when he was driving up the hill out of Atworth towards Bath he was aware of something thundering along beside him in the field but couldn't see anything when he looked directly at it. He became convinced after doing some research that it had been Dick Turpin that he had heard. Another witness had also heard about the same ghost and said that it had been seen or heard several times.

One man said that he had been told that the ghost of a man haunts the churchyard in Atworth. There is also an old track leading out of the village towards Stonar and both his own dog, and those of other people he had spoken with, were sometimes very reluctant to walk along there.

A36 BATH - towards Warminster

There is a story that along this road, close to Limpley Stoke, a ghostly face once appeared in the road in front of a car, causing all the dashboard gauges to fail at once.

A witness also told me that a side road off the A36 leading towards the tiny village of Hinton Charterhouse is known locally as Hangmans Lane, and is said to be haunted by a female ghost.

Also leading off the A36, closer to Bath, is Brassknocker Hill. There is an unknown beast said to roam the hillside here and two witnesses wrote in to say that they had seen it. One even had the presence of mind to whip her camera out as it ran between the car she was travelling in as a passenger and the car in front of them. It moved so fast though that her photograph only caught the tip of its long tail. She thought it looked a bit like a large monkey running on all fours.

A363 BATH – towards Bradford on Avon

This stretch of road, called 'Sally in the Woods', is famously haunted by the ghost of a woman variously said to be a gypsy woman who was murdered here, or a gypsy child who was locked in Brown's Tower and left there to starve to death. Some local witnesses told me that they had been told that the story relates to a child run over in the woods some years ago. Many people believe the road is named for this ghost.

This area was actually the site of a Civil War battle in 1643, and the word 'sally' means going forth in battle, so it is also speculated by some that this is the real origin of the name of the road.

One writer has conducted extensive research on the origins of the ghost and says she was actually Sarah Gibson, born in 1724 and died at the very great age of 100 years old in 1824. She was married to a gamekeeper on the estate and when he died, she was turned out of the tied cottage they shared. She took her possessions and went and lived in one of the huts in the woods which the gamekeepers used and managed to live out there on her own for the next 40 years. Not surprising then, that she became known as a witch.

A361 BECKHAMPTON

There are two standing stones beside the A361 a mile or so west of Beckhampton. Legend has it that they mark the grave of one Walter Leader, who was framed for the robbery of a stagecoach and the murder of the coachman. He was hanged for his supposed crimes but tragically, shortly after he died, the official pardon he'd been hoping for came. It had come to light that he had not, in fact, been part of the gang who had committed the crime.

Not surprisingly perhaps, he is said to still haunt this stretch of road. Unfortunately though he still gets listed as the 'ghost of a highwayman' which I expect is particularly galling considering he was an innocent man and not a highwayman at all! Alternatively, it perhaps *is* the ghost of one of the gang – endlessly remorseful for allowing an innocent man to go to the gallows in his stead.

Either way I could not find any accounts of recent sightings, although one correspondent did tell me that she had heard of a ghostly coach and horses around the same area, which is curious.

BOWERCHALKE – towards Woodminton

There is an old story that in the fields along the road between Bowerchalke and Woodminton, the ghosts of horses can sometimes be seen and the sounds of a fierce battle heard. The area is said to be the site of a battle between the Romans and the Britons. One source gives the location as Patty's Bottom – but I am not sure where that is. I was not able to find any accounts of actual sightings.

BULFORD

There are two ghosts which haunt the main road through Bulford. One is that of a lady who crosses the road and causes consternation to car drivers. She is supposed to be wearing an evening dress, and the source story claims that one driver (variously said to be either a car driver or a lorry driver) saw her cross the road and pass ***through*** a barbed wire fence.

There is also meant to be the ghost of a man wearing a wide brimmed hat. He is known as The Whistling Cavalier, because he whistles the tune 'Greensleeves'. That tune is certainly old enough – it is mentioned in Shakespeare's work in 1602 so clearly predates that. Many people attribute the writer as Henry VIII, although this is not known for certain.

The Whistling Cavalier was apparently last seen and heard by a teenager in 1995, who saw him from her bedroom window.

CALNE

There is an old story of a phantom man who stands at the side of the road as it passes through Calne. He was seen in 1965 by a driver who thought he had hit him, so stopped his car and ran back to check. He saw the man walking away and followed him intending to ask if he was OK, but the man simply disappeared right in front of his astonished eyes.

In 1968 two people in a car saw a figure in white standing in the road in front of them late one night.

When I asked locally, one person explained that the road between Calne and Derry Hill is called Black Dog Hill because it is haunted by a black dog, which is quite possibly another Shuck legend. Nobody came forward who had seen the male figure, though.

B4005 CHISELDON - towards Hodson

This lane is supposedly haunted by a strange looking entity which bounces up and down in the middle of the road. It is just an amorphous blob with no particular shape - but I was unable to find any actual sightings or witnesses. Interestingly though it's not the only bouncing type anomaly I've been told about, as there is one in my book 'The Ghosts of Marston Vale'.

A4 CORSHAM

The original source for this seems to be from 1990 so the story must predate that - but by how far is unclear.

It seems that a lorry driver had been driving along the A4 somewhere close to Corsham at around 2.30am one morning, when he saw a white figure in the road ahead picked out by his headlights. Puzzled by seeing someone apparently out so late, he watched the figure for a moment. As he watched, it suddenly 'blurred' as it rushed at great speed towards him and then seemed to be clinging to the side of his lorry. He said it seemed to be leering in at him through the window for a moment before dropping off the vehicle as he sped along.

Apparently he was so traumatised by it that it took him some months to be able to talk about it and when he did, he described it as a skull-like face clinging to the side of his lorry and grinning at him through the window.

HEYTESBURY - near Skew Railway Bridge.

The original story for this describes a couple driving home late one night in October 1965. It says they encountered a figure sprawled over the parapet of the bridge in such a way as its legs were protruding out into the road, and they had to swerve to avoid running the legs over.

They were worried they *had* actually clipped his legs, so screeched to a stop. The man got out of the car, which his fiancé was driving, and spent fifteen minutes searching for the figure but there was literally no-one about. They gave up and carried on with their journey. The lady dropped her fiancé off before returning along the same route to go to her own home. As she crossed the bridge again, she saw two figures wearing balaclavas and had to swerve again.

When I asked locally, I was told this had happened on the old A36 route between Heytesbury and Warminster, where it crossed the railway line by Norton Bavant. As best as I can tell, and from what the locals were able to tell me, it looks like this might be the road now called the B3414. It is a known accident blackspot. Several people were aware that it was said to be haunted by a figure standing on the bridge.

A350 HINDON - junction with A303

This crossroads just northwest of the village is said to be haunted by a phantom coach pulled by four matching grey horses.

A429 MALMESBURY - Burton Hill

In the early morning in January 1967 a driver reported seeing a pale grey figure appear in the road in front of him as he drove towards Hullavington on Burton Hill. The figure turned towards him as he braked sharply, revealing that it seemed to be wearing a bright buckle at its waist. The figure briefly raised its arm, stepped towards the verge, and promptly disappeared.

There is also supposed to be a ghostly carriage and horses along the same stretch, which allegedly crashed into the pool which used to be along here. One local resident told me that she remembered seeing a report, probably in the 1970's, of someone who had actually seen the coach. Several others had also heard the tale.

One lady recalled that her parents had been driving back to Malmesbury from Corston along that road in the 1960s when they saw a dark figure in the road. Her mother had been convinced the car had hit him, although her father was certain there had not been a collision. They turned the car around and went to check but there was no sign of the figure.

They then saw the same figure again a few years later and this is what finally convinced them they had in fact seen a ghost. They had been told on the second occasion that it was the apparition of a vicar who had been killed near there. Not surprisingly, my correspondent's mother was never keen to use that road at night again.

Another lady wrote and explained to me that her Aunt, who lives in Corston, said she once saw a grey lady in a long dress on the road close to this same spot.

A gentleman also wrote in to say that his brother-in-law used to live in the cottages at Burton Hill when he was a young man. He would tell the story of how they often saw the light of what looked like the lamps on a coach cross the road and disappear into the pond. My correspondent had himself walked the route on numerous occasions over the years and never actually witnessed anything, although he did find it had a spooky atmosphere.

And amazingly one local explained that according to her mother, this is the ghost of her own great-great-great-grandfather! He was travelling home on the stage coach which crashed and then rolled over into the small pond which used to be on Burton Hill (it is no longer there), trapping the passengers inside it. He died, and it is his ghost which wanders the road there.

A345 MARLBOROUGH - towards Pewsey

This stretch of road is alleged to have the ubiquitous headless horses and coach haunting it. Like the original writer, I too get astonished as to why there are so many headless horses in our folklore since we've never been a nation in the habit of beheading hapless innocent horses!

When I tried to see if anyone had ever actually seen it, some people thought it was at the crossroads from Pewsey to Wilcot (Wilcot Road), and others thought it haunted Cherhill, which is quite some distance away. One lady had heard it was seen close to Marlborough, on the old track near Granham Hill and Treacle Bolly.

A gentleman was aware that halfway along the road in question there is Oare and Huish, and he knew of stories of people riding their horses on the lanes around there and how the horses would 'play up' close to where there was once a gibbet.

Another correspondent told me that about 53 years ago (so probably 1965), she lived in West Kennett and was seeing a young lad who lived in Oare. He came to pick her up one winter's evening and was slightly later arriving than they had arranged.

When he arrived he was clearly very shaken and when asked what was the matter, he explained that he had seen a ghost on the Pewsey to Marlborough road. It was near the first turning to Clatford coming from Oare. He had seen a figure of a man standing in the middle of the road, who was dressed in modern clothing but a little outdated. The poor lad remained tense for a long time afterwards whenever he had to pass the same spot.

Another told how when she was a child travelling home on the school bus in the 1980's, she would always look out for the ghost of the headless horseman whom she had been told rode between Upavon towards Pewsey on the A345. Sadly, she never did see him, although some 'grown ups' at the time told her that they had.

I wonder if the gibbet was erected to mark the spot where a highwayman was hanged who attacked coaches - could that account for both sets of ghosts?

A4 MARLBOROUGH - Bath Road

One lady told me that one cold November night around 10pm, she and her friend were driving along Bath Road in Marlborough close to the Marlborough College, when they saw a dog-like creature run across the road in front of their car.

Even as it ran, it dissipated into thin air like a wisp of steam. She said it was the weirdest thing she had ever seen, and she braked sharply out of sheer astonishment.

MELKSHAM

There is one report of a man who was seen around midnight walking down Snarlton Lane with his umbrella raised to shield his head and face. As the witness approached, the man lowered his arm - revealing a headless body. The person who related the incident saw the figure three times in all and eventually stopped using the lane as a route home. A few people came forward to say that they had heard stories of Snarlton Lane being haunted, and one said she had been told it was a highwayman who was sometimes seen there.

When I asked locally at least two people had heard of a ghost who haunts the 'S' bend in the road past Lower Woodrow on the way to Lacock, where it joins Clink Lane. One said they never felt comfortable driving along there at night, although they had not actually seen anything themselves in the seven years they lived there.

Another correspondent told me that she had heard that if you drive round the 'S' bends, then the ghost of a man might appear sitting in the back seat of your car. Someone else said they had often experienced odd things there when driving home from work.

WORCESTERSHIRE

A448 HARVINGTON - the fields and roads surrounding Harvington Hall and the crossroads at Mustow Green

It is claimed that in the early 1700's the witch Mistress Hicks was found guilty of raising storms to ruin the crops of her enemies and making people vomit up pins and urine. She was executed for her alleged crimes and her body interred at the crossroads in Mustow Green. This was a custom often followed to stop someone's restless ghost from wandering around. It didn't seem to work in Mistress Hick's case, for the ghost of the hapless old lady has been seen wandering all around the local lanes and across the grounds of Harvington Hall itself.

Interestingly there are two historical pamphlets detailing the prosecution of witches, one dated 1705 and the other 1716. One of the pamphlets mentions Mistress Hicks and her daughter but states that the trials were held in Northamptonshire and Huntingdonshire.

Curiously though, some historical researchers suggest that these two pamphlets were much later 'retellings' (or complete fabrications) with some considerable embellishments of witch trials which actually took place a century earlier, but trying to pass them off as recent. One of the earlier trials which these two pamphlets seem to have taken as source material *was* in Herefordshire/ Worcester.

However, actual records show that the last witch to be executed in England was Alice Molland in Devon in 1684: so Mistress Hicks, whoever she was, cannot therefore have been executed in the early 1700's.

LENCHWICK - King's Lane

There is supposed to be a phantom coach, complete with headless coachman according to one local who had heard of it, which runs along this small stretch of lane.

YORKSHIRE

B1242 ATWICK

This lonely coastal road is said to be haunted by the spectre of a highwayman – headless of course.

There is also a holy well on the west side of the village, which would tend to suggest this was a more frequented road in times gone by.

AYSGARTH – The Straights – Road towards Woodhall

A lady dressed in Victorian attire is sometimes seen strolling along this road. She is most often seen in the early spring, around March, and it is assumed this coincides with the date of her death.

BAILIFF BRIDGE – A58/A641 Junction

This crossroads, where The Wyke Lion pub sits, is supposedly haunted by both a man on horseback and a phantom car. It's such a notorious accident blackspot, that it is called the Hellfire Crossroads. It was first called Hellfire Corner as far back as 1940, when a newspaper reported that a motorist had lost control of his car when he was distracted by a bright light rising up out of the woods.

Between 1977 and 1981 there were so many of these strange lights observed (and now dubbed UFO's) that the phenomena earned the nickname of The Wyke Woods Flap. (Flap being an old word for commotion).

A684 BEDALE – leading to Little Crakehall

The road leading west from Bedale is reputedly home to a grey misty figure. The mist is also said to haunt a nearby wooded area, although I wasn't able to find any actual sightings of it.

One person however did helpfully give me information about 'The Plague Cross' situated along this same stretch of road.

It is a stone socket supporting a short portion of a stone upright, and is also known as 'The White Cross', even though it is clearly no longer a cross.

It is supposed to mark the spot where villagers would meet between the boundaries of their neighbouring districts, to exchange food and buy goods at a 'safe' distance during the period of the Black Death. Money would be left in a bowl of vinegar in order to prevent the plague from spreading.

The Black Death, or bubonic plague, reached England in 1348 a.d. and caused widespread deaths. I wonder if there is any connection between the stone marker and the apparition.

BOLTBY

At around midnight one night in June 2012, a witness in a car saw a woman wearing an old fashioned party dress. They were immediately aware they were seeing something not natural as there was nothing to be seen below the area of the woman's knees and where her face should have been there was just a blurry shape. The apparition was also faintly illuminated.

CLUMBER PARK

Although not strictly a 'road ghost', I have included this entry just out of interest, as it was on one of the paths within the wonderful Clumber Park. It happened in 2010 to a correspondent who wrote to me, who was walking in the park with his girlfriend of the time and her nephew.

They were walking along beside the lake where the two curved stone benches sit. Ahead of them, they noticed an Old English sheepdog (popularly known as a Dulux dog due to its use in the television advert by that company) running ahead of a woman who was walking along. It ran down the path towards our witness, and then veered off into the bush at the side of the path. Although our witness and his lady friend watched the bush expectantly for several minutes as they walked, the dog never reappeared.

Had it been a small terrier of some sort, one might assume it had run down a rabbit hole or some such, but a large Dulux dog?

Curiously, the woman they had at first assumed was the dog's owner just carried on walking and never acknowledged the presence of the dog at all.

B6089 GREASBROUGH - The Whins

This is a classic road ghost story dating back to at least 1985. There is said to be the figure of an old woman seen along this road who steps out in front of passing cars, but when the worried drivers stop and search there is nothing to be found. I found another reference to her from 2004.

When I asked locally, someone mentioned that they remembered from their childhood being told that this road was haunted by the figure of a monk, which makes me wonder whether this is more a classic case of urban myth transforming over time.

KIVETON PARK - Packman Lane

One correspondent, Craig, wrote in to tell me of the experience he had on Packham Lane. Craig explained that it is common knowledge that you can encounter the ghost of a highwayman on his horse along this lane and that he will cross the road in front of your car if you drive up there at night. He is supposedly especially drawn to estate type cars, possibly because the shape is reminiscent of an old fashioned coach, which he would have been used to stopping and robbing in life.

At 23 years of age, Craig travelled there by car with two of his best friends. This would have been in the late 1990's. They had two girls in the car with them, so whilst the other two lads sat in the front, Craig sat on the back seat with the girls. He explained to me that it is a long stretch of road with no artificial lighting and is quite isolated although there is a farmhouse at the far end of it.

As they came to the big dip in the road, the electrics on the car suddenly ceased to function, making the engine stutter and die and the lights dim. The car's own momentum helped the engine to turn over and start up again, so that as they reached the bottom of the dip and started the ascent, they had their full lights on again.

There - caught in the beam of their headlights - was the figure of a man on horseback crossing the road. He was wearing a tricorn style hat and what looked like it might be a cape or cloak. Craig described him as sort of foggy silver in colour. The horse seemed quite large, but was not visible from the knee downwards.

The figure came from the direction of the copse of wood on the right and crossed the road into the woods on the left. It did not turn to look at them nor acknowledge them in any way, and the whole encounter was brief - no more than a couple of seconds. Today, the wood has largely been removed or cut back away from the road. The area where it happened now has a wind farm on one side and an open field on the other, although the lane itself still has a thin line of trees on either side.

Our witnesses carried on driving to the end of the lane where the farmhouse is and here they also saw a wispy, semi translucent, possibly female figure dart around the side of one of the buildings.

When I looked for corroboration of what Craig saw that night, I found several other accounts dating from the early 2000's and even later. One writer was even brave enough to park up and spend fifteen minutes searching the area for a natural explanation, to no avail.

There is speculation that the reason the horse's legs cannot be seen is because the level of the road has changed over the intervening years, and there is even some suggestion that this was an old Roman road originally. There is also mention of the ghost of a small boy who can be seen along this same lane. He is alleged to be the young son of a local farmer, who darted out in front of his father's horse and cart and was caught under the wheels and killed. I wonder if our original witness Craig actually saw him near the farm buildings, and only assumed it was female due to the slight stature of the form they briefly saw.

One writer had also heard that there was meant to be a troop of ghostly Roman soldiers who could be seen along this same stretch of road.

MASHAM COMMON

One gentleman wrote to me to say that he has heard of there being the ghosts of Roman soldiers who march across this piece of land - seen only from the waist up because they always seem to march when a ground mist is lying.

A close friend of my correspondent's had once seen the ghostly soldiers and told my correspondent that when he drove a little further down the road he saw another car driver stopped at the side of the road who was 'frightened to death' at what he had just witnessed. He had been told that they haunt this area because there used to be a Roman encampment here.

A684 NORTHALLERTON – towards Leeming Bar

There is a source story that two women were driving one night from Northallerton towards Leeming Bar. Suddenly, a large black dog darted out in front of the car. Knowing she was going to hit it and quite probably seriously injure or kill it, the driver closed her eyes in horror even as she performed an emergency stop.

The passenger, on the other hand, kept her eyes open and saw the dog actually pass through the bonnet of the car. As it did so, she had time to notice that it was shadowy in form rather than solid looking, and although she could see it had floppy ears she could not really make out what type of face it had.

When I asked locally about it, one person had heard the same tale and remembered that it came from around 2002. No-one else came forward to say they had seen it however.

STIRTON

Driving through Stirton one August night in 2009 at about 3.00am, four friends were concerned to see what looked like an older lady wearing white clothing and clutching a handbag standing on the grass verge at the side of the road. They were worried that something must be wrong for her to be there so late at night alone, so they stopped the car around 25 meters or so beyond where they had seen her and reversed the car up to see if they could offer help of some sort.

She had disappeared, and although they spent quite some minutes searching for her, there was no sign of her at all. Unfortunately, I wasn't able to find any other accounts of her.

A616 STOCKSBRIDGE BYPASS

This is a very well-known haunting, and it is really the land upon which the road was built that is affected but now the intrusion of the modern bypass has given the ghosts somewhere new to roam. The principal ghost is thought to be that of a monk, who centuries ago fell out with his mother church and was consequently buried in unconsecrated ground when he died, causing him to remain earthbound as a roaming spirit.

There are said to be many reports of him being seen at the side of the road and even some of him appearing sitting in the passenger seats of cars driving along this road at night. The bypass was built in 1987 and there are several reports from the construction workers who built it. They were adamant that they started to encounter strange sights and noises on the building site which would later become the road.

Then one night, they saw a group of children playing 'Ring'a'Roses' one night in the field.

The road is known as an accident blackspot and there is a lot of speculation that many of the accidents are caused by the sudden appearance of the monk.

In 2017 The Star carried an article with a video recording showing Phil Sinclair, a ghost hunter, terrified by a shadowy figure. He also captured the sounds of growling on tape.

My correspondent Craig (see Kiveton Park entry) told me that he had been travelling in the back of a minibus in May one early evening a few years ago along this stretch of road. As they drove along the bypass, he idly looked out of the window at the fields they were passing. He suddenly noticed something very dark black, with no particular discernible form, in one of the fields. Curious, he looked more closely at it, wondering what it was and a moment later it sped across the field as a sort of formless mist towards the road, before he lost sight of it.

A659 TADCASTER - towards Leeds

One elderly friend of mine told me that many years ago, he was working as a minibus driver in Yorkshire. He was driving along the A659 from Tadcaster towards Leeds when he suddenly saw, caught in his headlights, the misty, translucent form of a woman drift across the road in front of his bus.

He has never been able to come up with a rational explanation for what he saw that night, even though to this day he insists there are no such things as ghosts.

A64 TADCASTER

In 1993 a couple with their small child in the car were driving into Tadcaster from the York direction. There were still open fields beside the road as they had not yet reached their destination, when they were suddenly forced to brake sharply by the figure of a man wearing long knee high boots running across the road in front of them.

He was only a few feet away from their car, and they were able to register that he looked terrified - even though at the same moment they also registered that the figure was partially transparent. He carried on running for a second or two, then sort of shimmered slightly and disappeared.

A629 THURGOLAND

In September 1992 a family of five consisting of parents and their three children were driving down this road after dark. Suddenly, floating about three feet above the road in front of their car, was a figure wearing something which might have been a cape but it was indistinct enough for them not to be sure.

As soon as the figure appeared, their car engine stalled, giving them a moment of panic as whatever it was swept towards their car and then veered off and floated into the woods and out of sight.

The car then helpfully restarted.

TICKHILL - Wong Lane

Wong Lane is a perfectly straight urban street in this small town. It boasts its very own story of a spectral coach and horses though, which are said to charge down its length. When I asked about it locally several people had heard of the tale, some from when they were children. One thought it also came down nearby Wilsic Road, and Hangman's Hill.

A number of others pointed out that they had lived on or near to the road for many years - in some cases their whole lives - and had neither seen it nor heard tell of it. It would tend to suggest, therefore, that this is an old tale and a haunting which is no longer active if it ever was.

CHAPTER 2

SCOTLAND

A83 ACHADUNAN - just past the A815 junction

In the early hours of the morning in the early 1980's, two people were travelling by car along this scenic road on their way to catch a ferry.

They passed a man walking along the side of the road wearing a heavy dark coloured coat, a bowler hat, and carrying an umbrella and a suitcase.

They were curious about why someone so inappropriately dressed for the location should be out walking in the pitch dark, but didn't assume they had seen a ghost until some years later when they found out that the area was haunted by a figure whose description matched that of the man they had seen.

ARBIGLAND

There is a story that the area known as Three Crossroads in this remote coastal hamlet which overlooks the English Lake District on the other side of the inlet is haunted. The tale is that the daughter of the local well-to-do landowner fell in love with one of the stable lads.

One version I found claims that the two of them knew their love would never be allowed, and the lad committed suicide. Even at the time there was suspicion that her family actually murdered him and passed it off as suicide. His lady love then wandered away in sorrow, losing herself amongst the rugged terrain and was never seen again except in the form of a ghost which still haunts these crossroads. In other versions, it is *his* ghost who haunts the area.

One writer gives their full history and states that it was Helen Craik whose lover was murdered by a bullet to the head in 1792. As her father was the local Justice of the Peace, there was no hope of having the crime investigated and it was passed off as 'suicide'. Distraught, Helen moved away to Cumberland where she lived on as a spinster until her death at the age of 74.

There don't seem to be any accounts of either ghost being seen in recent times.

ARBROATH – old A92 disused road approaching Arbroath

This road is now actually called the ghost road – because it is a disused road, slowly becoming overgrown and disintegrating. It was replaced by the modern A92 and it now lies abandoned for a stretch. When it was still in use, one driver coming down it after dark encountered a woman standing on the roadside whose head was glowing slightly as if she was lit by the light from a lantern. Not surprisingly, he kept on driving.

Even with the road disused as it is today, it is said to still have a very heavy atmosphere at night and that the sounds of a scream and car crash can still sometimes be heard here.

BANCHORY – A93 and A980

There is a ghost monk who is said to walk the roads around this town – especially the older parts. He has sometimes been known to step out unexpectedly in front of cars.

A6088 BONCHESTER BRIDGE

Although some forty miles north of Hadrian's Wall, this village is said to host the phantoms of a 'Roman Legion', marching along the road into the village from the direction of nearby Chesters. Honestly, I'd be surprised if it was a full Roman Legion still marching along here because there were around 5,000 soldiers in a unit referred to as a Legion. The smallest unit in a Roman army was a Centuria and totalled roughly 80 to 100 men. You'd expect 5,000 ghosts marching along might get rather more witnesses than this haunting seems to.

The reality of course is that today people use the phrase 'Roman Legion' to mean any size group of Roman soldiers.

The old kirk near here also boasted the story of a ghost who was bound by the priest there to walk only a certain line 'between Hoddleswoodie and Howabank'.

CRAWFORD - Watling Street

Ten ghostly Roman soldiers are said to walk along this street, which presumably (given its name), is also an old Roman road.

A7 EDINBURGH - towards Stowe

This stretch of road seems to attract ghost vehicles. There is said to be a phantom lorry that is sometimes seen driving erratically along the A7 south of Edinburgh, and there was an account from 2010 of a spectral Austin car on the same stretch of road. When I asked locally for any sightings, one person said they had actually heard that the stretch is also haunted by a white lady.

FORTH ROAD BRIDGE - slip road on M90

There was a report from one early evening in summer 2002 when a driver saw, in clear broad daylight, an old style Austin Allegro.

Glancing to his left as he overtook the car, he noticed that it had sustained front end damage and was being driven by an elderly couple. The man driving the old car was wearing a grey coloured flat cap. The witness assumed they were vintage car enthusiasts, but was mildly curious about the front end damage to the car. As he completed his overtaking manoeuvre, he glanced back in his rear view mirror before taking up position ahead of them in their lane.

They had completely disappeared. There was no car on the road behind him and nowhere they could have stopped or pulled over.

GLASGOW – Dalmarnock Road Bridge

Dalmarnock Road Bridge is an attractive red iron and brick built bridge which provides transport and pedestrian access across the River Clyde. It joins Dalmarnock to Southern Rutherglen, and is famous for its 'suicide ghost'.

He is said to be dressed in reasonably modern attire, with black trousers and a three quarter length coat, and looks to be in his early thirties or so. He is seen looking down into the waters below before suddenly making the jump. Apparently people see his apparition fall a short distance, but then disappear even as it falls.

I was not able to find any actual sightings of him.

KILMACOLM

This large village is said by one report to be haunted by the ghost of a Victorian lady dressed in a black gown, who drifts ominously around the roads, floating a little way above the ground. With such scant detail to go on, I wasn't expecting to get many responses when I asked locally, but I did get one interesting response.

One witness wrote in to tell me of her own story. She explained that on this particular day, she and her sister had decided they would go on a power walk as part of their fitness regime. A friend had recommended that they walk the 'back lane', as it was a particularly nice route. Their route followed a path surrounded by trees and bushes and consisted of a man made wooden path raised slightly above the ground to keep it clear of the mud. Our witness was expecting to thoroughly enjoy the walk, as it is a pastime which usually brings her great peace and a sense of wellbeing.

On this day however, as soon as she and her sister began walking, she began to feel a bad energy around them which she really didn't like and which started to make her feel quite uncomfortable. Her reaction must have been palpable, as her younger sister asked her what was wrong several times and seemed genuinely puzzled as to why she seemed not to be enjoying their walk. She also noticed that she had lost phone signal and that increased her sense of discomfort since there is normally good mobile coverage in the area.

She started to feel like they were being watched, and the feeling became so uncomfortable that she stopped and said she wanted to turn back. Her sister, however, wanted to carry on to the next bend and see what was around it. Although her sister did carry on and look, our witness found herself rooted to the spot with a sense of dread.

When they turned around and headed back she described feeling enormous relief, and she felt like she could not get out of there quickly enough. A few days later, she was told by a mutual friend that the area was haunted by a man who wandered into the water there whilst inebriated and drowned.

A75 KINMOUNT STRAIGHT

The Kinmount Straight, as this stretch of the A75 between Carrutherstown and Annan is known, has another name in popular nomenclature: The Ghost Road. It really is an almost ruler straight stretch of road, passing through gentle, fairly flat rural countryside and in most places with open fields on both sides. On the face of it, it seems to be a very innocuous bit of road. However, there are numerous records of very strange sightings along it - of almost everything supernatural, from ghosts to cryptozoology to the just plain weird.

It boasts the 'usual' type of road ghost in the form of phantom people seen which the driver thinks they are about to hit, or did hit, but which disappear like a puff of smoke in the wind when the driver stops to investigate. One truck driver in 1957 experienced exactly this. He thought he saw a couple walking along the road right in front of his lorry and with no time to stop. When he nevertheless braked sharply, to his surprise they were suddenly nowhere to be seen.

A lady driver in 1997 saw a male wearing a red jumper and dark trousers leap out directly in front of her car and although she performed an emergency stop, the man had disappeared with no trace.

Some lorry drivers who have had to take one of their tacho breaks in a layby along the road have reported seeing small groups of bedraggled looking people walking through the night pushing old fashioned handcarts.

There have also been unusual looking animals seen along here, such as phantom dogs and even bears, as well as ghostly horses. There are several videos on line which show paranormal investigations along the road, as well as blogs detailing what paranormal researchers found.

There are so many in fact, that it would be pretty much a whole chapter of its own if I tried to repeat them all here. However, I was not able to find any direct witnesses to add anything new to the mix. It does seem, however, that it would be a reasonable assumption to make that this is a fairly active site in a paranormal sense.

KIRK O'SHOTTS - Newmill and Canthill Road

This tiny hamlet has a 15th Century church, and the road running past it not only has an unusually lengthy name (it's actually called 'Newmill and Canthill Road'), but is also said to be haunted. There is a story that on a foggy night a lady driving along here on her own had a horrible experience when a pedestrian seemed to appear out of the thick mist right in front of her car.

She had no chance to brake and when she hit him, he bounced over the bonnet and was thrown over the car. Shocked beyond measure and absolutely horrified, she braked to a sudden stop, looking behind her in the mirror as she did so. Her horror only grew when he saw that the man had landed on his feet behind the car, and was standing there stock still. Although scared, she knew she had a responsibility to check if he was hurt, so she reversed the car slowly back, intending to ask whether he was OK or needed hospital treatment. As she reversed she was watching him in her mirror when he simply vanished.

It seems that her experience is not unique as the report suggests that numerous other people have also seen the figure in the road here. Most report him as very tall, wearing a dark cape of some sort.

B869 STOER - towards Clachtoll

This lonely stretch of road in the very far north west of Scotland is said to be haunted by a dog-like entity, but which sometimes appears with a humanoid face and small horns. This isn't the first Shuck type creature to be said to have either a humanoid or monkey-like face, which in itself is quite curious.

One correspondent wrote to me with this account, "A friend of mine was walking back from Lochinver one night and as he reached Creag an Ordain (the rock that overshadows the road) he heard a splashing in the water of the loch and great back dog with eyes like burning peats came out of the water and up the bank towards him. It growled as it came out of the water and as it did so, sparks flew from its mouth. The poor man was terrified and fled along the road as fast as his legs could carry him.

"The dog, though, was faster and soon overtook him. As it turned to face him, he stood face to face with the beast. It was a terrifying sight with a half human face with horns on its head. It growled and snarled and the poor man was quaking with fear. but he kept on walking because there was nowhere for him to run.

"The dog belched fire and growled, but did not attack him. Just as suddenly as it had appeared it disappeared straight into the middle of the road. It was many days before he would walk that road again, even in broad daylight."

It's a very strange account, if true, as it has such a hint of the usual mediaeval type tales of how Black Shucks were likely to behave.

A858 MARYBANK, ISLE OF LEWIS - road alongside the Loch.

There is a source story I found which claims that the road alongside the Loch is haunted by a man who was executed in Stornoway for committing murder whilst out on a bird hunting trip. The local people that I corresponded with were able to tell me that this would either be Loch Airigh (occasionally spelled Airidh) na Lic, which is the one closest to Marybank, or Loch Cnoc a'Choilich.

I was put in touch with a local man who was known to collect many of the folklore stories from the region, and to spend much of his free time around the Lochs. He told me that he had never heard of such a haunting at either Loch, but he had heard that a ghost car haunts the road near what he knows as 'The Ghost Loch', or Loch Leiniscal on the A859.

A9 PITLOCHRY - towards Newtonmore

There is a rather strange tale associated with this stretch of road, according to one source. Apparently, a family driving along this road in 2002 saw a golden coach pulled by matching white horses travelling along the side verge of the road, heading into the oncoming traffic. No other vehicles seemed to notice it, which is apparently what alerted them to the fact that it was an apparition. The account doesn't say where it went - or whether they saw it disappear.

When I asked for any information, one man dryly pointed out that there must be better places to haunt than the side of the A9. Another person said they were aware of UFO sightings along this same stretch, which is interesting.

A87 SLIGACHAN, Isle of Skye - leading towards Portree

This road is quite famous for its ghost car. There are stories that drivers along here will see a car approaching them rapidly from behind but at the point at which it should overtake them, it suddenly disappears.

When I asked locally, several people remembered that it had been seen by the postman when doing his rounds in his van and that he was off work for a while afterwards suffering from shock. They thought the story ran around fifteen years ago. He had seen lights approaching him from behind at speed, so had pulled over to let the car pass - but nothing came. At first he didn't think much of it, until it happened several more times before he got to the end of the road.

One lady recalled that her mother had worked at Sligachan at the time and said that several people came in while she was working who said they had just encountered the ghost car. Apparently, the car was seen on the old road before the modern day A87 was built. This original road was apparently a much narrower road with passing places and went by a different route to the modern day road.

Certainly, one gentleman told me that his father and grandfather had seen the ghost car whilst travelling along the old road in the 1960's and that his father was a man who did not normally believe in such nonsense as ghosts, let alone talk about them.

Apparently, some people have theorised that it is a phenomenon caused by lights reflecting off the Loch. Others mentioned that the area seems to be a magnet for time slip type phenomena.

One witness told me that she was once on the A851 between Broadford and Kinloch when she saw headlights coming towards her and so pulled her car to the side and waited for the other vehicle to come past but nothing ever did. She had heard the ghost car is also seen there but at the same time wondered whether what she actually saw were her own headlights reflecting back off something.

Another witness told me that in the early 1980's he was driving from Luib to Sligachan Hill and was followed by headlights which suddenly disappeared in a way he found difficult to rationalise. One lady also pointed out that mysterious lights are also sometimes seen along the Lonmore to Colbost road (the B884).

Curiously, one lady remembered being told that the driver of a Co-op lorry had seen the ghost of a lady standing in the middle of the road about ten years ago (2008?) as he passed the Varragil bridge on the A87 when heading towards Sligachan. Interestingly, there was also some discussion on how, several of us had thought it funny when we were teenagers (me in the south, my correspondents up on the Isle of Skye) to switch off car lights on bright nights, and sneak up behind other vehicles before switching the lights on again... maybe the ghost car has a mundane explanation?

A82 SPEAN BRIDGE – towards Torlundy

One late evening in April 2016, two people were travelling along this road in their car. The passenger suddenly noticed a white ball of light hovering about a foot above the surface of the road which then floated into the roadside hedge and vanished. When they turned to the driver to ask if they had seen it too, the driver replied that they had seen nothing.

WALES

A4046 ABERBEEG

This stretch of road between Aberbeeg and Cwm is said to be haunted by the ghost of a policeman. He was murdered in the line of duty in July 1911, when he went to arrest a drunken man who was throwing stones. There was a scuffle between the pair, during which the drunk struck PC Pope with one of the large stones.

The PC, who tragically had only married 8 months earlier, fell to the ground mortally wounded and died at the scene within a few minutes of heart failure. His memorial is on the Gwent Police roll of honour.

Since then a ghostly figure has been seen along the road. Curiously, he is said to wear a tall hat – which was not part of the police uniform in 1911. Might this mean this ghost has been misidentified in urban myth?

Local residents agreed the road was spooky and that there were lots of tales pertaining to it, but none specifically mentioned the male ghost nor had anyone had any personal experiences along there.

A55 ABERGWYNGREGYN

There is an account that two university students walking along this road to find a bus stop late one evening in autumn 1975 encountered the ghost of an elderly lady. At the time the new road had not yet been built, so this was on the older road which has now largely disappeared.

As they walked along looking for the bus stop their friends had assured them was along there, they saw, outlined in the headlights of cars coming towards them, the figure of an elderly woman, somewhat stooped over, standing beside the road. They assumed she must be waiting at the bus stop they were seeking, so started to hurry towards her.

As the next set of car lights illuminated her as they got closer, she suddenly disappeared by dissolving towards the ground like a pillar of falling sand right in front of their astonished eyes.

BROUGHTON – Old Warren (Near Chester)

This stretch of road, just to the west of Broughton and just inside the Welsh border, was said to be haunted as far back as the 1930's when it was a quiet and lonely stretch of road. Today, it runs parallel to the busy North Wales Expressway, which perhaps makes it harder for the ghost to make his presence known.

It was said to be the ghost of a preacher wearing a cape and a clergyman's hat, very tall, and with a scowling face. I did find one report which said he would peer into any cars parked along the road, which might make for an interesting ghost hunt.

A40 CARMARTHEN – towards Llangathen

A source says that in summer 1981 a lorry driver trundling along this busy road saw a parked pick-up truck at the side of the road ahead of him.

There were three men standing around the truck and the lorry driver was wondering what the issue was as he passed them. Just as he drew level to them in his lorry, one man gave the other a hard shove, pushing him straight under the cab of the lorry!

Horrified, the lorry driver started to frantically brake, looking in his rearview mirror as he did so and fearing that his lorry would have either crushed or be dragging the victim.

He was possibly even more horrified to see that the men and the pick-up truck had all vanished without a trace.

LLANGENNITH

In the late 1990's a car driver travelling along the small main road running through this village, saw a misty ghost of a white lady who stepped out immediately in front of his car. I was not able to find any more detail anywhere about this haunting.

A470 LLYSWEN - just next to the bridge over the River Wye

In January 2008, according to one source, a gentleman was driving by this turning onto the bridge with a passenger in his car at around 7am in the morning. They both saw an older man standing beside the road and described him as quite tall and wearing a long grey coloured coat.

Weirdly, in the predawn half-light, they also noticed that his head was just a smooth oval in shape with no features, and was very faintly glowing. They only saw him for a moment as they passed.

MONMOUTH - Watery Lane

There is a tale that the lane is so named because a stream used to run along here, in which a man was once tragically drowned. Since then his ghost has been seen walking the lane.

On one occasion a woman mistook him for the postman and tried to catch up with him to chat, only to see him disappear in front of her eyes.

One lady wrote to me to tell me her own experience of the lane. She explained, "We moved to a house on the lane itself in 1983, but before then we lived at Tower View and our garden backed onto the lane, so I grew up knowing all about the reputation of the lane being haunted, as did many of the children around there."

She told me that there are various accounts of different hauntings of the lane and particularly the Bailey Pit farm which lies at the end of it, since Watery Lane is a dead end. She explained that when she was about 19 years old, she needed to deliver some flyers along the lane to every property. At that time, there were fewer houses than there are now, and she had finished all the ones on the lane proper and just needed to walk down to the end where the farm was and deliver one there. Since it was a bit of a trek to walk down to the farm, she had taken one of the family's pet dogs with her to give it a walk.

She said, "As we got near the old barn at the entrance, the dog stopped abruptly and absolutely refused to go any further. There had been no problem prior to that point, and up until then I did not feel anxious or anything, so I'm sure it wasn't a case of her picking up on my feelings. Anyway, despite all my efforts, she wouldn't budge and seemed quite agitated, so I gave up and walked her back to the house. I never did deliver that last flyer! So though I've not seen anything myself, I'm sure there was something there that she sensed."

A541 NANNERCH

There used to be a pub called 'The Rising Sun' along this stretch of road, which locals told me used to be next to where the modern day 'The Cherry Pie Inn' stands and which is now converted into flats.

There has long been seen the ghost of a woman wearing a long black gown and with a hood drawn up to conceal her face in the roadway outside The Rising Sun. She sometimes steps into the road before vanishing, or steps from the road into the dense undergrowth. The last recorded sighting of her that I could find was in the 1990's.

I spoke to a former barmaid from The Rising Sun, who explained that the ghost was well known when she worked there. She put me in touch with one of the waitresses who was there for 14 years until 1984.

This second witness recalled that the pub itself was said to be haunted, with the attic area which they used for storage being a particular problem. She remembered that one of the barmen had gone up there to fetch down some extra chairs one day and came down white as a sheet. He'd been inside the actual attic when the door suddenly slammed violently shut on him even though there was not a breath of wind.

Another gentleman wrote in to me and explained, "I was born in Nannerch Lodge, Waen Dymarch which is an old stone lodge approx 200 yards from the Rising Sun across the old railway line and up the lane. I lived there with my parents and sisters until we moved up to Nannerch village in 1963.

"Over the years the bad corner by these buildings has been an accident blackspot before and during my lifetime, with some fatal casualties. My family have lived in this area (Lixwm and Nannerch) since 1780 and a lot of stories have been passed down through the generations. There have been tales of ghostly figures approaching the corner of a woman crossing the road wearing a long dress with a shawl around her shoulders, they say coming from an old stone cottage situated close to the sluice gate that diverted water to the old mill waterwheel".

He also knew of another tale . It said that a team of horses had just delivered some barrels of ale to the pub, when something spooked them and they galloped off at full speed, completely out of control and dragging the barrel dray behind them. They careened into an old woman on the corner and killed her - and it is her ghost who now haunts the road. He said that his Grandfather and father used to travel back home by horse and cart from the pub before World War I broke out, and they both believed they had seen the ghost of the old woman.

A48 NANTYCAWS

A man driving along here late at night in autumn 2010 had to brake hard when the figure of a man suddenly ran out in front of his car. Before it had passed the halfway point of crossing the road, the figure simply vanished.

Something similar happened again in 2016, when someone else saw a dark figure vanish whilst it was crossing the road. I was not able to find any other sightings for this.

NEWPORT - Malpas Road

In November 2002, a paranormal researcher and podcaster was driving home late one night (or early one morning, depending on how you look at it), and drove down Malpas Road. As he passed St Mary's Church, movement from close to the graveyard entrance caught his eye and he glanced across.

There on the edge of the beam of his headlight was a young girl walking along alone. She looked to be in her late teens or maybe early twenties and was wearing a very short, dark coloured mini skirt and a much lighter bra or bikini style top. She was not wearing a coat, and given the time of the year her inappropriate dress for such a chilly night immediately caught his attention and he looked more closely at her - wondering if she was trying to get home from a nightclub or some such and whether she was OK.

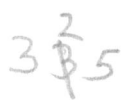

As soon as he looked more closely, she turned to walk into the graveyard and therefore out of his view – but not before he had noticed to his horror that actually, she was just floating along and there was nothing visible below her lower shins!

IRELAND

ANTRIM - Dublin Road, towards the Belfast international airport

There is an account that in 1991 a man driving to work suddenly saw a young girl wearing a long 1900's type dress cross the road ahead of him riding on an old fashioned bicycle.

When he got level with the spot where he had seen her, it immediately became apparent that there were no gaps in the dense hedges on either side of the road that she could either have emerged from or ridden into. Furthermore, even if she did somehow get through the hedge there were only deeply ploughed muddy fields on either side which would not be feasible to ride a bicycle across!

When the witness reached the point where he had seen her, he realised that there were no gaps in the heavy hedge rows and that on either side of the road deep ditches leading into heavily ploughed fields made it impossible for anyone to cross at that point.

BALLYMENA - Crebilly Road

Many decades ago, a rather daring highwayman decided to rob one of the wealthy houses along this road and tried to make his escape on horseback with his bag of loot. Unfortunately for him, the guards strung a piece of wire across the gateposts, so as he rode through at full gallop in his haste to get away, his head was severed clean from his body. Since then, his headless ghost, still on horseback, can sometimes be seen or heard roaming this road on Halloween.

One or two other versions of this tale seem to exist. The most colourful is that the local squire argued with his lover and tore away from the house on his horse. So angry was he about their quarrel that he did not wait for the gates to be opened but instead tried to force his horse to jump them but was flung from his mount and decapitated when he hit the spikes on top of the gate.

R407 KILDARE – outside Clongowes Wood College

This road is home to a phantom coach and horses, but more curiously, there is also a small child ghost who darts out in front of cars, or is sometimes seen standing at the side of the road as if waiting to cross. There is also a large phantom black dog, which mostly stays closer to the college buildings, but has been occasionally seen around the roads.

NEWTOWNABBEY – M2 slip road by Greencastle

In February 1993 a lady driving onto the M2 in the early evening, when it was of course already pitch dark with the time of year, suddenly saw a young girl of maybe 11 years old skip across the motorway lane ahead of her car and then disappear. The child ghost was wearing a long sleeved, tiered skirted white dress and had pale coloured hair.

BIBLIOGRAPHY

Boar and Blundell - World's Greatest Ghosts
Anne Bradford - Haunted Holidays
J.A.Brooks - Ghosts and Witches of the Cotswolds
Janet Cameron – Haunted Kent - 2012
Edward Charnell, Historian
Arthur C Clarke - World of Strange Powers 3
Adriana Cracun - Rebellious Hearts: British Women Writers and the French Revolution
Jason Day - Paranormal Essex
Gloria Heather Dixon - Strange Places: a Few Seconds behind Cotherstone
Andrew Greene - Ghosts of Today
Anthony D. Hippisley Coxe - Haunted Britain
Geoff Everett
Henry Farrar - CD Rom of Hurst
Joan Forman - Ghosts of the South
Sonja Francis - Horrible Haunted Thame
Jack Hallam - The Ghosts of London
Brian Haughton - Famous Ghost Stories - Legends and Lore
Helen Murphy Howell - Road Ghosts and Spirit Hitchhikers
Jason Karl - Great Ghost Hunt
Carmel King - Haunted Essex
Clive Kristen - Ghost trails of the Lake District and Cumbria
Clive Kristen - Ghost trails of Lancashire
Sue Law - Ghosts of the Forest of Dean
Rupert Matthews - Haunted Places of Bedfordshire and Buckinghamshire
Rupert Matthews - The Miser of Braishfield
Christine McCarthy - Some Ghostly Tales of Shropshire
Keith Nickson - researcher and Author
Wallace Notestein - A history of witchcraft in England 1558 to 1718
Damien O'Dell – Paranormal Bedfordshire – 2013
Damien O'Dell - Paranormal Cambridgeshire
Jenny Randles - Timestorms
Daniel Scott – Bygone Cumberland and Westmorland 1899

George Riley Scott – The History of Torture Throughout the Ages - 1959
J & A Spencer - Encyclopedia of Ghosts and Spirits 1 & 2
J & A Spencer - The Ghost Handbook
Daniel Stannard - Bedfordshire Ghosts 2006
Sarah Tarlow - The Golden and Ghoulish Age of the Gibbet in Britain
Elisabeth Thomas - Haunted Mid Herts
Peter Underwood - Where the Ghosts Walk
Michael Williams - Ghost Hunting South West
bedsarchives.bedford.gov.uk
Derby Telegraph
Eastern Daily Press
Eerieplace.com
Furnesshiddenheritage.blogspot.com
haunted-discoveries.co.uk
Hauntedhistory.com
HauntedIsles.blogspot
Hauntedwiltshire.blogspot
Hidden Wirral – Myths and Legends
Historic Assynt - Dave McBain
Horse and Hound
Houghton Regis Heritage
Luton Paranormal Society
The Manchester Mercury
Northampton Chronicle
Notes and queries fourth series, vol xi, p83
https://oxney.wordpress.com/
Paranormal Database
Peaklandheritage.org.uk
The Rose and Crown, Low Hesket, Cumbria
Wearesouthdevon.com
www.abertilley.net
www.bbc.co.uk/lincolnshire/unexplained
www.charlesworthtopchapel.co.uk
www.chilternsaonb.org
www.chroniclelive.co.uk/news/north-east-news/see-gateshead-drivers-spooky-video-9812147
www.hiddenhighgate.org

www.historyrevealed.com
www.roadghosts.com
www.strangebritain.co.uk
www.thegreyhoundinn.net
www.whaleybridge.net
www.wirralfire.net

List of places covered:

Bedfordshire
Aspley Guise
Bedford Tavistock Street
Bedford – All Hallows
Carlton to Harrold
A6 Clophill
Clophill Great Lane
Colmworth
Cranfield
Deadman's Cross
Harrold to Lavendon
Houghton Regis
Kempston
Markyate
A507 Millbrook
Milton Bryan
Pavenham
Riseley
Salford
B1042 Sandy
Sharnbrook
Stanbridge
Wood End

Berkshire
A329 Bracknell
Bracknell – Quelm Lane
A338 Hungerford
Hurst
A34 Newbury

Buckinghamshire
Bennetts End
A413 Chalfont St Peter
Cryers Hill

A40 Gerrards Cross
A418 Haddenham
A4128 High Wycombe
High Wycombe – Cock Lane
High Wycombe – Loakes Road
A404 High Wycombe to Amersham
Nash
Seer Green
A421 Tingewick
Turville

Cambridgeshire
Alconbury
B1052 Balsham
Horseheath
B1050 Longstanton
M11 Junction 13
A1 Peterborough
Peterborough, Sutton Heath Road
Snailwell
A142 Stuntney
West Wratting
Whittlesford

Cheshire
A529 Audlem
Bunbury
A50 Church Lawton
B5074 Church Minshull
Kingsley
Knutsford
Tarporley
A51 Wybunbury

Cornwall
Bude
A30 Bolventor
Calstock

Camborne
B3266 Camelford
B374 Carthew
A39 Davidstow
Helstone
Liskeard
A30 Mitchell
Penzance
B3314 Port Isaac
A3058 Quintrell Downs
B3306 St Just
A3071 St Just
A39 St Kew Highway

Cumbria
A6 Barrock Gill
Barrow in Furness
A685 Kirkby Stephen
Leece

Derbyshire
A511 Bretby
Burbage Bridge
A514 Castle Gresley
Charlesworth
Derby, Agard Street
Derby, AScot Drive
Derby, Chester Green
A623 Eyam
B6251 Eyam
Handley
B6001 Hassop
A6013 Ladybower Reservoir
B587 Lount
Smisby
Whaley Bridge
A6187 Winnats Pass

Devon
Cheriton Cross
A379 Gara Bridge
A386 Great Torrington
Holcombe
Lapford
A379 Shaldon Bridge

Dorset
B3157 Abbotsbury
B3081 Bottlebrush Down
A348 Bournemouth
Bradford Peverell
Briantspuddle
Bridport
B3162 Broadwindsor
A35 Charmouth
Chideock
Horton
B3078 Knowlton
Loders
Lyme Regis
Symondsbury
West Lulworth

Durham
B6278 Barnard Castle
A690 Brancepeth
A167 Newton Aycliffe
A688 Staindrop

Essex
Audley End
Basildon
Bradfield
Braintree
Canewdon

Chelmsford
Faulkbourne
Great Wakering
B1052 Hadstock
High Laver
A1060 Little Hallingbury
Mersea Island – Dawes Lane
Mersea Island – East Mersea Road
North Shoebury
Stanway
Thorpe le Soken
Tollesbury

Gloucestershire
Avening
B4226 Cinderford
Clearwell
B4632 Cleves Hill
B4228 Coleford
B4234 Coleford
A429 Fossebridge
A429 Moreton in the Marsh
A44 Moreton in the Marsh
B4068 Naunton
Rodborough Common
B4020 Shilton
A429 Stow on the Wold
A438 Tewkesbury
Upper Swell
B4234 Whitecroft
Winchcombe

Greater London
A116 Aldersbrook Road
A2 Bexley
Blackheath
Brownswood Park
A5200 Dartmouth Park Hill

Hampstead
Highgate
A41 Stanmore

Greater Manchester
Droylsden
Golborne
A57 Hyde
B6391 Turton Bottoms

Hampshire
Aldershot – Bourley Road
Aldershot – Alma Lane
Braishfield
Bramshott
Chalton
East Meon
Gosport
B1254 Southsea
Waterlooville – Lovedean Lane
Waterlooville – Hulbert Road
Winchfield

Herefordshire
A465 Bromyard

Hertfordshire
Baldock
Berkhamsted
Bulls Green
Burnham Green
B462 Bushey
Datchworth
B487 Hemel Hempstead
Hinxworth
St Albans
A41 Tring

A1170 Ware
Whitwell

Isle of Wight
A6054 Locks Green
B330 Nettlestone

Kent
Bearsted
A25 Borough Green
Brenzett
Charing
A299 Chilton
Cranbrook
East Malling
Grafty Green
Herne Bay
B2169 Hook Green
Lydd
B2160 Matfield
Meopham
A259 Old Romney
A258 Oxney Bottom
Rusthall
Sandhurst
A21 Sevenoaks
A262 Sissinghurst Castle
A28 Tenterden
Upper Dartford
Wye

Lancashire
Accrington
AShworth Valley
A675 Bolton
Fleetwood
A565 Formby
Freckleton

Newton le Willows
Stump Cross

Leicestershire
Broughton Ashley
Charley
B667 Evington
Knipton
Market Bosworth

Lincolnshire
Alkborough
A52 Friskney
A16 Grimsby
Kelstern
A52 Leverton
B1190 Lincoln
Louth
North Hykeham
A15 Ruskington

Merseyside
Bromborough
A5038 Liverpool
Liverpool - Higher Lane
Liverpool - Maryland Street
Liverpool - Queensway Tunnel

Norfolk
A47 Acle
A148 Bale
Blakeney
A1067 Fakenham
Gorleston
A12 / A47 Hopton
B1354 Horstead
A11 Norwich

Reedham
Shelfanger
A11 Thetford
A1075 Thetford

Northamptonshire
Bozeat
Cold Ashby
A4500 Ecton
Harrington
B672 Harringworth
Irchester
A508 Lamport
A5213 Northampton
Raunds
A6003 Rushton
Salcey Forest

Northumberland
A696 Belsay
B6309 Black Heddon
B6306 Blanchland
A1 Buckton
A1058 north Shields

Nottinghamshire
Calverton
A6075 Edwinstowe
Nottingham
Watnall

Oxfordshire
Aston Tirrold
A4095 Bampton
Burford
Denchworth
East Hanney

B4031 Hempton
A4329 Little Milton

Shropshire
Astley Abbots
Bomere Heath
B4373 Bridgnorth
Bridgnorth - Moat Street
Chatwall
Horsehay
Loggerheads
Longnor
Ludlow
A458 Much Wenlock
A442 Telford

Somerset
A38 Barrow Gurney
A372 Bridgewater
B3129 Bristol
B4467 Bristol
Bristol - Willsbridge Hill
Brockley
A39 Cannington
B3114 Chew Valley Lake
A30 Crewkerne
A396 Cutcombe
A30 East Chinnock
A39 Knowle
Nunney
A39 St Audries
Thornbury
A39 Street
A38 Taunton
B3170 Taunton

Staffordshire
Bobbington

Clayton
Fazeley
Great Haywood
M6 Lichfield
A460 Rugeley

Suffolk
Barnham
A146 Barnby
B1062 Beccles
bentley
B1074 Blundeston
A1065 Brandon
Bungay
Burgh
Chelmondiston
Corton
B1070 Hadleigh
A47 Hopton
Martlesham Heath
A1088 norton
Pettistree
Polstead
B1078 potsford Wood
Snape
Tuddenham

Surrey
A25 Betchworth
Chaldon
Dunsfold
A246 Effingham
A325 Farnham
B365 Hersham
A23 Horley
A3 Milford
A324 Pirbright
A31 Tongham

Sussex
A27 Arundel
A23 Bolney
Brighting Park
Brighton
Buckbarn Crossroads
Buxted
A259 Chichester
B2141 Chilgrove
Crowborough – Walshes Lane
Crowborough – Alice Bright Lane
B2169 Frant
A23 Handcross
A259 Icklesham
A21 Johns Cross
A286 Midhurst
A21 Robertsbridge
B2100 Woodhurst
A2270 Willingdon

Warwickshire
A428
A3400 Atherstone on Stour
Bedworth
A4141 Chadwick End
Coventry
A426 Dunchurch
A4177 Hatton
A5 Hinckley
A435 Kings Coughton
Ryton on Dunsmore
Westwood Heath
Whitacre Heath

Wiltshire
A365 Atworth
A36 Bath

A363 Bath
A361 Beckhampton
Bowerchalke
Bulford
Calne
B4005 Chiseldon
A4 Corsham
Heytesbury
A350 Hindon
A429 Malmesbury
A345 Marlborough
A4 Marlborough
Melksham

Worcestershire
A448 Harvington
Lenchwick

Yorkshire
B1242 Atwick
Aysgarth
Bailiff Bridge
A684 Bedale
Boltby
Clumber Park
B6089 Greasbrough
Kiveton Park
Masham Common
A684 Northallerton
Stirton
A161 Stockbridge Bypass
A659 Tadcaster
A64 Tadcaster
A629 Thurgoland
Tickhill

Scotland
A83 Achadunan

Arbigland
Arbroath
Banchory
A6088 Bonchester Bridge
Craford
A7 Edinburgh
Forth Road Bridge
Glasgow
Kilmacolm
A75 Kinmount Straight
Kirk O'Shotts
B869 Stoer
A858 Marybank
A9 Pitlochry
A82 Spean Bridge

Wales
A4046 Aberbeeg
A55 Abergwyngregyn
Broughton
A40 Carmarthen
Llangennith
A470 Llyswen
Monmouth
A541 Nannerch
A48 Nantycaws
Newport

Ireland
Antrim
Ballymena
R407 Kildare
Newtonabbey

Printed in Great Britain
by Amazon